Colin Wood.

THE BOYS' ENTERTAINMENT BOOK

THE BOYS' *Entertainment* BOOK

by ROBERT G. SMITH

A collection of snappy skits, shorties, stunts, games, dramatized songs, and ghost stories written for boy scouts, cub scouts, church and school youth groups, boys' clubs, and even girls' clubs, who are seeking new material and ideas for all types of entertainments, amateur shows, special programs, parties, and campfires.

Publishers

T. S. DENISON & COMPANY

Minneapolis

Printed in the U. S. A.

By The Brings Press

Library of Congress Catalog Number: 57-9455

To

MY MOTHER

A Friend to Boys

CONTENTS

FOREWORD

This book has been prepared for boy scout troops, explorer posts, cub packs, school and church organizations, boys' clubs and various other youth groups seeking new material and ideas for all manner of entertainments, amateur shows, special programs, parties and campfires. There is even some material in this book suitable for girl scouts and campfire girls.

Most of the material is original and published here for the first time. Its entire presentation, including a generous amount of pictures and drawings, is intended as a fresh and stimulating answer to the usual question, "What shall we do for our next affair?" I hope that you who seek the answer in these pages will find this material so suitable that you will be eager to tackle future programs with this wealth of new suggestions.

My own experience in program work, outside of my role as a story teller, has centered around Boy Scouts, particularly Troop 30 of Philadelphia, and this special interest is quite understandably reflected in the contents of this book. However, other youth organizations, girls and boys, schools, and many adult groups should find this volume a fruitful source when seeking help for various occasions.

I also like to think that the major part of this book makes good reading in itself. To this end I have tried to avoid a routine method of introducing and describing the different skits and stunts, indulging in some side remarks from time to time which I hope will not be taken simply as wisecracks. Incidentally, in my years of coaching boys as entertainers I have observed that such humorous asides, or comments, have often been picked up by the boys and used in their own roles as emcees or performers. Thus, these attempts at humor may serve two purposes, or "kill two stones with one bird."

Now for a few remarks about the several sections of this book.

SNAPPY SKITS contains thirteen original skits (or play-lets), some requiring a fair amount of costuming, props and rehearsals; others very little.

"Who Sneezed?" was first presented by the Turtle Patrol of Troop 30, and there appears to be some doubt as to who originated the idea. However, the Turtles agree that most of the credit belongs to Gus Clarson (Chairman, Troop Committee) and Jim Mealey (now an Explorer Scout.)

"A Picture of Spring" is my own modified and expanded version of an old skit, origin unknown. I also took some liberties with Johnny McGuckin's "Pot of Gold Quiz Show," but he is my friend and said it was all right.

I am the author of the other ten skits.

SHORTIES are dramatized jokes or peewee skits; also called blackouts or quickies. The Flaming Arrow's Johnny McGuckin contributed "No Deal," and "The Heavy Chif-fonier" was the brainchild of Bob Chantigian and Bill Schaffer of a former Flaming Arrow Patrol in Troop 30 some 25 years ago. They did such a good job of it I never forgot it.

"Smith Brothers Cough Drops" is another one I have remembered for more than 25 years, from the days when Norm Ryan staged it at Camp Kerodoki, Eaglesmere, Pennsylvania. I am responsible for the rest.

STUNTS and GAMES includes some 90 different stunts and audience participation games under 36 headings, many of which are not basically original with me although in most cases their development is. For example, the "Baby Bottle Contest" is an old "30" specialty which I dressed up with the baby bonnets, rattle and lollypops for a television show a few years ago and have subsequently used, with gratifying response, as an audience participation interlude during a program of stories.

On the other hand, a number of the stunts and games here described were dreamed up by this author and, therefore, are now making their debut in print; unless, of course, others have created them independently, there being no closed circuit on ideas.

DRAMATIZED SONGS consists of nine rather familiar melodies which are easily sung and which make it possible to get everyone "into the act," for instance, an entire boy scout troop, as I have done. These dramatizations are good fun for participants and spectators alike. Indeed, the latter may be strongly tempted to join in, even without any encouragement.

Strangely enough, the section on *Ghost Stories* is probably a unique addition to a book in this field. However, the demand for these stories by youth leaders, and the boys and girls themselves, must be very great, judging by my own experiences. It is really remarkable that ghost stories suitable for telling to youth groups, *and* acceptable to them, are just about unobtainable in print despite the fact they are unquestionably the most desired type of entertainment for campfires and many affairs of comparable nature held indoors.

Like all Gaul, *Ghost Stories* seem to be divided into three parts; those generally considered appropriate for youthful ears but which boys and girls spurn, adult horror and weird tales which definitely should *not* be told but which frequently *are* because of their availability in print, and, thirdly, what I consider to be the happy medium, although there will be considerable difference of opinion on this point. It is admittedly a difficult problem and one which I have approached with a very sincere desire to do what is right and best for the "kids."

Humorous ghost tales and stories which explain away any seemingly supernatural happenings are often recommended for campfires by well-meaning adults, but boys and girls do not agree. I have tried all types and now take my stand with the kids that ghost stories should have a "real creepy" or "Big Boo!" ending.

While such stories are not desirable for young children, and might unduly upset youngsters not emotionally stable, healthy boys and girls of camping age thrive on them just as they do on lots of noise and vigorous games. Ghosts are as much a natural heritage of youth as Santa Claus and the Easter Bunny are of childhood.

"Crooked Arrow" is the only ghost story I have ever told in the daytime. However, I told it four times one hot Saturday afternoon in Philadelphia's Fairmount Park to as many large groups of cubs, scouts, and parents and friends, holding the attention of all despite the competition of games, Indian dancing and other activities nearby.

"Troop 30's Ghost" was originally told in simpler form by the late Dr. William L. Fisher, lecturer at the Fels Planetarium in Philadelphia, founder and for twenty years Scoutmaster of Troop 30. Although the story is mostly imagination, there evidently was an "Old Bill" some sixty or more years ago, Troop 30 did camp in "The Haunted House on Darby Creek" from 1920 to 1938, and how proud we were that we had a ghost all our own.

The ghost story scare shared with one's comrades is a truly wonderful experience and one of the most remembered and cherished parts of camp life. Make no mistake about it, boys and girls often are really scared and some do have subsequent dreams, but how they do love their ghosts just the same. As one boy put it, "A good ghost story makes a campfire." It is a pity more adults cannot understand and sympathize with this age-old, perfectly normal craving of youth.

The two Indian stories in Section Six have been included in this volume because of the steadily growing interest on the part of many youth groups in the Red Man's tribal dances, costumes, ceremonies and activities. It is hoped that one of these stories may be just the thing to "complete" an Indian evening, or serve to round out a general program with an Indian number.

The manner of telling these stories makes it possible to offer a "moral" in a very acceptable form. Speaking of morals, I had better confess that the Towedo Tribe and its customs are purely my own imagination, although, I trust, not too far out of line with more authentic Indian lore.

Thus you can see this is definitely a different kind of program book but one which, I believe, will receive a warm welcome from youth groups, schools, libraries and many interested individuals.

I wish to express my gratitude to the scouts and explorers of Troop 30 (and the cubs of Pack 30) who have inspired the creation of much of the material in this book, particularly the ghost stories, and who have been so cooperative in helping me take the pictures used to illustrate various skits and stunts.

I especially want to thank Howard Dunlap for his friendly interest and many helpful suggestions, as well as for the preparation of all the preliminary drawings required for the illustrations.

Finally, I am deeply grateful to L. M. Brings, President of T. S. Denison and Company, who, on the basis of one skit, "The Courtship of Miles Standish," encouraged and guided me to assemble and rewrite other material I had in fragmentary form, and to keep creating more until I can now say, "Here is my book. I hope you like it."

Bob Smith

Section One

SNAPPY SKITS

Suggestions for the Leader

While *Snappy Skits* should be good fun for both audience and cast without too much study and rehearsal, they do require a certain amount of practice and most of them involve some memory work. Where lines must be learned they should be memorized as soon as possible because rehearsals are not too useful until everyone knows his part. It is only then that a director can really begin to help the actors get into their different roles.

And it is all important that each person in any production, even a crazy farce, have the right feeling for his part. All too often amateur actors talk with as little naturalness as robots. This is partly due to the normal tendency to concentrate on words with little regard for the emotions behind them, and partly the result of trying to assume a character not one's own without actually striving to understand the character.

The secret of successful acting, of course, lies in actually being the person one is supposed to be. Like the village half-wit who found the lost horse when everyone else failed. He explained that he simply imagined he was the horse, went where a horse would go, and there it was. Thinking oneself into a part, and sincerely trying to think and feel as that individual might, is what enables one to get realism into one's acting and speaking. I stress this point because these skits depend so heavily upon the way they are done; everything else—costumes, props and scenery—being more or less expendable.

Scenery, in fact, is unimportant, and these skits may be staged almost anywhere. Little or no furniture or other large props are required for most of them. Costumes are desirable in some cases, although the general idea of many parts can be conveyed with a little ingenuity in using clothing and materials available. The pictures and drawings in this section will give some idea of what can be done in the way of costumes and staging. A narrator can always ask the audience to imagine whatever is not too apparent.

Scene shifting is generally of a minor nature, mostly a matter of having actors and incidental props ready to move on quickly when the preceding scene ends. See Section Two's introduction for some suggestions for staging skits without a curtain.

Generally, where there are large items on the stage (furniture for "The Sore Toe and Other Ailments," a cliff for "Boat Down River," and door and windows for "Goodnight!") there is only one scene so that no shifting is necessary during the skits. The chairs used in the first and last scenes of "A Good Turn" can be pushed back against the rear wall of the stage for in-between scenes. The two doors for "The Lady Or?" can be on the stage during the first two scenes, covered by suitable material which may be quickly removed for the third scene.

Some of these skits may be staged at campfires. However, most of them are more adaptable to indoor production.

Here are two suggestions to directors:

1. Do not draft unwilling actors.
2. Do not try to put on a skit when the cast does not really want to do a good job of it.

Because unless the actors are enjoying themselves the audience will not. And skits are supposed to be fun for all.

However, you are more likely to have the same problem I usually have, more would-be actors than you can use.

THE COURTSHIP OF MILES STANDISH

This light-hearted farce of a historical (?) love triangle of Pilgrim Days at Plymouth, Massachusetts, is an excellent costume skit for many different organizations, whether boys or girls.
PARTS: 2 Males, 1 Female, 1 Optional (narrator)
COSTUMES: Pilgrim
PROPS: Easily improvised with the exception of a spinning wheel which may be omitted.

This little playlet requires some good "hammy" acting. There are three actors—Miles Standish, John Alden and Priscilla Mullen—and the Narrator.

Consult any pictures of Pilgrim Days for information regarding costumes. The actors, of course, should look their parts. Miles Standish needs a helmet, breastplate and sword; also a gun for Act III, which can be improvised from a pole or stick, a funnel, etc. He also needs a daisy. John Alden is not much of a problem. Priscilla is a demure maiden with a bonnet, a long gray dress and a white apron.

The essential props are a table, two chairs, a quill pen (feather) and inkstand, and a spinning wheel. This latter can have a bicycle wheel minus tire as its principal part, or it may be contrived from a barrel hoop.

Act III and One-Eighth is optional.

NARRATOR. After a great deal of reading and research, none of which had any connection with the subject at hand, it is our pleasure to present for your confusion tonight, "The Courtship of Miles Standish." It may be of interest to note that this is probably the first recorded two-men and one-girl love story of the white race in America. The poet, Henry Wadsworth Longfellow, wrote a long poem about it, but we are going to present to you this evening the *true* story as it *really* happened. *(Holds up a hand with two crossed fingers and clears his throat.)* Anyhow, our characters are: *Miles Standish,* soldier of fortune and commander of the military forces, if any, of the Plymouth Colony; *John Alden,* carpenter and part-time secretary to Miles Standish; and—the beautiful *Priscilla Mullen,* with whom both men are secretly in love. That is, neither of them has told Priscilla, or each other, as the curtain rises on the first act of *The Courtship of Miles Standish.*

ACT I

(Miles paces up and down while John works at the table)

JOHN *(Looks up.) Must* you tramp up and down so, Captain? How can I write with you shaking the whole doggone house?

MILES. I'm sorry, John, but I am facing a fearful crisis.

JOHN *(Alarmed.)* Don't tell me the Indians are on the warpath!

MILES. Oh, no! Nothing that simple. *(Sighs deeply.)* I'm in love.

JOHN *(Really startled.)* In love? You?

MILES. Yes, I'm in love. There's no law against it, is there?

JOHN *(Fervently.)* I should hope not.

MILES *(Strikes a pose with his hand on his sword.)* Ah, yes! *(Shifts his hand to his heart.)* Yes, John, I am head over heels in love with the *beautiful Priscilla.*

JOHN *(With dismay.)* With Priscilla! You mean Priscilla Mullen?

MILES *(Blissfully.)* The very same.

JOHN *(In a very small voice.)* Oh!

MILES *(Looks sharply at John.)* Oh what?

JOHN *(Sadly.)* Just "Oh!" *(Gulps.)* When are you going to tell her?

MILES. I'm not. You are.

JOHN *(Exclaims.)* Me! *(Jumps up and faces Miles.)* You want *me* to tell Priscilla that *you* love her?

MILES. But of course! *(Moves closer to John.)* You're much better at that sort of thing than I am. I'm a soldier, accustomed to fighting battles and stuff like that, while you are a man of letters, who knows how to say all those sweet things the ladies go for.

JOHN. I am? I do? *(Aside.)* Why hasn't somebody told me that before this?

MILES *(His hand on John's shoulder.)* Certainly! You are just the man to make love to Priscilla for me.

JOHN. But don't you think each man should do his own courting?

MILES. I suppose so, but when a man is not so hot at making pretty speeches, and he has a good friend like you . . .

JOHN *(With gulps.)* A good friend—like me?

MILES *(Both hands on John's shoulders.)* Yes, John, a good, true, loyal friend like you.

JOHN *(Sadly.)* When you put it that way, Captain, you got me.

MILES. Swell! *(Slaps John on his back so hard he almost jars his teeth loose.)* I knew I could count on you.

JOHN *(Aside.)* Another blow like that and you could count me out.

MILES *(Briskly.)* Now you go tell Priscilla the good news, and everything will be just dandy. *(Pushes John toward the door.)*

JOHN *(Moves as slowly as he can.)* Yes, Captain Standish. Everything will be— *(Gulp.)* —just dandy.

(CURTAIN)

NARRATOR. And that is the end of Act One. Poor John

Alden! What a fix to be in! As Act Two begins we find him dragging his reluctant feet toward the home of the beautiful Priscilla Mullen.

ACT II

(The curtain opens on Priscilla seated at a spinning wheel, maybe singing or humming a tune to herself. Can be a modern love song.)

JOHN *(Approaches the door.)* Fine thing! On my way to win the girl I love for somebody else. How did I ever get into a mess like this? *(Shrugs his shoulders.)* Oh, well! Here goes nothing. *(Knocks on the door.)*

PRIS. Who's there?

JOHN. Me. *(Enters.)*

PRIS. Why, John Alden, how nice to see you!

JOHN *(Abruptly.)* Say, Priscilla, how would you like to get married?

PRIS *(Gets up; flustered.)* Well, this *is* a bit sudden, John, and—I—uh—

JOHN. To Captain Miles Standish.

PRIS *(In dismay.)* To Captain Miles Standish!

JOHN *(Manfully.)* That's right. To Captain Miles Standish. Our fearless leader! That noble gentleman! That great warrior! Gallant defender of Plymouth! Our fearless leader . . .

PRIS. You said that before.

JOHN. So I did. Anyhow, Captain Standish loves you deeply and he has sent me to . . .

PRIS *(Indignantly.)* Well, if Captain Standish loves me so much, why does he not come and say so himself?

JOHN. Aw, Priscilla, you know how it is with the Captain. He's right on the ball when it comes to mixing it with the

Indians and things like that, but he's a little bashful about making love.

PRIS. He's not the only one.

JOHN. Huh? *(Aside.)* Wonder what she meant by that crack. *(To Priscilla.)* Anyhow, Priscilla, Captain Standish is a mighty fine man, and any girl in Plymouth—any girl in England, for that matter—would be very fortunate to get him for a husband.

PRIS *(Firmly.)* In that case, I would not think of depriving all those girls of the pleasure of Captain Standish's hand in marriage.

JOHN *(Shocked. Raises his arms to a horizontal position and parallel toward Priscilla as he speaks so that she is just between the tips of his fingers.)* But, Priscilla! I'm telling you the Captain *loves* you.

PRIS *(Steps forward between John's outstretched arms.)* Why not speak for yourself, John?

JOHN *(Startled.)* Who, me? *(His face lights up and his arms go around Priscilla.)* Oh, boy! *(Priscilla puckers expectantly but John stops within an inch of a kiss and claps his hand to the side of his head.)* Oh, Golly! What'll I tell the Captain?

PRIS *(Opens her eyes, registers extreme annoyance and whatnot.)*

(CURTAIN)

NARRATOR. John sure is in a mess now, but a very nice mess, if you should ask me. However, here is Act Three coming up with John Alden returning to report to Captain Miles Standish the result of his love-making expedition. He anticipates considerable displeasure on the part of his good friend, the Captain.

ACT III

(The curtain opens on the Captain pulling petals from a daisy, saying . . .)

MILES. She loves me, she loves me not, she loves me, she loves me not, she . . . *(As John enters.)* John! You're back!

JOHN *(Slowly.)* Yes, Captain, I'm back.

MILES. Well, don't just stand there, man. Tell me . . . *(Sudden alarm at John's downcast face.)* Why, whatever is the matter. John? Don't tell me she doesn't want to get married!

JOHN. No . . . I mean, yes, Captain. Priscilla likes the idea of getting married.

MILES *(Much relieved.)* Well, then, everything is hunky-dory.

JOHN. That all depends on who you are.

MILES. What do you mean by that?

JOHN. I mean Priscilla would rather marry me.

MILES *(Amazed.)* Marry you? Why, that's ridiculous!

JOHN. I wouldn't say that.

MILES. Do you mean to stand there and say Priscilla Mullen said she would rather marry *you* than *me?*

JOHN. Well, not exactly. But she said she *wouldn't* marry you, and that I should speak for myself.

MILES. Well, how do you like that?

JOHN *(With a blissful smile.)* I like it.

MILES *(With anger.)* That's not what I meant, you double-crossing, stabber-of-a-friend-in-the-back, you.

JOHN. But, Captain, can I help it if all the girls go for my wavy hair?

MILES. You could get a crew haircut. Just imagine it. My girl marrying my friend.

JOHN. I did the best I could for you, Captain. Honest Injun!

MILES *(With sarcasm.)* So it seems.

JOHN. Anyhow, as long as things have turned out the way they have, how would you like to be my best man?

MILES *(Explodes.)* What! Me be your best man! Standing idly by while . . . *(Turns toward the gun.)* Where's my gun?

JOHN. N-now, Captain, d-don't go d-doing anything y-you, or . . . *(Gulp.)* . . . I m-may be s-sorry for.

MILES *(Gets the gun.)* Oh, don't worry. I can take it. *(Strides to the door.)* I'm just going out to shoot a few bears and wildcats—to calm my nerves. *(Exits.)*

JOHN. Poor Captain Standish. He's really a good kid. *(Shrugs his shoulders.)* But, if you haven't got it, you just haven't got it.

(CURTAIN)

NARRATOR *(Holds up a hand.)* Hold everything, folks. It's not over yet. We really did a lot of research on this one and are proud to offer you our exclusive discovery in Act III and ONE-EIGHTH.

ACT III AND ONE-EIGHTH

(The curtain opens on John Alden writing at a table. Priscilla approaches and knocks on the door.)

PRIS. Knock, knock!

JOHN *(Looks up.)* Who's there?

PRIS. Butch and Jimmy.

JOHN *(Goes to the door.)* Butch and Jimmy who?

PRIS *(Enters.)* Butch your arms around me and Jimmy a kiss. *(John does so.)*

(CURTAIN)

NOTE: *If the part of Priscilla is played by another boy, the curtain can open again to show both boys wiping off a kiss and making wry faces, or, if boy and girl, to show them still kissing. The curtain quickly closes again, as though its opening was an error.*

John Alden returns to break the news to Captain Miles Standish with Jimmy Cameron as John Alden and Dick Selwood as the Captain.

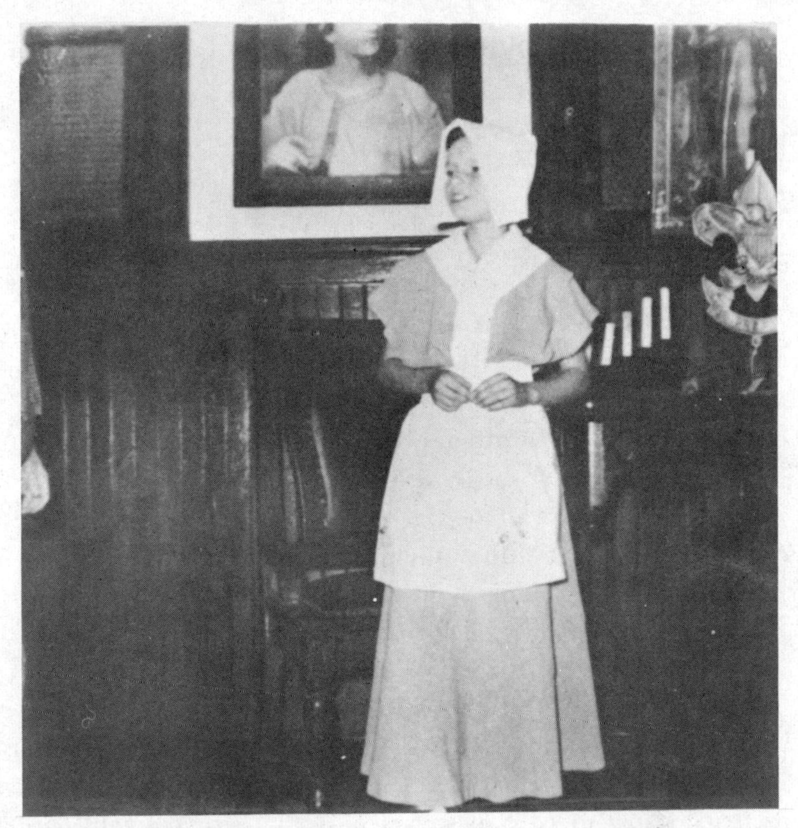

Lovely Priscilla Mullen as played by Dave Sterling.

WHO SNEEZED?

A brief satire on life in the happy land of the Comrades. This is a good campfire number, requiring a minimum of rehearsal or preparation.

PARTS: 6 to 8 males
COSTUMES: Easily improvised
PROPS: 1 toy gun; appropriate farm tools optional but not recommended unless very careful attention is given to the safety factor.

This skit calls for six to eight characters who could be either men or women. However, men would probably seem more appropriate and a group of girls putting on the skit could be dressed accordingly.

The lead and only speaking role (with one tiny exception) is played by a tough-looking commissar or "comrade officer" who is armed with a tommy gun or some other gentle persuader. He is facing a group of five to seven "comrade farmers" who are dressed in nondescript outfits so as to appear as sad sacks of the collective farm.

OFFICER. Comrade farmers, I must tell you that *The Party* is displeased with your work. You have not produced your assigned quota of cabbages. Not only that, but the cabbages you have produced were small ones and with worms in them yet. *The Party* does not like to have worms in the cabbages. So, it is my duty to warn you that you must produce more cabbages, bigger cabbages, better cabbages, cabbages without worms, cabbages of which *The Party* can be proud, cabbages in which you, the comrade farmers, can take pride, cabbages . . . *(Near the end of this speech, one sad sack farmer, not immediately in the officer's line of vision, sneezes "ka-choo." The officer stops. There is deep silence for a few seconds. Then the officer speaks.)*

OFFICER *(Sharply.)* Who sneezed?

FARMERS *(Continue to stand as a group of sad sacks. There is deep silence, their faces without expression.)*

OFFICER *(Louder and more sharply.)* Who sneezed?

FARMERS *(As before, although their eyes may move just a trifle to left or right.)*

"Once More, Who Sneezed?"

Comrade Tony Devine lies across Bruce Hillier as Comrade Officer, Jim Mealey, threatens Comrades Bob Hack, Jimmy Trainor, Ray Hack, Johnny McGuckin and Howard Dunlap.

OFFICER *(Slowly and ominously.)* Who sneezed?

FARMERS *(As before.)*

OFFICER. So! Nobody speaks! Very well, then, I will keep asking, "Who sneezed?" Every time I ask and nobody speaks, somebody . . . *(Taps his weapon significantly and looks hard at each farmer. He's a real toughie.)* Now! Who sneezed?

FARMERS *(As before, with a possible slight movement of their eyes.)*

OFFICER *(Aims the gun at one farmer and fires. It's no "cowboy" bang, though. Make it a more modern weapon sound.)*

FARMERS *(One victim tumbles forward in a heap. The others remain frozen. There is no sound.)*

OFFICER *(Changes his voice each time he asks question by talking lower, louder, slower, faster, etc.)* So! You see! Now then, who sneezed?

FARMERS *(As frozen as ever.)*

OFFICER *(Takes aim at another farmer and shoots. The farmer falls backward. And so it goes until every farmer but one is dead, making a heap around the last, the saddest sack of the bunch. Officer looks at him and asks for the last time.)* Who sneezed?

FARMER *(In a scared, squeaky voice.)* I did!

OFFICER. Gesundheit!

(CURTAIN)

A PICTURE OF SPRING

A lovely thing indeed, with the narrator doing most of the talking, the actors generally restricted to pantomime. It can be staged with a minimum of rehearsal and, thus, is a campfire possibility.
PARTS: 2 Males, 1 Female, 8 Optional
COSTUMES: Ordinary play or everyday clothes
PROPS: Few and small.

This skit calls for eleven participants, including the narrator.

NARRATOR. I should like to paint for you this evening a glorious living picture of Spring. Any resemblance between this picture and art, or anything else for that matter, is just too bad. . . . Ah, Spring! Just imagine a lovely day in March . . . *(Takes out a handkerchief and blows his nose loudly.)* . . . maybe we better make it April when the weather is a bit warmer. *(A boy sneaks up and hits him in the face with a squirt from a rubber bulb.)* What's this? April Showers? *(With a forced laugh.)* It is a beautiful day in *May*, with the golden sun smiling down on us all. *(A boy appears with a sign suspended from his neck, reading, "Son of Mr. and Mrs. Golden." The boy stands on a box and smiles sweetly down on the audience. From time to time his face can assume a normal expression and then be pulled back into a smile by the use of index fingers at each corner of the mouth.)* In the right foreground we see a sturdy old oak tree. *(Large boy enters with one arm bent upward and one downward to simulate branches.)* . . . that has braved the wind and the rain. *(The boy with the rubber bulb enters to make like wind with a fan; the tree bends before the wind. The boy takes out the rubber bulb and squirts the tree in the face; the tree retreats to the left background, mopping his face with a handkerchief.)*

As I was saying, in the *left background* stands a sturdy old oak tree, with a little bird singing in its branches . . . *(A small boy enters, flapping his arms, and hops up on the back of the tree, and sings "Tra-la-la, tweet-tweet.")*

Lover Left Out

Photographer got everyone and everything but one of the lovers. Johnny LaMonte is Rabbit; Jim Mealey, the Babbling Brook; Bob Hack, the Rustic Bridge; Wayne Rensch, the Barefoot Boy; Ray Hack, the Sturdy Oak Tree; Jack Page, the Little Bird; Jimmy Trainor, the Golden Sun; and Barbara Kerr, the Girl; while the Boy, Ronnie James, is represented only by his right foot.

While a cute little bunny rabbit comes hippity-hop . . . *(A boy hops in as a rabbit.)* . . . as happy and carefree as only a rabbit can be. *(The rabbit winks or smiles at the audience and uses his hands as waggling ears.)* Through this lovely woodland scene a babbling brook winds its way. *(A boy crawls in, winding around.)*

BROOK. I babble, babble as I flow, to join the brimming river, for men may come and men may go, but I go on forever. *(These lines are spoken in a sing-song voice. The brook then comes to rest with his head supported by one hand.)* But, gosh! It sure gets tiresome!

NARRATOR. Over this babbling brook, we see a quaint little rustic bridge . . . *(A boy takes his place on his hands and knees over the brook. The head of the brook is toward the audience with his body on a slight diagonal toward the rear of the stage; thus the bridge is alwost sideways to the audience and the barefoot boy can face toward the audience.)* . . . and on this bridge, at peace with all the world, sits a barefoot boy, fishing. *(A barefoot boy, with large white bow bandage on his big toe, sits on the bridge with his feet hanging over the brook. He has a line on a short pole so that the line may drop close to the hands of the brook. The brook can then take a toy fish from his pocket and fasten it to the line.)* And now our Picture of Spring is complete. *(Looks sideways.)* Oh, no! Not quite! For here, arm in arm, come two happy hearts that beat as one. *(Two lovers enter, arms twined around each other's waists, heads close together.) Ain't Love Grand? (The boy kisses the girl with a loud smack. The bird bends to kiss the tree on the cheek. The tree dumps the bird and bolts off, with the bird in pursuit, flapping his arms. The rabbit hops over and kisses the brook, who jumps up to chase the rabbit, spilling the bridge and barefoot boy. All run off except the lovers who are oblivious of everything else, and the sun who turns the sign up to cover his face, after registering shocked surprise at such goings on. The back of the sign reads: "It ain't over yet, but I am." The sun exits.)*

LOVER. Ah, my dearest, you are a lovely flower and I a busy little bee in quest of honey. *(He begins to buzz and circle the girl who closes her eyes, tilts her face up and puckers expectantly. As the bee buzzes close, the boy with the rubber bulb enters and gives the bee the business. The bee, or lover, chases the boy. The girl opens her eyes, makes an angry face, and clenches her fists. The lover chases the boy around the girl and back past her. She starts to chase the lover.)*

NARRATOR *(Holds up a hand for silence if necessary.)* It is now May, but the sap is still running. *(The lover comes around again with the girl still after him. The girl stops, looks at the audience, and raises her right fist for emphasis.)*

GIRL. But, I'll get him by June. *(Runs off.)*

(CURTAIN)

NOTE: *With an all-boy cast, or an all-girl cast, wearing slacks, there is no problem of casting; however, with a mixed cast some ingenuity becomes necessary. To even things up somewhat the narrator can be a girl, of course, and such changes as the following can be made:*

1. Small girl can have a rubber bulb.
2. Rabbit can easily be girl in slacks or shorts.
3. Bird can be a girl as above.
4. Sun can be a girl, with a second sign suspended from first to read: "Daughter of Mr. and Mrs. Golden. Sonny has the measles."

THE GOOD TURN

Longer and calling for more actors than the others, *The Good Turn* is a good skit for boy scout troops, schools and other organizations numbering scouts among their membership. *The Good Turn* idea is put over effectively with plenty of humor.
PARTS: 11 Males, 5 Females, 1 Optional (narrator)
COSTUMES: Scout uniforms, adult clothes and play clothes
PROPS: Easily assembled.

Cast of Characters

Bud (Patrol Leader)
Dave (Asst. Patrol Leader)
Frank, Larry, Martin, Al,
Freddy, Shorty (Scouts)
Mr. Grouch
Mrs. Bundles
Dear Old Lady
Grocer
Little Girl
Tough Kid
Kathy (Frank's Sister)
Kathy and Frank's Mother
NARRATOR

In this skit eight different scenes follow in fairly rapid succession. However, props are at a minimum so that, except for picking up the spilled bundles, oranges, and the kitchen sink in their respective scenes, it is merely a case of shifting actors. The chairs needed for the first and final scenes can be pushed back out of the way for intervening scenes, for which no furniture is required. A small table with white paper thumb-tacked over it and a few dishes on it, plus a dish towel should be sufficient for the dish-washing scene. There can be a crate to go with the oranges, if you want to get fancy. Otherwise, a half dozen oranges and a storekeeper's apron on the grocer should fill the bill.

The scouts are not in uniform for the first patrol meeting after school, nor for the good-turn scenes, with the exception of Frank, who has changed into his uniform before attempting to help with the dishes. Thus, all the scouts should have time to get into uniform for the final patrol-meeting scene.

NARRATOR *(Before the curtain.)* You know, if there is one thing that everybody knows about the Boy Scouts it is that each and every scout is supposed to do a good turn every day. But *do* they always? After all, boy scouts are only human too, and a good turn every day is asking a lot of anyone. Well, suppose we find out what happens when Bud Jenkins, Patrol Leader of the Silver Fox Patrol, calls a special meeting of the patrol right after school about this very subject—Good Turns.

SCENE 1

(The curtain opens on the Silver Fox Patrol assembling with school books. Several are seated while others are still standing or entering.)

DAVE. Say, Bud, what's the big idea of calling a patrol meeting now when we're meeting tonight anyhow?

AL. Yeah, how come, Bud?

LARRY. What's the hot dope? *(All seated by now.)*

BUD. Well, it's like this. Mr. Watkins asked me last night if we Silver Foxes were really doing Good Turns. So I said, "I guess so." And then he said, "But do you know so?" So I said, "No, I don't." So he said, "Why don't you find out?" So I said, "All right, I will." And so that's what I want to know—are we?

MARTIN. I guess so.

FRANK. Most always, or anyhow, sometimes.

FREDDY. My mom says I do her a *wonderful* good turn *every day*—when I go to bed. *(Laughter.)*

BUD. That's what I mean. For instance . . . *(Real stern to Shorty.)* Did you do a good turn today, Shorty?

SHORTY. W-well, now that you ask me—*No!*

BUD. See!

DAVE. Aw, give the kid a chance. The day isn't over yet, and besides, did *you* do a good turn today?

BUD. *No.*

DAVE. Then why jump on us? *(Murmurs of agreement.)*

BUD. I'm not jumping on anyone. I just want to suggest we all make an extra special effort to do a good turn between now and patrol meeting tonight, so that when we do meet . . .

MARTIN *(Dramatically.)* Each trusty boy scout can raise his right hand to the position of the scout sign and say, "I have seen my duty and I have done did it."

BUD *(Grins.)* That's the idea. What about it, fellers?

DAVE. Okay, Bud.

AL. You can count on me.

LARRY. And me.

FRANK. A good turn or bust.

FREDDY. Good-turn Freddy, I was known as.

MARTIN. Never let it be said that Martin Addleson failed the Silver Fox Patrol in its hour of trial.

BUD. Swell! Looks like it's unanimous. *(Looks at Shorty.)* Or is it? Shorty, are you in on this?

SHORTY. W-well, I'd like to be, but it's hard to see how I can work anything else in today. I've got so doggone much to do now.

DAVE. You can't be too busy to do a good turn.

SHORTY. I dunno. I got about all I can handle, but I'll try. *(Laughter.)*

BUD. Well, try your hardest, Shorty, and so will the rest of us. *(Real snappy.)* Patrol, attention! *(The boys snap to attention.)* Scout sign! *(The boys raise their right hands to the scout sign.)* Third point of the Scout Law!

SCOUTS *(Unison.) A Scout is Helpful.* He must be prepared at any time to save life, help injured persons and share in the home duties. He must do at least *one good turn to somebody every day.*

BUD. Patrol dismissed! *(The boys start horseplay.)*

(CURTAIN)

NARRATOR. Sounds like great stuff. The Boy Scouts to the rescue, and all that, but let's see what happens as our heroes sally forth to do their daily good deeds. First, let's watch little Freddy in action. Freddy doesn't like to be told so, but he's a real cute kid, with that curly blond hair and big blue eyes that really get the girls. *(Change the description to match the boy.)* Shh! Here he comes now—and he sees a dear old lady about to cross a busy street. What more could any boy scout ask?

SCENE 2

(The curtain opens on a dear old lady about to cross the street. Freddy approaches.)

FREDDY *(Courteously.)* May I walk with you across the street, Lady?

D. O. LADY. Why, certainly, my little man. How long have you been waiting to get across?

FREDDY. B-but, but, I meant . . .

D. O. LADY. It's quite all right, little boy, just take my hand. *(She takes his.)*

FREDDY *(As she starts across, pulling him close to her.)* But I'm a boy scout and I . . .

D. O. LADY. Now, sonny, you mustn't be ashamed of asking for help. My goodness, an old lady like me is only too happy to help you little boy scouts. Just stay close by my side and nothing will happen to you. *(She holds him close to her while Freddy looks as embarrassed as any boy scout would in such a situation.)*

(CURTAIN)

NARRATOR. Was Freddy ever embarrassed? Oh well, those things will happen. But why don't we check on Dave? He's the gallant protector type, you know.

SCENE 3

(The curtain opens on a little girl crying. She has a broken doll. Dave approaches.)

DAVE. Aw, what's the matter, little girl? *(Kneels to comfort her.)*

GIRL. My dolly! *(Holds it up.)* She's all busted. *(Cries harder.)*

DAVE. Aw, that's too bad, but don't cry. Maybe I can fix it. *(Takes the doll.)*

TOUGH KID *(Approaches.)* Hey, you! Whatcha doin' to my kid sister?

DAVE *(Stands up, with the doll.)* Why, nothing, I was just . . .

KID. Oh, so ya busted the kid's doll? Now ain't that brave?

DAVE. Hey! Now wait a minute! I couldn't help it—I mean I didn't do it.

KID. Oh, yeah? Well, I'm doin' this. *(Quick one-two to eye and jaw. Dave bites the dust. Sound effects for the one-two punches desirable.)* That'll learn you. Come on, Sis. I'll fix your doll.

(CURTAIN)

NARRATOR. Wow! What a one-two punch! A left to the eye and a right to the jaw. Poor Dave! He made out worse than Freddy. However, Martin and Larry might have better luck as they hurry to pick up some oranges that spilled and rolled into the street at the *Better Buy Fruit and Vegetable Market.*

SCENE 4

(The curtain opens on Martin and Larry hurrying to pick up oranges.)

MARTIN *(Stooping.)* Good thing we came along just now.

LARRY. Yeah. A truck mighta run over some of these and . . .

GROCER *(Running up.)* Hey, you kids! What do you think you're doing?

LARRY. Why, we're picking up . . .

GROCER. Stealing oranges, huh?

MARTIN. No, sir. We're only picking them up for you.

GROCER. For yourselves, more like it. Well, you don't steal my oranges and get away with it.

LARRY. But we're boy scouts.

GROCER. Then you ought to be ashamed of yourselves. *(Snatches the oranges from the boys.)*

MARTIN. But we're doing our good turn . . .

GROCER. Good turn, is it? *(Snorts.)* Well, I'm thinking I'll do a real good turn by turning you two over to the police. *(Drops the oranges in his apron, which he gathers up with one hand to hold them. Starts to reach for Martin.)*

MARTIN. Come on, Larry, let's scram. *(Takes off.)*

LARRY. Right with you. *(Runs off.)*

GROCER. Hey, you kids, stop! *(Runs after them.)* Stop those kids!

(CURTAIN)

NARRATOR. Gosh! Martin and Larry really did get themselves into something. This good turn business isn't going so good. What next?

SCENE 5

(The curtain opens on a lady carrying packages and an umbrella. Bud approaches from the rear.)

NARRATOR. Uh-oh! Here comes Bud, the Patrol Leader, who started it all. It will be interesting to see how he makes out as he hastens to assist a lady with a heavy load of bundles.

BUD *(Politely, as he comes up from the rear.)* Pardon me. I'll just take this big bag.

LADY *(With indignant surprise.)* Oh, no you won't! *(Pulls away.)*

BUD. But I only want to relieve you of part of your load.

LADY. And don't I know it. I'm wise to your tricks.

BUD. No, lady, you don't understand. I'm only . . . *(Tries to get the bag.)*

LADY *(Sharply.)* Go away! *(Hangs onto the bag.)*

BUD *(Still trying.)* Please, lady, I've got to do my . . . *(Bundles tumble to the ground.)*

LADY. Now see what you've done! Well, I can handle the likes of you. *(Starts hitting Bud on the seat of his pants with the umbrella. Bud flees with the lady in hot pursuit.)*

(CURTAIN)

NARRATOR. So Bud failed, too! Guess this just isn't the Silver Foxes' day. Still, their luck may change as opportunity comes knocking at Al's door, so to speak. At least things can't get any worse. Or can they?

SCENE 6

(The curtain opens on Al and the Tough Kid approaching each other.)

KID. Say! You're a boy scout, aren't you?

AL *(Suspicious.)* Yeah. What about it?

KID. Well, ain't you guys supposed to do good turns for people?

AL. Yeah.

KID. Did you do yours today?

AL *(Still wary.)* N-no, but . . .

KID. That's swell! Maybe you can help me. I'm in an awful jam.

AL *(Relieved.)* Well, I'll try to help you. What's your trouble?

KID. That Mr. Grouch in there *(Jerks his thumb toward an imaginary house.)* took my new football and if I go home without it my old man—uh, I mean, my father will beat me.

AL *(Indignant.)* Why, he can't do that.

KID. Sure, he can. He's bigger'n me—oh, you mean Mr. Grouch. Well, I told him he couldn't keep it but he said he wouldn't give it back until somebody pa—I mean, he wanted to know if I was responsible for brea—Well, I said—I mean, he says I gotta be responsible for . . .

AL. I understand. He thinks it isn't really your football and you're not responsible for it.

KID. Yeah! That's it. He thinks I'm not responsible for brea—for the football.

AL. Well, I'm a scout, and he'll believe me. Just wait here and I'll get your football for you.

KID. Gee, you're swell! *(As Al approaches the house.)* What a dope!

AL *(Approaches the house, knocks on an imaginary door. Mr. Grouch comes to the door.)* I came to get that football you're holding.

GROUCH. Oh, you did! And are you the one that's responsible for . . .?

AL. Yes, I'll take full responsibility.

GROUCH. That's all I want to know. *(Grabs Al and calls into the house.)* Call the police, Jezebel. I've got the rascal who broke our window.

(CURTAIN)

NARRATOR. Poor Al! He is in a jam for fair! And when he meant so well, too! Well, keep your fingers crossed and we'll see how Frank does. Seems he tied a ribbon to his finger to help him remember, and then forgot anyhow, until after supper while changing into his Scout uniform. Now here he comes to the kitchen where his sister, Kathy, is doing the dishes.

Scene 7

(The curtain opens on Kathy drying dishes. Frank hurries to her.)

FRANK. Take a powder, Kathy. I'll dry the dishes.

KATHY. Oh, no you don't, smarty pants. Your turn is tomorrow night.

FRANK. I know but I'm doing them for you tonight.

KATHY. Yes, and then I'll have to do them tomorrow while you get off early for the movies. Well, you don't get away with it.

FRANK. I'm not trying to get away with anything. I only . . . *(Reaches for the towel.)*

KATHY. Don't worry! You're *not* getting away with anything. *(Jerks the towel away.)*

FRANK. Aw, what's the use o' talking? *Gimme that towel. (Grabs hold of the towel.)*

KATHY *(Hangs on.)* I won't. *(They struggle. Kathy calls.)* Mother! Make Frank leave me alone!

MOTHER *(Enters.)* Frank, please let Kathy be.

FRANK. But, Mom, I'm just trying to help her.

KATHY. And I don't want your help. *(Yanks the towel away and takes a dish.)*

MOTHER *(To Frank.)* Why must you always start these arguments with Kathy? Every night it's the same story—argue, argue, argue.

FRANK *(Disgusted.)* I give up! You just can't win.

KATHY *(Sticks her tongue out at Frank.)*

(CURTAIN)

Kathy and Frank battle over the dish towel. Parts played by Anne and Bob Ormsby.

NARRATOR. So it seems. Well, that's everybody—except Shorty. Wonder where he got to. He's the one who was going to be so everlastingly busy. Remember? Anyhow, it is now time for patrol meeting, so let's drop in to see what the fellows have to say about their afternoon of good turn adventures.

SCENE 8

(The curtain opens on a sad-sack looking bunch of boy scouts, flopped or flopping into chairs, discouraged, disgusted and dejected. Dave has a black eye. Al remains standing.)

BUD *(Kicks a chair so it points more toward Al.)* Have a seat, Al?

AL. No, thanks. *(Rubs himself.)*

FREDDY *(Stands up to imitate an old lady.)* Certainly, my little man; take my hand and come with me. *(Shifting from his conception of the old lady's voice to a disgusted*

Freddy voice.) You and your good turns! *(Flops back into the chair.)*

DAVE. Yeah! Just look at my eye! *(Points to his eye.)* It's all your fault, Bud.

MARTIN. Larry and me almost got arrested on account of you.

LARRY. Boy, I never ran so fast!

FRANK. Just try to do a good turn for a kid sister.

DAVE. Don't mention kid sisters to me. *(Feels his jaw.)* I still think my jaw's busted.That Bud and his bright ideas!

MARTIN. I'm telling you, Bud, you really goofed this time.

BUD. Aw, lay off. How do you think I felt when the lady thought I was a hit-and-run package snatcher? I could have gotten arrested myself.

AL. Well, I *did* get arrested. And my father had to pay six bucks for a new window. And then that darn kid said I swiped his football, and his father punched my father in the nose, and that's why I don't feel like sitting down. *(Rubs himself again.)*

MARTIN. Well, now! Shorty himself arrives. *(Shorty enters, stands just inside the door.)*

LARRY. Let's hear his tale of woe.

DAVE. Yeah. Spill the dirt, Shorty. What went wrong with your good turn?

FRANK. Did you just get out of jail?

AL. Or didn't they catch you?

SHORTY. Didn't do no good turn.

DAVE *(Indignantly.)* You mean you didn't even try!

SHORTY. Just didn't have time.

MARTIN. You had as much time as we did.

FREDDY. You could at least try.

FRANK. Yeah, I tried.

LARRY. Me, too!

BUD. How come you didn't even try, Shorty?

SHORTY. It's like I said, I just didn't have time. When I left you guys this afternoon I went over to do errands and stuff for Mrs. Whitely—like I do every day—'cause she's sort of crippled up and can't get around so good. Then I got some things out of the cellar that Mrs. Jones was giving to the Good Will—I promised her I would. Then I remembered I had some old toys and things myself, so I ran home and got them. Then I had to beat it over to Billy Myers' house. He's the new kid in our block and he don't know nobody yet hardly, and he's sick. So I took him some games and comic books. Then I did some errands for his mother. She's kinda busy, sort of. Then I kidded Billy into taking his tonic—had to take some myself first and did it taste awful. *(Makes a face.)* Then Billy looked so sad when I started to go, I stayed and played with him until I was almost late for dinner, so I had to rush home and gobble up my dinner—Mom was mad as anything—but I wanted to finish another ash tray for the veterans I've been making things for when I go to the Veterans' Hospital this Saturday morning—I go every two weeks, you know, to visit with 'em. And then it was time for patrol meeting so I dashed over here, and I hope it don't take too long because I'd like to fix my sister's skates before I do my homework. *(Stops, out of breath.)*

DAVE. Holy mackerel!

AL. No time, he says!

FRANK. A one-man scout troop!

MARTIN. What's he call a good turn?

LARRY. Too busy! No wonder!

FREDDY. Oh, brother!

BUD. Goodnight!

(CURTAIN)

THE LADY OR?

A beautiful princess, a poor but honest lover, and a mean old king affair, with an unexpected slapstick climax.
PARTS: 3 or 4 Males, 2 Females, 2 Optional (narrator and "Or?")
COSTUMES: Improvised
PROPS: Double-door arrangement requires some effort, the "Or?" is easy.

This little skit calls for seven or eight characters, including the narrator, king, princess, poor but honest lover, beautiful maiden (?), one or two guards, and someone to handle the "or." The costumes are improvised to suit the parts, the poor but honest lover wearing something that can stand messing up as indicated in scene three. The principal prop consists of two doors side by side. These can be of heavy cardboard on a wood framework. However, there must be a divider between them on the inside as well as the walls at each end to give the effect of two vestibules. The side walls and divider can be of cloth, cardboard, etc. One other very essential prop is described at the end of act three.

INTRODUCTION BY NARRATOR

Some years ago Frank R. Stockton wrote a story entitled "The Lady Or The Tiger," which stirred up quite a fuss in its day. Very briefly, a half-barbarian king in days gone by instituted a most unique punishment for various crimes or personal enemies. The populace would gather in a special stadium and, at a signal from the King, the victim would be thrust into the arena where he would have his choice of two doors to open.

Behind one door would be a beautiful maiden dressed for a wedding and behind the other a large tiger that hadn't eaten for several days. No matter which came forth, the people considered it a great show. If it happened to be the beautiful maiden, the victim was promptly married to her regardless of whether or not he already had a wife and family. If the tiger came out, well . . . draw your own conclusions.

Now this semi-barbarian King had a beautiful daughter, the Princess, who had a poor but honest lover. The King discovered the luckless lad making love to his daughter and promptly condemned him to face the Lady or the Tiger. The young man knew the Princess knew which door was which, so, when he stood before them and had to make the fateful choice, he glanced up at the Princess who indicated which door he should open. He opened the door and that's the end of the story. Because, as Stockton explained, he just did not know how the mind of a semi-barbarian Princess worked. Would she rather sacrifice her lover to another woman than see him be a tiger's dinner, or would she prefer to let the tiger have him than see him in another woman's arms? Frank Stockton didn't know the answer and neither has anybody else in all the years since. Now, at last, we intend to find out, once and for all, by re-creating the characters and circumstances, and letting nature take its course. Ladies and gentlemen, we give you . . . The Lady Or?

ACT I

(The curtain opens to reveal a poor but honest lover on his knee before the princess.)

LOVER. Oh, my radiant Princess, I adore you. I love you with all my poor but honest heart. I swoon before your matchless beauty. Gee, kid, I think you're swell.

KING *(Enters.)* How dare you make love to my daughter, the Princess!

LOVER. But your majesty, I do love her.

KING. Oh, you do, do you? Then you must face the Lady or the Tiger.

LOVER. Oh, no!

PRINCESS. Oh, no!

KING *(In true villain style.)* Oh, yes! *(The guard or guards enter and drag the hapless lover out as the princess kneels to her unrelenting papa. Curtain.)*

NARRATOR *(Before the curtain.)* It sure looks bad for our poor but honest lover. However, a complication seems to have arisen. Suppose we see what it is.

ACT II

(The king is seated on the throne or simply standing, looking real regalish.)

GUARD *(Enters and bows.)* Your Majesty!

KING. Well! Are the Lady and the Tiger in their stalls?

GUARD. The Lady is, your Majesty, but the Tiger . . .

KING. Yes?

GUARD. Well, you know what the price of meat is these days, and you know how hard it is to get meat anyhow . . .

KING. So?

GUARD. Well, you know the roast you had for dinner . . .

KING. Yes, very tasty. *(With sudden consternation.)* You mean . . . Not the Tiger!

GUARD. The very same.

KING. Oh, what a mess!

GUARD *(Smacks his lips.)* But, it was a very tasty tiger.

KING. Never mind that! What'll we do now?

GUARD. I don't know, your Majesty.

KING *(Real villainous.)* Well, you better find out, because if you don't have *something* behind that other door, we'll serve *you* for supper.

GUARD. But what *can* I get?

KING. That's your headache, but if you fail me . . . *(Draws an imaginary knife across his throat with a suitable sound effect, and exits.)*

GUARD. Woe is me! *(Claps his head between his hands, a picture of despair. Then suddenly he smiles as a great light dawns. The curtain closes.)*

NARRATOR *(Before the curtain.)* It would seem he has a bright idea. For his sake, let's hope it works, because that King sure is a mean customer. Anyhow, now we will find out what a semi-barbarian Princess would really do when faced with such a fearful choice. Watch carefully, folks, as we bring you the stupendous, electrifying conclusion to this dramatic, romantic story from out of the past.

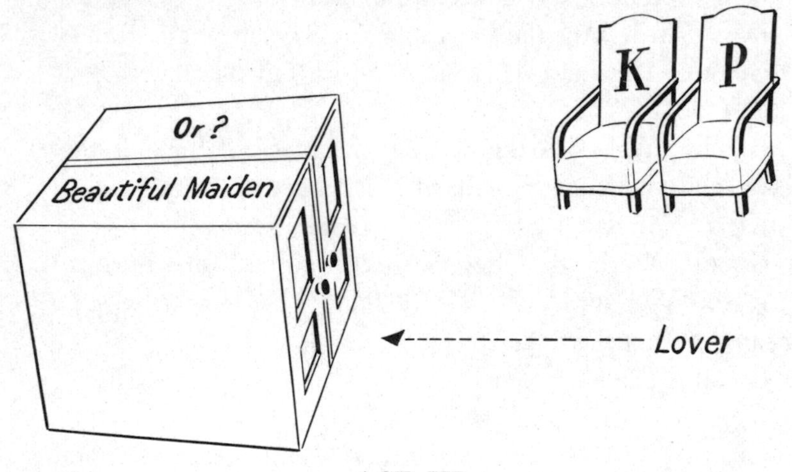

ACT III

(Two doors in the center stage are at an angle to the audience so that the audience can see what transpires. The King and Princess are on one side.)

LOVER *(Thrust in by the guards on the opposite side from*

the Princess, he comes forward slowly to face the two doors. He looks to the Princess for a signal. She indicates a door. The Lover approaches the door, hesitates and again looks at the Princess; she nods. He opens the door. Out comes a maiden painted and dressed fit to kill, or even worse.)

MAIDEN *(Shrieks.)* Lover Boy!

LOVER. Oh, no! *(Places a hand firmly in the face of the maiden and pushes her back through the door, closing it. Opens the other door and gets hit in the face by a plate of instant vanilla pudding or something equally gooey. The Lover turns around to face the audience. His tongue comes out and licks at the pudding. Curtain.)*

(FINIS)

AUTHOR'S NOTE: *Use a paper plate for the pudding and make sure you don't splatter the audience with it. I refuse to assume any responsibility for anything that happens.*

DANIEL BOONE'S ESCAPE

A highly imaginative exploit of the great pioneer for those who have Indian costumes or enjoy improvising the same with feathers and blankets and such.
PARTS: 6 to 8 Males, 1 Optional (narrator)
COSTUMES: Indian and one pioneer
PROPS: Incidental except for fire (wood and red paper, etc.) and bows which can be fashioned from branches and cord.

This little historical farce is written for pantomime, all lines being spoken by a narrator. However, the actors may take lines, if desired. The actors are Daniel Boone, Indian Chief Stands-Around-in-Woods, and four to six braves.

Essential props are an imitation fire, a box of marshmallows, a toasting stick, a leather thong or piece of rope, a tent stake, and a roll of scotch tape on a small dispenser, plus costumes, of course.

NARRATOR *(Appears before the curtain on one side of the stage.)* Daniel Boone, peerless pioneer, fearless frontiersman, the daddy of them all, had many thrilling adventures and stirring experiences. Tonight it is our pleasure to portray one of his most narrow escapes from death by burning at the stake. As our play opens we see Daniel seated before his little fire, deep in the Kentucky wilderness, cooking his frugal meal.

(The curtain opens. Daniel is toasting a marshmallow, a box of marshmallows beside him.)

There's nothing like a well-done marshmallow to nourish one's weary body after tramping all day through the woods. Oh well, Daniel Boone will soon be eligible for his Boy Scout Hiking Merit Badge.

(Daniel eats a marshmallow, smacking his lips. He yawns, stretches, and gets up.)

Daniel can use a little shut-eye, and no wonder. It takes a bit of doing to wrestle a big black bear out of a pine tree, tumble eighty feet to the ground and arrange to have the bear on the bottom when you arrive. Please note that like the good camper he is, Daniel puts out his fire.

(Daniel lifts the fire, carries it a short distance, opens an imaginary door, places the fire outside, and then shuts the door. He stretches again, scratches himself hither and yon, and lies down, using the box of marshmallows for a pillow.)

But while our bold, brave Boone browses — I mean "drowses"—his Indian foes steal stealthily upon him. Such a sneaky business!

(Indians approach in a single file, holding bows in their left hands. The first Indian stops, holding a finger to his lips. The second Indian bumps into him, the third into the second and so on until all have bumped. The first Indian points to the fire and then proceeds on tiptoe, leaning well forward. The others do the same, holding the bows well to the left, their right hands raised with one finger to their lips to indicate the need for silence. The first Indian bumps into the door, the others piling into him. The second Indian thrusts the first Indian aside and opens the door. The others follow him in, each carefully wiping his feet before entering. They surround Boone with drawn bows. No arrows, please, or you will be reported to the National Safety Council.)

One of the Indians prods our dauntless Daniel with his foot.

(The Indian does so. Daniel awakens to see the Indians lined up on each side of him.)

"One move and you are a dead duck," says the Indian to Daniel's left.

"The name's Boone," says Daniel. "Daniel Boone that is."

"On your feet," says the grim-faced warrior on Boone's right. *(Boone starts to comply.)*

"Don't move!" says the brave to Dan's left. *(Daniel freezes.)*

"Get up!" says the Indian on the right. *(A slight motion by Dan.)*

"Don't move, I said," says the left-hand brave, drawing the bowstring taut. *(He does so, likewise the Indian to Daniel's right. Daniel looks at each of them and they look at him.)*

Daniel is in a tough spot, and that's for sure, but his natural sense of backwoods hospitality does not fail him. "Have a marshmallow," he says.

(Daniel reaches for the box. The Indians relax and Daniel gets up and offers marshmallows to all. When the Indians are happily munching marshmallows, Boone leaps to the door, pulls it open and runs out, slamming the door behind him, so that the Indians, in pursuit, pile into it and each other. Boone trips over the fire and falls. The Indians rush out and seize him, tying his wrists together with a thong or rope. They lead Boone offstage. Curtain.)

Too bad! Daniel made a good try, but it just goes to show you how important it is to make sure your campfire is really out so that it can't cause any trouble. Anyhow, our second and final act opens. *(The curtain opens to reveal the noble Indian chief shading his eyes with a hand, crouched forward.)* Chief Stands-Around-in-Woods gazes down the trail, wondering what has happened to his brave braves. They should have been back with the bacon—that is, Boone—long before this. *(The Chief looks at his wrist watch and shakes his head.)*

"Ah—I mean, 'Ugh!'" he exclaims, as he sees his braves approaching with Boone.

(The Chief assumes a dignified stand with his arms folded over his chest. Suddenly he realizes he has covered up a totem painted on his chest; lowers his arms so that they cross over his stomach and thus shows the totem. If no artist is handy, the totem can be a picture of an animal or bird fastened to the chest with scotch tape. The Indians bring Boone before the Chief. They hand the Chief marshmallows. The Chief tries one, chewing it thoughtfully, nods approval and hands the box to one of the Indians who stands by with it so the Chief may help himself as desired.)

The Chief tells Daniel Boone that he is a very brave man, but that now the Indians will inherit his courage and skill, since they will burn him at the stake and dance in the smoke, so that Boone's spirit, escaping in the smoke will give his courage and skill to them. The Chief sends a brave for a stake.

(The brave exits. The Chief takes another marshmallow and refolds his arms on his chest, remembers the totem and lowers his arms again to his stomach. He repeats this sequence as often as practicable during the skit. The brave returns with a tent stake.)

"Not tent stake, Wooden Head!" yells Chief-Stands-Around-in-Woods. *(The Chief takes the tent stake and throws it down.)* "I meant . . . say, 'Wooden Head;' that's good. We use him for stake."

(The brave tries to flee but is seized and held by two Indians while the third Indian swings an imaginary mallet. The victim's knees bend with each blow until he is on his knees, supposedly sunk in the ground that far.)

"Now tie Boone to stake," the Chief orders, but Boone says, "Wait, O Noble Chief Stands-Around-in-Woods! If you would capture my courage and skill, why depend upon the old-fashioned, uncertain smoke method? Why not be modern and up-to-date? Do it by electro-magnetism."

"How we do that thataway?" asks the Chief.

"A good question," replies Boone. "Let me show you."

(Boone takes a roll of scotch tape on a small dispenser from his pocket and connects the Indians together as he talks by binding their index fingers with scotch tape. The Chief is at the rear of the circle, facing the audience.

Boone starts with him, connecting the braves on each side of him to the Chief. Boone stays inside the circle, moving from one side to the other until all are connected. Boone talks while he does this, stretching out the following speech to cover the period of fastening the Indians together.)

By joining you and all your brave braves together, O Noble Chief Stands-Around-in-Woods, I will make heap big medicine. With these strips of magic deerskin, from the deer one could see through if one could but can't because the deer is never where one looks when one looks there since it was somewhere else all the time, I join you, one by one, Great Chief and braves, with the Chief at one end and I at other. *(Boone pretends to fasten himself in the circle facing the Chief, but he actually fastens the two Indians together, index fingers and thumbs both, keeping his own arms crossed before him, and thus hiding the fact that the braves are bound together.)* You will observe my arms are crossed before me as I bind myself to your braves. This is done, so that when all is ready and the Chief gives command, I will try to hold in my courage and skill while you and your braves try to pull them from me by electro-magnetism. Do you think you have enough pull, O Chief?"

"Ugh!" says the Chief. "Plenty pull."

"Ugh!" say all the braves. "we got plenty pull."

"Then pull," says Boone.

"Don't pull until I say 'Pull,' " says the Chief, "and when I say 'Pull' pull. Pull."

(The Indians pull and Boone lifts his own arms from over those of two Indians, raises his right arm in a gesture of farewell, and departs. The Indians, after some

tentative pulling, swing into a dance, pulling and what-not, as they sing, "Daniel Boone was the daddy of them all," or they may indulge in a few war whoops.)

(CURTAIN)

THE SORE TOE AND OTHER AILMENTS

Or "The Doctor's Bad Day," and it is that, requires more stage setting than the others but there is no scene shifting; a few more patients like these and we would be fresh out of doctors.
PARTS: 5 Males, 2 Females, about 4 Optional (patients)
COSTUMES: Everyday clothes except doctor and nurse
PROPS: Furniture, doctor's items, incidentals.

For this playlet the stage should be set up as a doctor's office, including a waiting room, a nurse's cubicle and a doctor's examining room. These three rooms must, of necessity, be in a row across the front of the stage, being divided by folding screens, curtains or other improvised separators. Imaginary doors can connect the various rooms at the front of the stage. Chairs will be needed, plus a small table for the nurse and a desk for the doctor (which can also be a table.) You can go as far as you like with additional props or stick to the bare essentials.

A small table in the waiting room with magazines would be in order, also a lamp. The nurse should have some papers on her desk, a small three-by-five card file, a pen, a telephone, etc. A toy telephone will do nicely. The doctor will need some imposing-looking books on his desk and any other material appropriate for an examining room. He might have a stethoscope made from a small rubber plunger, two small ropes or lengths of wiring, and baby bottle nipples. Since the weight of this exaggerated instrument, plus its lack of tension, would cause it to fall to the floor, a piece of rubber can be used to hold it by going around the head at the ears, or it can be held by a piece of cord going over the top of the head. Let your imagination be your guide in dreaming up as much other stuff as you wish.

When the curtain opens, the nurse is seated at her table,

and the waiting room is full of patients, reading magazines, etc. There should be at least two or three more patients than the cast of actual actors calls for.

The doctor, with a bag, enters the waiting room from offstage, briskly opening and closing an imaginary door, nods to the patients, and opens the door to the nurse's office and closes it.

NURSE. Good morning, Doctor Guff.

DOCTOR. Good morning, Miss Stake. Any telephone calls?

NURSE *(Consulting memorandums.)* Yes, Doctor. Mrs. Worrywart called again. She wants to know if you are absolutely certain Mr. Worrywart has pneumonia. She says she met a woman whose husband was being treated for pneumonia but died of typhoid fever.

DOCTOR. Well, you can tell her to put her mind at rest. Her tongue too, for that matter. *(Quickly.)* No, don't tell her that. Just say there's nothing to worry about. When I treat a man for pneumonia, he dies of pneumonia.

NURSE. Yes, Doctor. Then there was a call from a Mr. Thomas Happy. He wanted to let you know how much he benefitted from your treatment.

DOCTOR *(Puzzled.)* Thomas Happy! But we don't have any patient by that name.

NURSE. That's what I told him, Doctor, and he said he knew that, but his late uncle, Alexander Greenbacks, was your patient, and he is sole heir.

DOCTOR *(Snorts.)* Young whipper-snapper! *(Clears his throat.)* Is that all?

NURSE. No. Mrs. Swallow says she heard of a new wonder drug called "Maze-In." Wants to know if she should take some for her . . .

DOCTOR *(Emphatically.)* Absolutely not! Why, that drug

is so powerful, no one should take it unless he is under thirty and in perfect health. *(Starts toward the office.)*

NURSE *(Picks up another paper.)* There was one more call, Doctor.

DOCTOR *(Turning.)* Yes?

NURSE. Miss Spinster says she is afraid she is having a relapse.

DOCTOR. Nonsense! *(Purses his lips and knits his brows.)* Tell her that some after-effects are normal in cases like hers, but that young people get over them more quickly than older folks. That'll snap her out of it.

NURSE *(Laughs.)* Oh, Doctor, you understand us women, don't you?

DOCTOR *(Smiles or chuckles.)* Oh, I suppose so, but there's one woman who has always baffled me.

NURSE. One of your patients?

DOCTOR. No, my wife. *(Opens the door to his office.)* You may send in the first patient, Miss Stake. *(Goes in and closes the door, puts the bag on his desk, puts on a stethoscope and sits at his desk.)*

NURSE *(Picks up a card on the table, gets up and opens the door to the waiting room.)* Let's see. *(Consults the card.)* Mrs. Lotsakids is first. The doctor will see you now. *(The mother gets up as does her son. They go into the nurse's office. The nurse closes the door, then opens the door to the doctor's office and closes it after them.)*

DOCTOR. Well, well, Mrs. Lotsakids . . . *(Waves her to the chair by the desk and gets up to move over the second chair for the boy.)* . . . and Tommy . . .

BILLY. Freddy!

DOCTOR *(Placing the chair.)* Yes, of course, Freddy, and how's the little . . .?

BILLY. Freddy is all over the earache.

DOCTOR *(Confused.)* But, but . . .

MOTHER. This is Billy.

DOCTOR *(Bluffing.)* Yes, indeed, Billy. I was just teasing you. And what's your trouble, Billy?

BILLY. School! It makes me sick!

DOCTOR *(Laughs.)* Yes, yes, but I mean what are you really sick of?

BILLY *(More firmly than before.)* School!

MOTHER. He has a stomach ache.

DOCTOR. Tsk! Tsk! Just like a boy!

BILLY *(Pointing to the stethoscope.)* You gonna listen to me?

DOCTOR *(Chuckles, if the chuckling type.)* No, not today, Billy, we'll just . . . *(Notes the look of disappointment on Billy's face.)* Hmm! Perhaps we should at that. *(Winks at the mother.)* Let's listen to what's going on in that stomach of yours. *(Billy, without urging, opens the bottom of his shirt, pulls up the undershirt and thrusts his tummy forward.)*

DOCTOR *(Places the stethoscope to the stomach and listens gravely, then moves the stethoscope and listens some more, and clucks his tongue.)* Hmm! *(Removes the stethoscope and gets a tongue depressor.)* Now stick out your tongue. *(Billy sticks out his tongue between his teeth, making a face.)*

MOTHER *(Sternly.)* Open your mouth, William! *(Billy does so.)*

DOCTOR *(Places the depressor on the tongue.)* Now say "Ah!" *(Billy starts to say "Ah!" and then gags as though about to upchuck. The Doctor hastily removes the depressor.)*

Well, well, there's nothing to worry about. We can fix you up with a dose of castor oil and orange juice so you can't even taste it.

BILLY. Good! I hate orange juice!

DOCTOR *(Laughs uncertainly.)* Miss Stake will prepare it for you, Mrs. Lotsakids. *(Opens the door as she gets up, and ushers the mother and boy into the nurse's office.)* One glass of tummy fix-upper, Miss Stake. *(Closes the door behind them.)*

NURSE *(To the mother.)* Just be seated, please. *(Hands her a magazine, then opens the door to the waiting room.)* Mr. Dimwitty.

DIMWITTY. That's me. I'm Dimwitty. *(Comes forward.)*

NURSE. Come right in, please. *(Ushers him into the doctor's office. She speaks to the mother.)* I'll be back in a minute. *(Exits.)*

DIMWITTY *(His head heavily bandaged with thick pad over his forehead.)* Hi, Doc! *(Takes a chair.)*

DOCTOR. My, my! What's happened to you?

DIMWITTY. I bit myself.

DOCTOR. On the forehead? Impossible!

DIMWITTY. Yes, it is. I stood on a chair.

DOCTOR *(Gives him a queer look.)* Hmm! Well, suppose we look at the damage. *(Starts unwinding the bandage which goes around and around his head. Another bandage is underneath and several gauze pads and adhesive tape under that. Take plenty of time to allow for action in the nurse's office.)*

BILLY *(Billy has seated himself at the nurse's table and is investigating cards, etc., while the conversation takes place in the doctor's office. Let's face it, this kid should be a good actor. When the doctor starts to unwind the bandage, the telephone rings on the nurse's desk. Billy answers it, using a falsetto voice.)* Doctor Guff's office. *(Pause.)* Yes, Mrs. Onions. Just a minute. *(Pause; deepens his voice.)* Doctor Guff speaking. *(Pause.)* Yes, Mrs. Onions. You say Dickie has one of those moods again? *(Pause.)* Well, I'll tell you, Mrs. Onions, if I know your Dickie . . . *(Holds hand over the mouthpiece and looks toward the audience.)* . . . and do I know that brat! *(Into the mouthpiece again.)* . . . he is suffer-

ing from nervous exhaustion. *(Pause.)* Yes, Mrs. Onions, all the other children are really tired of Dickie—I mean, the other children are tiring your Dickie. You know, Dickie is a very sensitive, highly-strung little stinker—that is, thinker. *(Hand over the phone.)* I was right the first time. *(Hand off the phone.)* Yes, Mrs. Onions, you keep Dickie in the house for the next several weeks after school and see that he reads good books—no television—especially cowboy programs—and lots of green vegetables—they're so soothing, you know—and no pie, cake, ice cream or candy. That should fix him good, Mrs. Onions. *(Pause.)* Not at all, Mrs. Onions. Goodbye. *(Hangs up the phone.)* Boy, I'll say I fixed him good! *(Gets up hastily as the nurse returns with two glasses.)*

NURSE *(Hands a glass to Billy.)* Here you are, Billy. *(Hands the other glass to the mother.)* And I thought you would like a nice glass of ginger ale.

MOTHER. Why, how nice! *(About to drink when the nurse speaks.)*

NURSE *(Sitting at the table.)* That will be three dollars, Mrs. Lotsakids.

MOTHER *(Setting the glass down on the table and opening her pocketbook.)* Oh, yes! *(Fishes out money after considerable searching among all sorts of contents. Billy, while the mother is searching for money and the nurse is busy recording information on a card, takes his mother's glass and substitutes his own. Mother pays the nurse.)* Here you are. *(Picks up the glass and looks gaily at her son.)* Well, here's to you, son.

BILLY. Here's to you, Mother. *(Both drink. A queer look comes over his mother's face.)*

MOTHER. Why, what an odd taste!

NURSE *(Looking up.)* Did you say something?

MOTHER *(Another drink.)* Well, I . . . *(Looks startled.)* I think we better be getting home. Come, Billy. *(They exit.)*

DOCTOR *(As the last bandage comes off.)* Why, this cut is all healed up!

DIMWITTY. It is? Oh, yes, it is. But there's something wrong with me.

DOCTOR. I can believe that.

DIMWITTY. Oh, now I remember. My ear hurts. And I can't hear so good, neither.

DOCTOR. Well, let's look into it. *(Gets a large flashlight from his bag and peers into the ear away from the audience.)* Hmm! *(Gets a large spoon and pretends to dig into the ear. He fills the spoon with dirt from a cloth bag which he has thrust up the other sleeve while getting the spoon from his kit. The mouth of this bag can be held by two smaller fingers while the thumb and the other fingers hold a flashlight above the spoon. Thus dirt can be emptied into the spoon as the head of Dimwitty is between the doctor and the audience. The doctor empties dirt from the spoon on a paper towel on the desk in view of the audience. He does this two or three times.)*

DIMWITTY. How is it, Doc?

DOCTOR. Well, I think we'll strike pay dirt soon. *(Sees something.)* Ah! *(Gets a pair of pliers and pretends to work with them. Places a dime between the ends of the pliers, steps into plain view of the audience and takes the dime from the pliers.)* Well, no wonder your ear hurt. You had this dime in it.

DIMWITTY. That's right, Doc. I did.

DOCTOR. You mean you knew it?

DIMWITTY. Why, shure! I put it in there two months ago.

DOCTOR *(Astonished.)* You did? But why?

DIMWITTY. Just wanted to see if it would fit, and it did. Then I couldn't get it out.

DOCTOR. But, good heavens, man! Why didn't you come to me before this?

DIMWITTY. I didn't need the money.

DOCTOR *(Sighs.)* I see. *(Shakes his head.)* Or do I? *(Opens the door.)* This way out.

DIMWITTY. Thank you, Doc. May I have the dime?

DOCTOR. Yes, you may. Even if I did mine it. *(Hands Dimwitty the dime.)*

NURSE. Three dollars, please.

DIMWITTY. Here's a dime toward it. *(Hands the nurse the dime.)* I'll pay the rest when I get it. *(Goes out through the waiting room.)*

DOCTOR *(As the door closes.)* One more patient like that and I'll blow my top. *(Returns to his own office.)*

NURSE *(Opens the door to the waiting room.)* Next, please. *(A man gets up and starts for the door, but a boy beats him to it, going past him and the nurse to the doctor's office. The nurse looks confused as she closes the door.)*

MAN *(To the other patients.)* Guess I'll just go home and die a natural death. *(Exits.)*

DOCTOR *(As the boy enters.)* Well, my boy, what seems to be your trouble?

BOY *(Sitting down.)* I got a sore toe.

DOCTOR. What's the matter with it?

BOY. It hurts.

DOCTOR. Yes, I understand. Now which toe is it that hurts?

BOY. The one that's sore.

DOCTOR. We're not getting anywhere. Suppose you take off your shoe. *(The boy does so, removing his right shoe and a long stocking. The doctor gets a magnifying glass.)* Now, which toe is it that hurts?

BOY. None of these. It's the big toe on my left foot.

DOCTOR. Then why did you take off your right shoe?

BOY. It's the only one I had on and you said take off my shoe. I got a slipper on my left foot.

DOCTOR *(Sighs.)* All right. All right. Take off the slipper. *(The boy does so, also the long stocking. Doctor, as the boy is removing the slipper and stocking.)* Have you any idea what is wrong with your toe?

BOY. Yes. It has a nail in it.

DOCTOR. Great Scott! You haven't been walking around with a nail in your toe, have you?

BOY *(As the stocking comes off.)* Sure, I always do. It's a toe nail! *(Holds up the foot.)* See, Doc! Ha! Ha! That's one on you. Now, how do you treat that?

DOCTOR. Like this. *(Seizes the boy and turns him over his knee and proceeds in the most approved parental manner, with considerable vigor. The boy yells like the dickens. The patients look startled. A nervous one can exit.)*

NURSE *(Runs to the door to the doctor's office and looks in.)* Why, Doctor Guff. It's simply marvelous how you get to the seat of the trouble. *(The boy, whose yells cease long enough for the nurse's line, now yells louder than ever.)*

(CURTAIN)

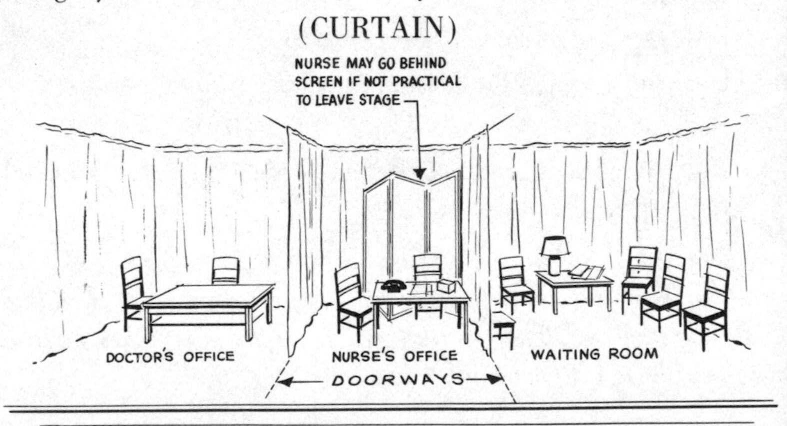

NO TELL LIE

A mischievous Indian boy gets his reward in the end, where boys so often get it. A very easy skit to prepare, if you have the costumes.
PARTS: 5 Males
COSTUMES: Indian
PROPS: Indian ceremonial pipe.

This little skit calls for five actors—four chiefs and one Indian boy. The Chiefs should wear headdresses, leggings, breechclouts and moccasins, with ornaments, vests or war-shirts optional. The boy wears a breechclout, moccasins and a headband with a feather. The only property actually required is an Indian ceremonial pipe. However, Indian or woodland props may be used to suggest either an indoor or outdoor setting.

The curtain opens on four Indian Chiefs seated cross-legged in a small semi-circle with a Chief at one end holding a pipe. The Indian boy, unnoticed by Chiefs, watches from one side. The boy's face indicates he has been up to mischief and is now gleefully awaiting results. His pleasure increases as each Chief exits, placing a hand over his mouth to restrain mirth, etc. The Chiefs exit on the opposite side of the stage from the boy.

The first Chief extends the pipe solemnly toward heaven, then toward earth, and then takes a long puff. He is handing the pipe to the second chief when a startled look appears on his face. He claps one hand over his mouth, gets up hastily, claps the other hand over his stomach and exits quickly.

SECOND CHIEF. No stomach!

THIRD CHIEF. Ugh!

FOURTH CHIEF. Ugh!

The second Chief holds the pipe to heaven and earth, takes a longer puff than the first Chief, hands the pipe solemnly to the third Chief. Suddenly a startled look appears on his face, he claps a hand over his mouth, gets up, claps a second hand over his stomach, and exits quickly, partly bent over.

THIRD CHIEF. Stomach like frog!

FOURTH CHIEF. Ugh!

Two Down and Two To Go
Ronnie James, as Indian Boy, watches Third Chief, Howard Dunlap, smoke pipe of obnoxious tobacco. Fourth Chief is Bob Clarson.

The third Chief holds the pipe to heaven and earth, takes a very long puff, slowly and proudly hands the pipe to the fourth chief and begins to fold his arms across his chest with great dignity, when, suddenly, he claps his hand over his mouth, leaps up, claps the other hand over his stomach and runs out.

The fourth Chief slowly sniffs the pipe very suspiciously, turns his head and sees the boy. The boy turns quickly and starts to tiptoe off.

CHIEF. Chipmunk! *(The boy freezes with his head pulled down like a turtle. The Chief speaks more sternly.) Chipmunk!*

BOY *(Half turning his head. Meekly.)* Yes, Father.

CHIEF *(Very sternly.)* Chipmunk! *(The boy slowly turns around and see the Chief who beckons with his right index finger. The boy slowly approaches until he is standing before the Chief who points to the pipe.)* Talk!

BOY *(Innocently.)* Something wrong, Father?

CHIEF. Talk!

BOY. Well, you see, Father, uh . . . *(He draws himself erect, looks squarely at his father.)* Father, I cannot tell a lie. I made special tobacco of old bird's nest, dried-up lizard and skunk cabbage.

CHIEF *(Kneels on his right knee with the left knee horizontal and points at the left knee.)* Bend!

BOY. But, Noble Chief, my father, have you not heard of how white boy, name of Wash-Many-Stones, spoke truth to his father, and his father did not punish white boy because he speak truth about cherry tree chopped down with tomahawk?

CHIEF. Paleface heap fool! Bend!

BOY. But, Father . . .

CHIEF *(Very sternly.)* Bend! *(Decisive motion toward the knee.)*

BOY. Yes, Father. *(Bends over the knee.)*

The Chief raises his hand. The boy turns his head with an imploring look. The Chief firmly turns the boy's head toward the ground, lifts up the backdrop of the boy's breechclout and applies his hand, seemingly with considerable force, while the boy yells, "How! How! How! Ow! Wow! Wow!"

The curtain closes.

The curtain opens far enough to show the Indian boy rubbing his buttocks. He gives the audience a dirty look and says, "Tain't funny!"

(CURTAIN)

BOAT DOWN RIVER

The boy scouts get some good-natured spoofing but still have a chance to demonstrate signaling proficiency, the use of a bowline knot and rowing technique.
PARTS: 5 Males
COSTUMES: Scout uniforms or hiking clothes, one farm boy
PROPS: Hiking gear, signal kits, improvised cliff.

Four boy scouts (or other hikers) and one farm boy are required for this skit. The action begins with the entrance of three of the hikers, who arrive at the bank of the river where there are two imaginary boats. On the far side of the river there is a narrow beach and a cliff. This cliff can be the stage or platform itself with the action beginning on the floor of the room if this is practicable. Otherwise, the cliff must be improvised or imagined.

One hiker is very fat (pillow) and all have such hiking gear as packs, canteens, axes, and, by all means, rope and signal kits. It won't hurt if the fat boy is cluttered up with all sorts of paraphernalia.

JOE. Well, here we are, and here are the boats, but where, oh where is Ol' Slowpoke?

PETE. If you're asking me, I'd say about a mile or so back thataway. *(Jerks his thumb back the way they have come.)*

BILL *(The fat boy.)* You mean we have to wait for him? *(Pulls out a bandanna handkerchief to mop his brow.)* If I can keep up, anybody can.

JOE. You can say that again.

BILL *(Agreeably.)* Okay. You mean we have to wait for him? If I can keep up, anybody can.

JOE *(Tries to cut him off but Bill continues and Joe's voice trails off when Bill finishes.)* All right, all right! Never

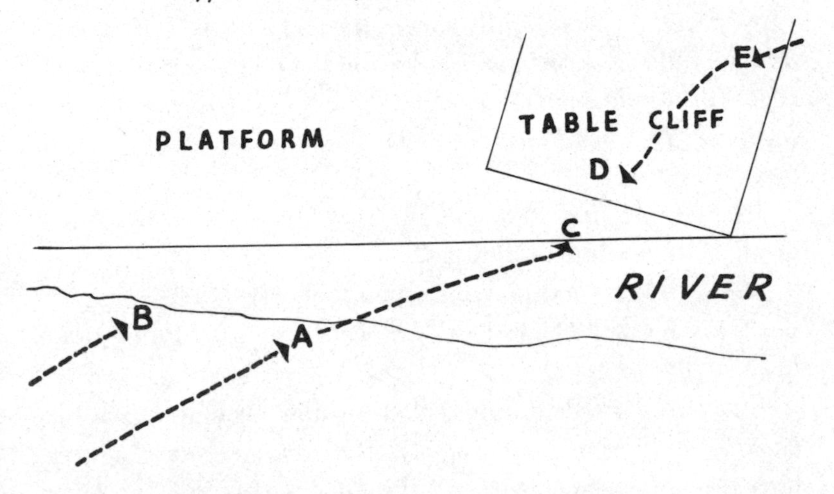

Stage Setting for "Boat Down River"

A—Where first three scouts take boat
B—Where Ol' Slowpoke appears up river from second boat at "A"
C—Where scouts land at base of cliff
D—Scouts on top of cliff
E—Farm boy appears

mind! You know I didn't . . . Oh, poof!

PETE. Why wait? The three of us can take one boat and leave the other for him.

BILL. Second the motion. I'll row. *(Starts to get into the boat.)*

JOE *(Hauls him back.)* No, you don't. You can be ballast.

BILL *(Protests.)* But that's what I always am.

PETE. Well! *(Bills looks insulted.)*

JOE. Pete, you take the stern.

PETE. Whatever you say, Joe. *(Gets in the boat, moves carefully to the stern while Joe steadies the boat, partly crouching to give the impression of sitting, and reaches for the oars.)*

JOE *(Gets in and takes the bow seat, also stooping, reaches for the oars.)* Okay, Bill, shove off and hop in. *(Bill, with a mighty heave, leaps into the boat with the grace of a wounded buffalo, plunges into Joe, who struggles to keep from falling over. Joe and Pete rock with the boat and steady it with their oars.)*

JOE *(As he and Pete get the boat under control.)* Good grief, Bill! Want to swamp us?

PETE. Boy, you'd make a hippo look graceful!

BILL. Well, I offered to row. *(Joe and Pete back water with the oars.)*

JOE. Hold it, Pete, and I'll bring her around. *(Does so, backing water with one oar and pulling on the other. The boys turn around together to head the boat toward the far bank, boys having their backs to it.)* Now, dig! *(Pete and Joe row, boys moving slowly in stooped positions.)* Keep a lookout, Bill, and let us know when we're getting close.

BILL *(Turns at his waist to watch, sees a bird and stares up, looking ahead suddenly and yelling.)* Land ho! *(The boat hits the land immediately afterward, boys tumbling backward. Pete and Joe struggle up to steady the boat with the oars.)*

PETE. That's what I like. Lots of warning.

JOE. All right, Hippo, all ashore that's going ashore.

BILL *(Lurches out, Joe and Pete swaying and steadying the boat with the oars. Bill turns after regaining his balance.)* I'll pull you up. *(Leans down to seize the boat.)*

JOE *(Tries to forestall him.)* Just a min . . . *(Bill heaves and Joe tumbles back against Pete.)*

BILL. What did you say?

JOE *(Disgusted.)* Never mind. *(Gets out, followed by Pete. They pull the boat up on the bank. Joe studies the cliff.)* Now we have to get up this cliff.

PETE *(Surveys it.)* Then let's get. *(Pete and Joe climb the cliff, making quite a project of it. Bill tries even harder but in vain as he keeps sliding back down. Gives up.)*

BILL. Hey! Throw me a line!

PETE *(Looks at Joe.)* Should we?

JOE. Hmm!

BILL. Aw, come on! I can't get up.

PETE. After all, how much weight can one cliff hold? *(Joe grins.)*

BILL. Please, fellers!

JOE. Oh, well! *(Uncoils the rope and lets one end down to Bill.)* Can you tie a bowline around your chest?

PETE. Or a slipknot around your neck?

BILL. Knots to you! *(Ties the bowline around his chest.)* All right! Heave ho, and *don't let go! (Joe and Pete heave while Bill struggles valiantly. Pete grabs him by the seat of his pants to pull him over the edge.)*

PETE *(As Bill lumbers to his feet.)* Well, here we be up here, and still no Slowpoke over there. *(Sees Slowpoke coming.)* Whoops! Spoke too soon. There he comes. *(Points to*

Slowpoke arriving on the far bank up river from the boat, which he doesn't see.)

BILL. How do you like that? He's not even on the right trail.

JOE. And he doesn't see the boat. *(Motions toward the boat down river, Pete and Bill likewise. Slowpoke just shrugs his shoulders.)*

PETE *(Sighs.)* Looks like this is a good time to try some signaling. *(Gets out a Morse flag.)* I'll send "Boat Down River" in Morse. *(Does so, but Slowpoke merely shrugs his shoulders.)* Just as I thought. He doesn't know his code.

JOE. Well, I can try semaphore. *(Gets out the semaphore flags, sends the same message. Slowpoke shrugs his shoulders.)* Nope! He doesn't know semaphore either.

BILL. Maybe if we sorta drew pictures. *(Pretends to shove the boat into the water, gets in, picks up the oars, backwaters, turns around and rows over; then points down river. Slowpoke looks confused, scratches his head, and finally shrugs his shoulders once more.)* Can you tie that for thickheadedness?

JOE. It's no use. We'll have to go get him. He probably can't row anyhow.

PETE. Well, let's leave Bill here. No use hauling him up the mountain again.

FARM BOY *(Comes up.)* What seems to be the trouble?

BILL. Ol' Slowpoke over there *(Points.)* got so far behind we took one boat and left the other for him. Now he's on the wrong trail and doesn't see the boat down the river.

PETE. And I sent him a message in Morse code, but he doesn't know his Morse code.

JOE. And I sent him a message in semaphore and he doesn't savvy that either.

BILL. And I even demonstrated for him but the stupe just can't understand nothin'.

PETE. So, we just have to go get the dummy.

FARM BOY. Is that all? *(Cups his hands to his mouth.)* Hey, you over there!

SLOWPOKE *(Also cups his hands and shouts.)* Yeah?

FARM BOY. Boat down river! *(Points.)*

SLOWPOKE *(Looks down river.)* Thanks! *(Joe, Pete and Bill look embarrassed and mortified.)*

(CURTAIN)

GOODNIGHT!
(Otherwise known as "Goodnight!")

A part of the world is given an opportunity to love two young lovers but at that hour of the night the desire to sleep in peace is stronger.
PARTS: 4 Males, 4 Females
COSTUMES: Regular clothes (lovers), night clothes (neighbors)
PROPS: Improvised windows and door.

Cast of Characters

Boy, Girl, Father (of Girl), and Neighbors: Snoopy (Female), Romantic (Young Female), Grumpy (Male), Stuffy (Female), Sleepy (Male).

Properties

Door: Can be made of cardboard and scrap lumber, with a curtain, divided in the middle, covering the upper half as though it were glass.

Windows: One per neighbor. Large cartons can be placed on tables, or piled on top one another to attain sufficient height, tops and bottoms being cut out and cartons fastened together so that actors can stand on chairs, etc., inside and look out the windows. Windows are of the type that part in the middle, thus being easy to open and close. Windows for Snoopy and Romantic can be fastened open, with curtains optional.

The scene opens on the young couple approaching the door in the center of the stage. They walk slowly, holding hands, and turn to face each other in front of the door, with hands toward the door. They really must act thataway about each other and put a lot of inflections and meaning into their "Goodnights."

GIRL *(Softly.)* Goodnight!

BOY. Goodnight! *(Looks at her and sighs.)*

GIRL *(Looking soulful or something.)* Goodnight!

BOY *(More of the same.)* Goodnight! *(Snoopy and Romantic open their respective windows, or look out if they are fastened open. One is on each side of the stage. Snoopy snoops, "tsks" and so forth throughout the skit. Romantic sighs, smiles, rests her head on her hands and so on. They react in character to remarks of the other neighbors.)*

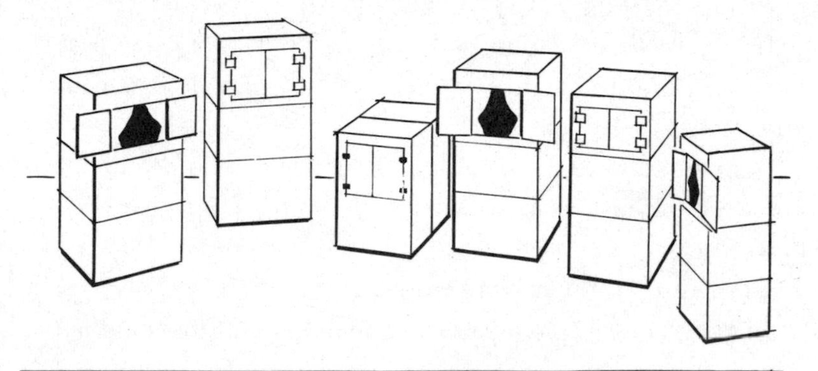

GIRL *(Pulling gently as though to release her hand.)* Well, goodnight!

BOY *(Holding on.)* Goodnight!

GRUMPY *(Opens the window and yells.)* Goodnight! *(Closes the window.)*

GIRL *(Hand lightly on the boy's chest as he edges closer.)* Goodnight!

BOY *(Takes her hand so that he holds both.)* Goodnight!

GIRL *(Looking down, softly.)* Goodnight!

BOY *(Releases one hand.)* Goodnight!

STUFFY *(Opens the window, tartly.)* How is a body to sleep if you two are going to keep that up all night?

GIRL *(To the boy.)* I can't go in if you won't let me go.

STUFFY. Then please let her go.

BOY *(Does so forlornly.)* Now I'll have to go home.

STUFFY. And about time! Goodnight! *(Closes the window.)*

GIRL. I'll have to go in now. *(Makes a feeble pretense.)* Goodnight!

BOY *(Shuffling his feet.)* Goodnight!

GIRL. Well, I have to go in. *(More pretense.)*

BOY. Before you do, would you . . . may I . . . could you . . .?

SLEEPY *(Opens the window.)* Look, bud, kiss her and go home, so the rest of us can get some sleep. *(Closes the window.)*

GIRL *(Softly.)* You were saying . . .

SLEEPY *(Opens the window.)* Goodnight! *(Closes the window.)*

BOY. Well, I . . . that is, I thought . . . well . . . *(Father peers through the curtain, his face purple. The curtain closes.)*

GIRL *(Expectantly.)* Yes . . .

BOY *(Looking down, his hand in his pocket, he does not see the door open. The girl is pulled in by father. Father stands in the doorway, glaring at him.)* Well, before I say "Goodnight" . . . *(With a sudden resolution, he straightens up and kisses father with a loud smack. Then he sees who it is and exclaims.)* Goodnight! *(Exits, but fast. Father looks the way a father would look who had just been kissed by his daughter's boy friend.)*

(CURTAIN)

(The curtain opens and the boy comes back on stage to say . . .)

Boy. The title of this little show was . . . *(The door and all windows open and all say . . .)* Goodnight!

(CURTAIN)

(The curtain opens to reveal the girl in the boy's arms about to be kissed. They turn faces toward the audience and say . . .) Goodnight! *(And then they turn to each other again as the curtain closes. The entire cast shouts from behind the curtain . . .)* Goodnight!

"POT OF GOLD" QUIZ SHOW

By JOHNNY MCGUCKIN

In view of the way quiz shows are going this take-off may not be so far off, but perhaps the sponsor should be the one to get the ax.
PARTS: 5 Males
COSTUMES: Regular clothes and improvised guard uniforms
PROPS: Pot of gold and incidentals.

Five actors are needed: Quizmaster, Contestant, Question Custodian, and two Guards. Props required: Several envelopes with a list of questions inside (the same list in each envelope), a hatchet, a box with lock and key, and a pot of gold (black iron pot preferred with anything to serve as a filler to within two or three inches of the top where gilded rocks can be piled up to give a "pot of gold" appearance.)

(The skit opens with the Quizmaster introducing a contestant.)

Q.M. Good evening, folks. This is the Pot of Gold Quiz Show where anyone can win a genuine Pot of Gold. *(Holds up the pot, making believe it is very heavy.)* As you know, we have our contestant from last week who won the silver lining for his last year's hat and is now trying for the Pot of Gold. Ladies and gentlemen, Mr. Melbatoast Ban Schurd, 3rd. *(Melba comes forward and bows to the audience.)* Of course, you can't have a quiz show without questions, so where is our Question Custodian, Mr. Dumptruck?

D.T. Right here, Mr. Boch. *(Comes forward carrying a locked box and flanked by two guards.)*

"Questions, please," says Quizmaster Johnny McGuckin to custodian Howard Dunlap as Bob Hack and Tony Devine stand guard. Contestant Ronnie James looks on and the Pot of Gold waits patiently on the floor.

Q.M. Very good! As you can see, we keep our questions under lock and key, and I have the only key. *(Holds it up and then unlocks the box.)* And now, Melbatoast, if I may so address you, just reach into the box and select an envelope.

MELBA *(Reaches in the box and feels around, looks puzzled, and feels around some more.)* The box is empty.

Q.M. Impossible! *(Looks in the box.)* By George, it is empty! *(Looks real stern.)* Can you explain this, Mr. Dumptruck?

D. T. Yes, Mr. Boch. *(Takes the envelopes from his pocket.)* You had the only key, you know, so I couldn't get the questions in the box.

Q.M. *(Relaxing.)* That's different. *(To the audience.)* So you see, folks, that I have the only key and nobody else can get into the box. Thus, the safety of our questions is beyond question. *(To Melbatoast.)* And now, Melbatoast, if you will select one of these envelopes. *(Fans them out for selection.)*

MELBA *(Chooses an envelope.)* I'll take this one.

Q.M. Very good! Now we must safeguard the other envelopes. *(Locks the box.)* First I carefully lock the box. *(Puts the key in his pocket.)* Then I pocket the key. *(Hands the envelopes to Dumptruck.)* And then I entrust the envelopes to Mr. Dumptruck. *(Mr. Dumptruck puts the envelopes in his pocket and marches off between the guards, carrying the box.)* Now before we begin the questions, let me repeat the conditions of this quiz. If you win, you get a genuine pot of gold *(Holds up the pot, with effort, then sets it down.)* . . . but if you fail to get every question *all right*—not half right, but all right, you lose *everything*. Let me repeat, you lose *everything*. Do you agree to these conditions, Melbatoast?

MELBA. I do.

Q.M. Very good. Now for the questions. *(Opens the envelope and takes out questions. These can be: "What color was General Washington's white horse?" "When do we celebrate the Fourth of July?" "How many bananas in a dozen?", etc., with Melbatoast getting each correct with considerable effort, including a hint or so, until . . .)* You are wonderful, Melbatoast, and it certainly looks as though you will win the Pot of Gold. However, let me warn you once again that if you do not get this last question all right—not half right but all right—you lose *everything*. Are you ready for the last question, Melbatoast?

MELBA *(Confidently.)* Ready, Mr. Boch.

Q.M. Bravo! And here it is. Who is buried in Grant's Tomb?

MELBA *(Smiling.)* That's easy. General Grant.

Q.M. Sorry!

MELBA *(Quickly.)* General U. S. Grant.

Q.M. No, I'm very sorry, you are only half right. Both General and *Mrs.* Grant are buried in Grant's Tomb. *(Dramatically.)* So, Mr. Melbatoast Ban Schurd, 3rd, you have failed and must pay the penalty. Your money, sir. *(Melba hands over his wallet.)* . . . and your watch *(Melba hands over his watch.)* . . . and your Mickey Mouse ring *(Melba gives him the ring.)* . . . and your coat *(Takes off his coat.)* . . . tie *(Takes off his tie.)* . . . shirt *(Off comes his shirt.)* . . . and *(Shrugs his shoulders.)*

MELBA *(Anxiously.)* Is that all?

Q.M. Not quite. We said you lost *everything*, remember? Right this way. *(The guards appear to escort Melba out. The Quizmaster picks up a hatchet. Offstage.)* Now, if you will place your head upon this block, sir. *(A loud blow and a scream is heard. The Quizmaster comes running back on and looks at his watch.)* Next contestant, quickly, before the police arrive.

GRANNY AND THE GUPPIES

The Terrible Guppies, the baddest of them all, terrorize Coyote County until they come up against fearless, fast-drawin' Granny Perkins. A narrated, pantomime production made to order for a large group looking for something easily and quickly prepared.
PARTS: 11 to 13 Males, 4 Females, 1 Optional (narrator)
COSTUMES: Western, of course
PROPS: Express wagon and incidentals.

Cast of Characters

Granny Higgins
Meany and Moreso Guppy
Miners—Joe and Jake
Burro, the Burro
Jimmy, the Boy Ranger
Pony, Jimmy's Pony
Bank Teller
Mrs. Flintheart, Bank President
Stagecoach Driver
Two Lady Passengers
Four Coach Horses
Narrator

This narrator-pantomime Western farce is for a large group and does not require much rehearsal, the actors picking up their cues from the narration for the most part, although the action may get a little ahead of the narration in some spots, particularly the final fight between Granny and the Guppies.

If shy a few actors, some parts can be doubled or a couple of the stage coach horses may be eliminated.

Costumes are easily improvised in keeping with the parts. Paper bag heads for the Burro, Jimmy's Pony and the Stagecoach Horses are optional. However, these can readily be made as per the drawing and will add to the fun. The Guppies and Granny use broom or mop horses with rope reins. These may be tricked up as desired. An express wagon will do for the stagecoach, on which the driver and passengers must perch as best they may. Rope harness is needed for the team of horses and can be fastened to their shoulders. The driver carries a toy rifle.

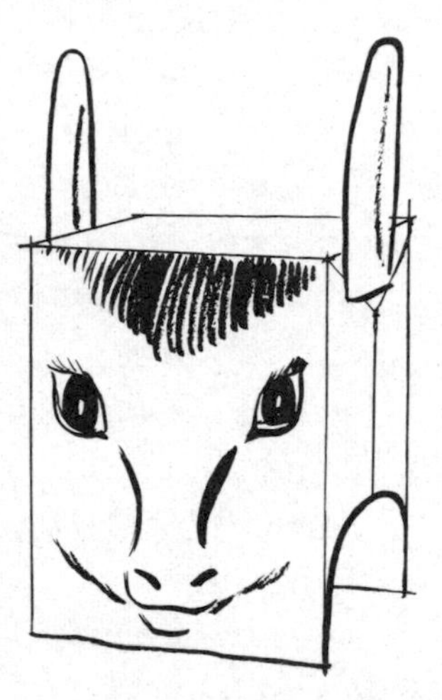

Lady passengers wear a flock of rings and necklaces and plenty of lipstick. The miners have a large burlap or paper bag stuffed with crumpled paper and tied together at the neck. They also have a "claim," a large piece of brown paper with "Claim No. 237" printed on it in large letters, and folded so as to go into Joe's pocket. Joe also has a pair of comic-type glasses.

Each Guppy needs a lollipop and Meany a small paper bag. The bank teller has a fair-sized bag of gold (stuffed with crumpled paper) and some stacks of newspaper money which can rest on a chair beside him when he is in his teller's cage, the rest of the cage being imaginary. The bank teller wears a tight-fitting stocking hat, flesh colored to give the imitation of a bald head, over which he wears a toupee which can be made of rope, etc.

Granny wears an old-fashioned dress, a white apron, a lace bonnet and a shawl held on her shoulders by means of a brooch in front. She should wear the most extravagant pair of six-guns and fancy belt. Her broom horse should look like a "Goodie" horse. The Guppies, Jimmy and Mrs. Flintheart also have guns.

All actors pantomime their "speeches" with exaggerated

mouth motions. The action calls for plenty of hamming.

NARRATOR. Ladies and gentlemen, hold tight to your chairs as we plunge you willy-nilly into the raw, reckless, ropin', ridin', rootin', tootin' Wild West of yesteryear, where men were quick on the draw or else—they just weren't, period. Yes, sir, here we go to Coyote County where a couple of hard working miners, Joe and Jake, are ready to take their precious bag of gold to the bank in town on their faithful old burro, named Burro. *(Jake, Joe and Burro come into view at one side of the stage. Jake has a bag of gold over his shoulder. Joe walks beside the burro.)*

"Well, Jake, Old Pal," says Joe *(Talking to the Burro.)* "we sure made a good haul this month."

"Correction, please," says Burro, the burro, "I'm Burro; Jake's ahead there with the gold." *(Joe stops, places both his hands on the burro's shoulders, and swings him around so as to study him face to face. Jake stops and waits for them.)*

"Just 'cause my old eyes are gettin' a mite weak don't think you can poke fun at me, Jake. We two have been pals too many years for that."

"Now look, Joe," says Burro, "I ought to know whether I am Burro or not." *(Joe reaches in his pocket and takes out glasses, wipes them with a bandanna handkerchief, puts them on and studies the burro some more.)*

"Well, I'll be doggoned," says Joe at last, "you are Burro, sure enough. Jake has a longer beard and shorter ears. But why aren't you carrying the gold like you're supposed to?"

"Oh, Jake's doing okay with it, isn't he?" asks Burro.

"That is not the point," Joe admonishes him. "Everybody knows that miners always have a burro to carry their gold to town and their supplies back. You should be ashamed of yourself, that's what you should be. *(Burro hangs his head.)* Now you march right straight over to Jake, apologize, and relieve him of the gold." *(The Guppies ride up quietly during this speech. Behind them comes Jimmy, the Boy Ranger, riding a pony. Jimmy dismounts on the far side of the stage and watches the Guppies approach the miners and Burro.)*

"Never mind," says Meany Guppy, as they both draw their guns. "We'll relieve Jake of the gold."

"Oh, no, you don't," says Joe. "This is our hard-earned gold and you ain't gonna take it from us."

"I," says Meany, "am Meany Guppy, and this is my brother, Moreso." *(Both remove their hats and bow with a flourish.)* "And now, *(Real nasty-like.)* up with your hands." *(Joe, Jake and Burro raise their hands, Jake, of course, dropping the bag of gold, which Moreso picks up.)* "Not you, Crowbait," says Meany to Burro. "What a stupid burro!" *(Burro hangs his head.)*

"From now on," says Meany to Joe and Jake, "we're gonna be your partners in this here mine, 'cause we're jumpin' your claim but we're gonna let you two keep on workin' it. Put your hands down, partners." *(Joe and Jake take their hands down.)*

"You can't jump our claim," Jake protests.

"Sure we can," says Meany. "Let's see it." *(Joe takes the claim from his pocket and hands it to Meany who opens up the claim to full size, holding it so that the audience can see the printing. He then spreads it out on the ground.)* "Now you will see how easily my brother, Moreso, can jump it." *(Moreso, with the bag of gold over his shoulder, goes up to one side of the paper, makes several practice bends as for a stand-*

ing broad jump and then makes a mighty effort at a jump, coming down on the far edge of the paper.)

"See! You can't do it!" Jakes gloats.

"That's because he was carrying that heavy bag of gold. I'll relieve him of it. *(Takes the gold from Moreso.)* Now I'll show you how easy it is." *(Meany takes his place at the edge of the paper, makes practice bends and jumps with the gold, landing on the paper as his brother did.)*

"See!" says Jake, "can't neither of you do it."

"That's because of these heavy guns," says Moreso. *(Both Guppies remove their guns, handing them to Joe and Jake to hold. Then both go up to the claim, holding the bag of gold between them, take practice bends and jump clear over the claim together.)*

"See!" they shout in triumph. "We jumped it!"

"Shucks!" say Joe and Jake. "They sure enough did."

"Now," says Meany, "each month we'll call for our share of the gold which you will put in this bag, *(Holds up the bag of gold.)* and you'll get your share, which goes in this bag. *(Pulls a small bag from his pocket and hands it to Joe. Jake is folding up the claim.)* Fair enough?"

"Why, sure!" says Joe. "A bag apiece is fair enough." *(Guppies start to ride off.)* "Just a minute," Joe calls, "you forgot your guns." *(Guppies feel their hips.)* "You're so right," says Moreso. *(Guppies return and get their guns, put them on and ride off.)*

"You know, Joe," says Jake, "I think we've been robbed."

"Could be," says Joe, scratching his head. "But they had the guns and we were unarmed, so what else could we do?"

"Nothin', I guess," says Jake. "Anyhow, it was sure nice of them to make us fifty-fifty partners. Come on, we better get back to work." *(Joe and Jake turn and go off.)* "And I'm supposed to be the donkey," says Burro. *(Burro follows Joe and Jake.)*

"You know, Pony," says Jimmy, the Boy Ranger to Pony, his pony, "I think they *were* robbed."

"I wouldn't say that," protests Pony. "The Guppies did jump their claim all right, and they had that heavy bag of gold between them when they did it. You saw that yourself."

"Yeah," says Jimmy, "but do you think it was a fair divide?"

"They get a bag of gold and the Guppies get a bag of gold," says Pony. "What can be fairer than that?"

"I dunno," replies Jimmy. *(Scratches his head.)* "I think we better follow them—the Guppies, I mean."

"If you ask me, this Boy Ranger stuff is going to your head," says Pony, as Jimmy mounts him. "And me with a lame back." *(Jimmy rides him out.)*

(The curtain closes, if there is one. Otherwise, the bank teller simply moves the chair with the gold and money on it on the stage and takes his place in an imaginary teller's cage at one side of the stage.)

And now our story takes us to Deadhead City where the Bank Teller of the Deadhead Bank and Bust Company is counting money. *(The curtain opens on the bank teller counting on his fingers. After each count of ten he turns one finger down.)* Jimmy, the Boy Ranger, rides in, looking everywhere for the Guppies. *(Guppies ride in on the far side of the stage from the bank teller, right behind Jimmy. Jimmy dismounts and shakes his head in discouragement.)*

"Here, Sonny, hold our horses," says Meany, as Jimmy turns in surprise. *(They hand the reins of their horses to Jimmy, and cross the street to the bank and go in.)* "We're drawin' out everybody's money," says Meany. "I'm Meany Guppy and this is my brother, Moreso."

"Yeah," says Moreso, "we'll take your money or your life."

"You mean I have a choice?" asks the Bank Teller. *(He turns and calls.)* "Oh, Mrs. Flintheart!"

"What is it?" asks Mrs. Flintheart, the Bank President. *(She comes on the stage, looking real mannish with six-guns at her waist.)*

"It's the Guppies, and they want my money or my life."

"Well, if it was *your money*," snaps Mrs. Flintheart, "I'd give it to them, but it happens to be *my* money, so let them have *your* life. It's all you've got."

"Mrs. Flintheart," snarls Meany, real mean-like, "we'll trouble you for that thar money."

"Try and get it," she replies, drawing her gun. But Moreso beats her to the draw—Bang! Bang! Bang!—and Mrs. Flintheart drops her gun, clutches at her heart and slowly crumples to the floor.

"Now," says Meany, "we'll have that money." He seizes

the bars of the teller's cage, and with one mighty heave, pulls them apart, reaches through and grabs the frightened bank teller by the hair of his head. "Hand it over," he orders. The now terrified teller does so. *(As the bank teller stoops to get the bag of gold and packs of newspaper money, he leaves his toupee behind in the clutch of Meany Guppy, coming back up under the toupee again as he hands over the gold and money. Meany releases the toupee and takes the money. Guppies exit, covering the teller with their guns. They hurry over to where Jimmy is holding their horses, holstering their guns as they go.)*

"Thanks, kiddo," says Meany to Jimmy, taking his horse. "You are a fine lad. Have a lollipop." *(Gives Jimmy a lollipop.)*

"You, too," says Moreso to Pony. *(Hands the pony a lollipop. The Guppies then mount their horses and ride off.)*

"You know, Pony," says Jimmy, the Boy Ranger, to Pony, his Pony, "I think they are the Terrible Guppies and that they have robbed the bank."

"Let's not go jumping to conclusions," protests Pony. "Baddies wouldn't give us lollipops, would they?"

"But you heard those shots, and they had their guns out when they came out, and one of them was smoking, and they had that bag of gold and all that money."

"Purely circumstantial evidence," argues Pony. "The way I see it . . ."

But before he could argue the case any further, the bank teller comes running out, shouting, "The Guppies have robbed the bank and shot Mrs. Flintheart as dead as a mackerel."

Jimmy, the Boy Ranger, looks reproachfully at Pony, his Pony.

"So I was wrong," says Pony. "Now what?"

"We must ride like the wind and get Granny Higgins. She will stop those Terrible Guppies."

"But, Jimmy," protests Pony, "can't someone else go? Every time we ride like the wind, *I* do all the galloping. *You* just sit."

"Well, sitting is what I'm supposed to do, and the galloping is your job. So let's get at it," and with that Jimmy jumps on Pony.

"Oh, why was I ever born a pony?" moans Pony. "Oh, well—Heigh-o! Pony, A-way!" And off he gallops like the loyal little pony he is. *(The curtain comes down, the* bank *teller goes off, and the curtain comes up.)*

In the meantime our story shifts to the road into Deadhead down which the stagecoach is now thundering. *(The express wagon comes into view drawn by horses who pull it slowly around the stage, with much jumping up and down during the subsequent action, finally milling to a halt when the driver falls.)* But what's this? *(Guppies gallop on, their guns blazing.)* Those Terrible Guppies are shooting up the stage. The brave driver whips his fiery steeds on to greater speed and then takes up his trusty rifle and fires back, while his fair passengers wring their hands. What a battle! What a racket! Such bang-banging! *(Guppies and the driver keeping up the banging.)* Has anyone got an aspirin?

The stagecoach driver is hit. He's dropping his rifle. He's tumbling off the stage. The Guppies ride up and stop the horses. "Whoa! Whoa!" says Meany.

"All ashore that's going ashore," says Moreso. "I mean get down outa that stage before we fill you full of lead."

The stage door opens and two beautiful but badly frightened ladies step down.

"Well, now," says Meany, "what have we here? Two lovely ladies, anxious to be relieved of all their heavy jewelry. We are at your service, ladies. I am Meany Guppy," and he bows gallantly.

"And I am Moreso Guppy," says Moreso, and he bows.

"And now, ladies," says Meany, "we'll give those pretty fingers a rest by taking off those heavy old rings." *(Moreso takes off his hat and collects rings from the ladies.)*

And thus the frightened ladies are robbed of the cherished tokens given to them by their loving admirers.

"You will regret this high-handed robbery when the Goodies get here," the ladies tell the Guppies. "And the Goodies will soon be coming."

"What makes you so sure of that?" asks Meany.

"Because they always come galloping when you rob a stagecoach on TV," reply the ladies.

"Well, this ain't TV," says Moreso, "and the Goodies ain't comin' 'cause we done shot every last Goodie in Coyote County."

"That's right," says Meany. "There's nothin' left but Baddies and a mess of In-betweenies. Get their necklaces, Moreso."

"Necklaces comin' off," says Moreso, holding his hat as the poor ladies remove their necklaces and drop them in. *(Both take off about six necklaces.)*

But unbeknownst to the Guppies, Jimmy, the Boy Ranger, has done his duty well—with Pony's galloping, that is, and here comes Granny Higgins a-ridin' to the rescue. *(Granny rides on the stage on a broomstick horse.)* Granny fires her gun in the air and the battle is on. *(Moreso drops his hat full of jewelry and both draw their guns, as the ladies duck down and crawl under the express wagon where they watch Granny and the Guppies shoot it out. Granny gallops up, banging away, dismounts, and ducks back and forth, crouching and firing, with Guppies doing the same.)*

Oh, what a battle! Granny and the Guppies, face to face at last. What a tale to tell our kiddies of a winter's evening, if we ever live through it. The Terrible Guppies, the baddest of them all, and Granny, of whom, of course, there is nobody gooder. Get 'em, Granny. Shoot them thar polecats!

Ah, Meany's guns are empty now, but he doesn't throw them away like they do on TV. No, indeed, he holsters them because he knows he can get ten cents apiece for empties at the super market. And now he goes to get the fallen stagecoach driver's rifle. And now, Granny and Moreso have also emptied their guns and holstered them so they can get their refunds.

Woe is us! If Meany gets the rifle, Granny is a goner. Poor, brave, old Granny! But what have we here? Why, it's Jimmy, the Boy Ranger. *(Jimmy gallops up and gets the rifle. If possible, Pony holds fast to his legs while Jimmy leans down and picks up the gun. Otherwise, Jimmy dismounts and gets it.)* Jimmy quickly swings around to cover the Guppies, but the stagecoach horses are in between and the Terrible Guppies attack Granny with their fists. What chance has a dear little old lady against those two ruffians? *(A terrific mock battle ensues with the narrator following it as best he may, such as . . .)*

Meany drops Granny with a terrific blow to the jaw, but Granny bounces up and sends Meany staggering with her right and knocks Moreso down with a body shattering left. *(Etc., etc., until . . .)*

There goes Meany down again, and this time it is for

keeps. He's had it. And so goes Moreso. *(Granny brushes off her clothes and wipes her hands, as the ladies crawl from under the express wagon and the driver carefully comes to life.)*

"You were magnificent!" say the ladies. "You must be none other than Granny Higgins!"

"'Twarn't much!" says Granny with her customary modesty, as the Boy Ranger rides over and dismounts. "Jimmy, here, is the real hero. He is the one who rode like the wind to bring me the word, and if he hadn't risked his life getting that rifle, well, I guess there wouldn't be no more Granny Higgins."

"Oh, you wonderful boy!" exclaim the ladies as they embrace the bashful lad. *(Jimmy struggles to escape as the ladies hug and kiss him. Pony laughs. Jimmy wrenches himself loose from the ladies.)*

But, Jimmy, modest youngster, gently frees himself from their tender embrace, and says, "Pony deserves all the credit. He is the one that did all the galloping. All I did was sit." *(Pony turns to flee but the ladies grab him and embrace and kiss him. The paper bag head can come off while he struggles vainly to escape their affection. Jimmy and Granny wink at each other. They shake hands. Jimmy prods the Guppies with the rifle. They struggle to their feet and are marched off by Granny and Jimmy, leaving Pony struggling with the ladies.)*

(CURTAIN)

THE HAUNTED CASTLE

A skit is the perfect way to have fun with a ghost and the success of this farce will amply repay you for the effort put into preparing same. The "Here Comes the Ghost" parody of "Old Black Joe" will quite likely be sung some more after the skit is over, and you can have more fun with the headless ghost from time to time.

PARTS: 2 Male, 2 Female, 2 Optional
COSTUMES: Ghost, crowns and—better read the script
PROPS: Crypt, piggy bank (rather special) and—same advice as above

---

Cast of Characters

King, Queen, Prince, Princess, Headless Ghost, Narrator

PROPS: Hand mirror
- Dried peas and bowl
- Bubble gum
- Pirate eye patch, head scarf and cardboard cutlass
- Pirate comic book
- 4 Crowns—made of cardboard and decorated
- Old sheet with piece of cheesecloth sewed in for face
- Box headpiece to go under sheet (see drawing)
- Glass fish bowl disguised as piggy bank
- Long cord or fishline
- 4 sets of night clothes (pajamas, nightgowns, bath robes, etc.)
- 1 crypt—cardboard
- Several chairs and a table

A scout or cub neckerchief or any colored cloth of triangular shape will do for the pirate headpiece. The eye patch can be cut out of black cloth. Considerable imagination may be used with the crowns. However, the King's should be the most elaborate.

A cardboard box about the breadth and thickness of the ghost's body, fitted for the head is needed to go under the sheet so as to give an impression of a headless ghost. This box can rest on the shoulders, with the front cut out for the face as per the drawing. An old sheet is draped over the entire body with a patch cut out where the ghost's face comes and cheesecloth sewed in. White sailor pants may be worn and plain white sneakers or white cloth cut to fit over the shoes. The cheesecloth insert is needed for seeing and breathing since there should not be any eye or nose holes. The sheet should be large enough to permit the arm motions described in the skit.

A glass fish bowl, either round or with two flat sides, roughly the size of a human head, can be painted to resemble a piggy bank, a piece of white cardboard or paper taped over the top, with a slit cut for coins. A smooth piece of white cardboard should be securely cemented to the bottom with a piece of fishline or a strong white cord inserted between the glass and the cardboard with a loop barely accessible at one side. The rest of the cord or fishline can be attached to this loop at the proper time.

The crypt can be fashioned from large cardboard cartons. It must be long enough and wide enough for the ghost to lie down in, with space to spare for the piggy bank head. It should be about two feet high with a cardboard slab as a lid. If it can be covered with white paper, such as is used for table coverings at church banquets, it will look fine. At the head of this crypt a small door is cut, just large enough for the piggy bank head, the cardboard itself serving as the hinge.

Now I think we are ready for the narrator to set the stage for "The Haunted Castle."

NARRATOR *(Before the closed curtains.)* Once upon a time there was a King who lived in a haunted castle. His wife, who was the Queen, because she was his wife, also lived in the haunted castle, because she lived with the King, since he was her husband.

They had one son, a boy, who also lived in the haunted castle because he was their child, and liked to be with his mother and father, besides which he had nowhere else to go. He would have been their only child except that they also had one daughter, a girl, who was the prince's sister and also the princess; which really isn't very complicated, once you figure it out. Anyhow—

One night the King and the Queen and the Prince and the Princess were all in the castle living room acting very Kingly, Queenly, Princely and Princessly, as they always did.

ACT I

(The curtain opens on the living room scene. Three chairs and a small table are the only essential furniture. Toss in anything else you want for the looks of things, but you will have to move it all out again for act three. The piggy bank is on the table. The King is seated in a chair with his crown on lopsided and blowing bubble gum. The Queen is seated near him, spitting dried peas at a bowl on the table, displaying considerable pleasure or chagrin with regard to hits and *misses. The Prince is down on the floor on his hands and knees, bottom up, reading a pirate comic book. He has a pirate's patch over one eye and a pirate headpiece under his crown, and is holding a cardboard cutlass, which he sometimes grips between his teeth. The Princess is perched in a chair making faces at herself in a mirror.)*

GHOST *(Faintly, offstage.)* Where's my head? *(Everyone pauses to listen.)*

QUEEN. Oh, dear! He's out looking for his head again. Wouldn't you think he would remember where he put it?

KING *(Looks at the Queen in mild reproof.)* He didn't put his head anywhere, my Queen. It was taken from him.

QUEEN. Then whoever took it should return it. Goodness knows, I return everything I borrow. *(The King sighs, opens his mouth to speak, but closes it again.)*

PRINCE *(Jumps up and runs to the King.)* Daddy King, tell us again about how he lost his head.

PRINCESS *(Jumps up and runs to the King.)* Yes, Daddy King, tell us again about how he lost his head. *(The Prince and Princess sit on the King's knees if practicable. Otherwise, as close to the King as they can conveniently get.)*

QUEEN *(Sighs and removes any dried peas still in her mouth.)* Yes, Husband King, suppose you tell us again how he lost his head.

KING. Well, it happened a long time ago when—Once upon a time there was a King who lived in a castle . . .

PRINCE. This castle, Daddy King?

KING. This very castle. And this King ruled his kingdom with an iron hand . . .

PRINCESS. Why, wasn't he married?

KING. Hush! Now this King was an old meany, if there ever was one, and whenever he wanted something that belonged to one of his subjects, like a horse, or cow, or . . .

PRINCE. Bicycle?

KING. There were no bicycles in those days.

PRINCE *(Pouting.)* Nor in these days as far as I can see.

KING *(Sternly.)* That will be enough out of you, young man. *(Clears his throat.)* Anyhow, whatever the king wanted, and he was always wanting something that belonged to somebody else, he just sent his soldiers, and they took it. And if the person from whom his soldiers took whatever it was they took that the king wanted, complained to the king, he would just laugh and say, "Try and find it." So, after awhile the people got so mad they came to the castle . . .

PRINCESS. Uninvited?

KING. You can say that again. And they grabbed the King and chopped his head right smack off. Then they hid the head and said, "Now, let him try to find his own head for a change." Well, that old meany of a King has been trying to find his head ever since.

QUEEN. Now that's what I call a nice cheerful bedtime story, so let's all go to bed and have pleasant dreams. *(All get up as though to retire, saying "Goodnight, Daddy King, Mama Queen, Son Prince, Daughter Princess, Husband King, Wife Queen, Brother Prince, Sister Princess," as the case may be.)*

(CURTAIN)

(Narrator invites the audience to get in the act by singing "Where's My Head" to the tune of "Old Black Joe.")

WHERE'S MY HEAD?

Here comes the ghost,
The King without a head;
Five hundred years
He hasn't stayed in bed,
'Cause he keeps lookin' for it everywhere
I hear his ghostly voice a-callin'
"Where's my head?"

Chorus: He's coming, he's coming,
He's a-lookin' for his head;
I hear his ghostly voice a-callin'
"Where's my head?"

Make sure your own
Head's on secure and tight,
Or he may take
It in the dead of night;
And you'll be him, the ghost without a head;
I hear his ghostly voice a-callin'
"Where's my head?"

(Chorus)

If you would save
Your own head from the King,
Just make a face
As mean as anything;
He'll be so scared, he'll wish that he was dead;
I hear his ghostly voice a-callin'
"Where's my head?"

(Chorus)

(The words can be printed on a blackboard, thrown on a screen, or reproduced on slips of paper which can be passed out to the audience. By the time arrangements have been made for singing and everyone is warmed up, the actors may be ready for act two without the necessity of singing the third verse. In this case it can be saved until the end of act two. The narrator can introduce the second act by suggesting that those present with weak hearts close their eyes until it is over.)

ACT II

(The curtain opens on the same scene as before but without anyone being present. If possible, the stage should be dark.)

GHOST *(Still faint but louder than before.)* Where's my head?

PRINCESS *(Offstage; frightened.)* Daddy King! Daddy King! *(Comes running on the stage.)* Help! Daddy King! He's after me!

PRINCE *(Running on the stage.)* I'm after you and stop screeching like that!

GHOST *(Louder and closer.)* Where's my head?

PRINCESS *(Throws her arms around the neck of the Prince.)* Oh, Brother Prince, save me!

PRINCE *(Trying vainly to untangle himself.)* If you don't stop strangling me, I'll need artificial respiration.

KING *(Enters.)* What ho! What gives? And stuff like that. *(He brings a lamp or candle as does the Queen who also enters.)*

QUEEN. Heavens to Betsy! What's all the fuss? *(The coming of light reveals all in their night clothes: pajamas, bathrobes or old-fashioned nightgowns. It would be fine if the King, particularly, had on a nightgown and night cap.)*

PRINCESS *(Still hanging onto the Prince.)* Save me, Daddy King, save me!

QUEEN *(Puts the light on the table as does the King.)* Now, Princess Daughter, let's not get excited. We must . . .

GHOST *(Very close.)* Where's my head?

QUEEN *(Throws her arms around the King's neck.)* Oh, Husband King, save me!

GHOST *(Enters. The King, Queen, Prince and Princess huddle together facing him.)* Ah! Four heads! One of them should be mine, but which? *(The King, Queen, Prince and Princess each point at another's head, making a circle of head-pointing.)* We shall see!

PRINCE. With what?

GHOST. Silence! *(Picks up the mirror the Princess was using before, then points at the Princess and beckons with an index finger three times. The Princess, as though in a trance, comes slowly to the Ghost while the others watch. The Ghost indicates the Princess is to stand on a chair or stool as may be best suited to their respective sizes. He then stands in front of her with his back to her so that her head appears where he has none. She leans forward to emphasize the placing of her head on his shoulders. He then studies the mirror; she makes faces. He shudders, turns and indicates she is to return to her place. He then points at the Prince and beckons three times with his index finger. The Prince comes forward and takes his place as directed. The Prince already has on his pirate headpiece and quickly puts on the eye patch; also a mustache if he has one, takes the cutlass between his teeth and looks real fierce when the Ghost sees him in the mirror. The Ghost cowers and turns to direct the Prince to his place. He then summons the Queen in the same fashion. She slips some dried peas in her mouth and, when he looks into the mirror, lets fly with a volley at the mirror. The Ghost jumps and grabs his chest as though shot. He sends her back and summons the King. The King blows bubble gum at him and the Ghost brings up his hands before his face, if he had a face, and sends the King back. The Ghost looks around and sees the piggy bank.)* Ah, I see a head! *(Goes for the piggy bank.)*

PRINCE. Lay off! That's my piggy bank! *(The King grabs the Prince as he starts forward and holds him, clapping one hand over his mouth. The Prince struggles in vain during the following.)*

GHOST *(Makes sure his shoulders are on straight, places the piggy bank on where his head should be, and looks in the mirror.)* At last! I've found my head! I'd know it anywhere! *(Can either exit with the head on his shoulders or lift it off and carry it out. If it falls and breaks some nice ad-libbing will be in order. There should be some money in it so that it will rattle.)*

PRINCE *(As the King releases him.)* He swiped my piggy bank!

KING. Better your piggy bank than one of our heads, son Prince.

QUEEN. Yes, better your piggy bank than one of our heads, son Prince.

PRINCESS. Yes, better your piggy bank than one of our heads, brother Prince.

PRINCE *(Sulking.)* I want my piggy bank.

(CURTAIN)

(The narrator returns to lead the audience in singing "Where's My Head?" again, calling their attention to the third verse, in case they ever meet the King without a head. Suggests that those who frighten easily give their heads to their neighbors for safe keeping during the third act.)

ACT III

(The curtain opens on a bare stage except for a crypt in center rear. The Ghost is lying down in the crypt, the piggy bank head in position, just inside the small door, which the Ghost can easily open from inside.)

PRINCE *(Ghostly voice, offstage.)* Where's my piggy bank? *(The Ghost lifts the lid or otherwise starts to peek out of the crypt when the Prince is heard again. Hastily lies down again.)*

PRINCE *(Very close.)* Where's my piggy bank? *(Enters in pirate regalia, looks all around, examines the crypt, goes to the far side of the stage, facing the small door at the head of the crypt. Whistles. Someone offstage pulls on the cord which has been fastened to the loop at the bottom of the piggy bank and laid along the rear of the stage where it will not be seen by the audience. The Ghost opens the door and the piggy bank comes out and slowly moves across the stage to the Prince, following him offstage.)*

GHOST *(Gets out of the crypt, setting his shoulders straight.)* Bring back my head. *(Starts in the direction the Prince departed.)*

PRINCE *(Returns.)* Now, just a minute, that was my piggy bank, not your old head. By the way, how long have you been looking around here for your head?

GHOST. Five hundred years.

PRINCE. Then it's time you looked somewhere else, and I've got an idea. *(The Prince then directs the Ghost to the place where the show is taking place, telling him there are plenty of heads there and he should find one to suit.)*

GHOST. Why, that sounds like a wonderful idea. I shall go there at once. Thank you very, very much.

PRINCE. Not at all. Good night and good luck.

GHOST *(Turns to go.)* Where's my head?

(CURTAIN)

NARRATOR. Well, that's the third act of the play but thanks to that double-crossing little Prince, there may be a fourth act, and *we may be in it.*

GHOST *(Offstage.)* Where's my head?

NARRATOR. Great Scott! Here he comes! Just don't lose your head, folks, and everything will be all right.

GHOST *(Enters and goes among the audience looking for his head. Undoubtedly those whose heads he threatens to take will make faces and the Ghost will shy off. After two or three attempts by the Ghost to get a head, the narrator comes down to talk with him. The narrator tells the Ghost he can do much better if he goes to (Giving a name) some other or-*

ganization since they have heads they never even use. This should be a rival organization. Or he can direct the Ghost to a summer camp the group attends, some cemetery, etc. Ghost thanks him and exits.) Where's my head?

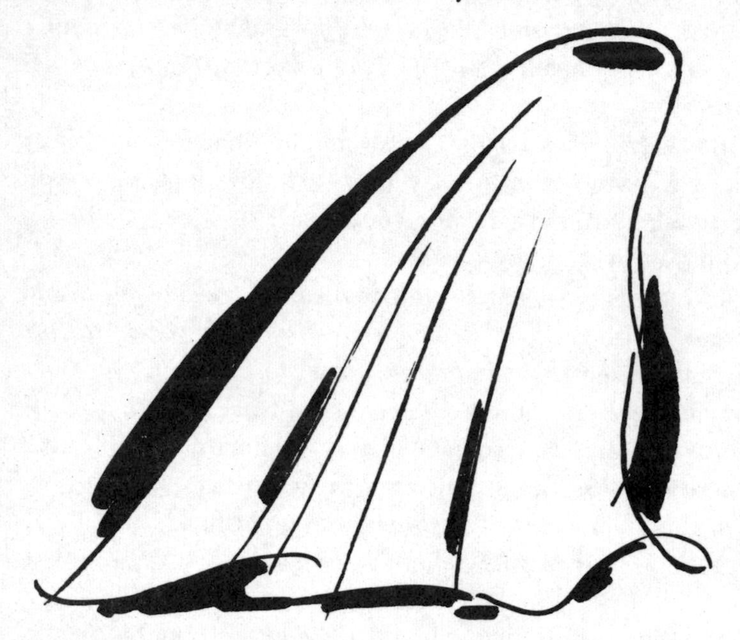

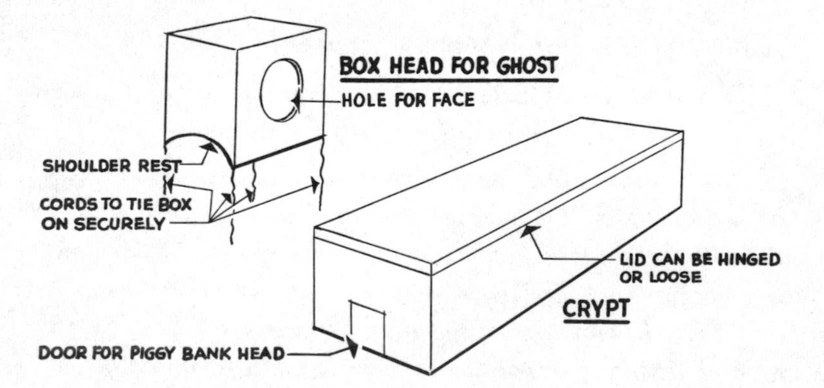

Section Two

SHORTIES

In staging "shorty" skits the key words are improvisation and imagination. That is, you "make do" with what you have and ask your audience to imagine the rest.

To begin with, you may not have any curtains and it may not seem worthwhile to rig up any. In such a case a blanket or other suitable fabric can be carried on and off the stage by two stage hands with scene shifting moving on and off behind same. A sheet through which shadows may be seen can be used if there is no real reason (such as surprise element) to conceal the scene shifting and some extra laughs may be secured by means of this shadow business.

Or, you may simply pretend you are using curtains with stage hands acting as though they were opening and closing same, and the narrator referring to them. Usually no curtains are used at campfires although it is quite possible to make some arrangement, such as a wire between two trees with blankets suspended by blanket pins.

This may not seem too important. On the other hand, too often little or no thought is given at campfire circles to the need for some kind of a stage area. As a result, some performers come close to tumbling into the fire or the audience. That is why it is a good idea to leave one section of the campfire circle open for entertainment purposes, which also has the advantage of not putting anyone in back of those performing, leading the singing and so forth.

A long, thin log may be used to mark the front of this stage area, and, if desired, some large cans may be partially sunk in the ground on the stage side of this log as footlights. A part of the can may be cut away for this purpose with large candles serving as the lights.

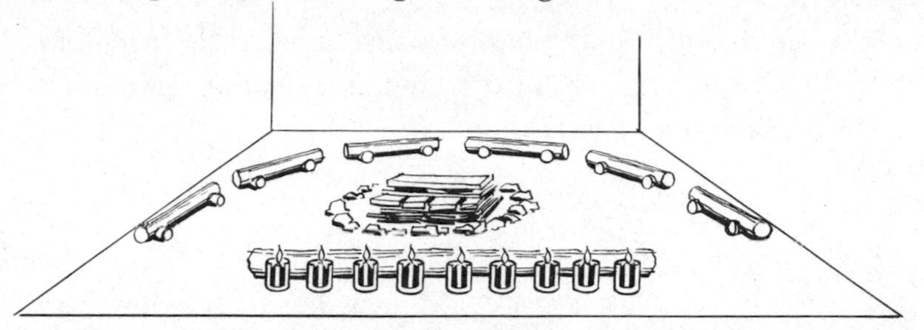

All of these "shorties" can be done almost anywhere, indoors or out, and where suggested props are not practicable, do the best you can, or tell the audience, "You will have to imagine . . ."

In some cases, as indicated below each title, the parts may be either male or female even though the skit may specify one sex or the other. In other cases, you may be able to change the sex, if desired, as, for example, in "Sweet Revenge" where the statue could just as well be Pocahontas (with a tomahawk), the Pioneer Mother (with a rifle), etc., and the Mad Scientist and Reporter women instead of men.

However, boys can always take the parts of girls and vice versa. Certainly a bunch of girls in blue jeans and plaid shirts can have as much fun as boys playing "Comrade Justice."

You may want to increase or decrease the number of parts in some skits, whether by tossing in extras, such as two more moving men in "The Heavy Chiffonier" or having someone take two parts.

One final admonition—while these "shorties" do not require a lot of rehearsal and nobody expects anything like perfection in their execution, you should try to put on a good show, be it ever so brief. This means some real effort. Generally speaking, last-minute, throw-together skits do not quite come off, whereas a little practice makes all the difference in the world.

Therefore, learn your lines, practice, use a little ingenuity in getting props and costuming, put imagination and spirit into your part, and—have fun.

BE PREPARED

(For 2 males or 2 females)

All you need for this is one scout leader, who can double as narrator and one young boy scout with five or six merit badges on the sleeve of his shirt. It does not really matter whether these include the badges mentioned in the skit since the audience will not be able to see the difference, if they know it. This skit can easily be used by a girl scout leader and girl scout.

LEADER. Please imagine you are attending a Big Scoutcraft Meet where several hundred boy scouts and explorers are demonstrating their skills. I am one of the officials and, while going around observing different groups of scouts, I meet a young lad with half a dozen merit badges on his sleeve and decide to test his knowledge. *(The Leader and the Scout approach each other.)* Say, there, son, I see you are a Star Scout with some interesting merit badges on your sleeve. *(Examines the sleeve.)* Oh, yes, you have the Cooking Merit Badge. Tell me, how would you prepare a rice pudding?

SCOUT *(Looks down, fidgets, and finally says.)* I don't know how to make a rice pudding.

LEADER *(Surprised.)* That's odd. But how about astronomy? You should be able to tell me what you would do if lost in the woods at night without a compass. *(The Scout looks all around, studies his feet, and shakes his head. The Leader becomes impatient.)* Now, look! There is no sense in having merit badges unless you know something about the subject. I see you also have a First Aid Badge, and that is very important. So! I have cut an artery in my leg and am bleeding to death. Now, what are you going to do?

SCOUT *(Completely miserable, he blurts out.)* You're going to bleed to death, Mister, 'cause this ain't my shirt.

* * * *

A SLIGHT MISUNDERSTANDING

(For 1 male, 1 female, 1 optional)

This stunt is done by pantomime and a narrator until the closing lines. The only props needed are a card (a shirt cardboard will do nicely) with the word "SUC-COR" on it, a couple of chairs or boxes or a chair and a table to serve as "the rock," and a book.

NARRATOR. Now, children, we will have our English lesson, so let's all pay close attention.

Our new word for today is *(Holds up a card.)* "Succor." This word can be used as a noun, meaning—"help, relief, aid, assistance," or "one who or that which succors;" or it can be a verb, meaning—"to help or relieve in difficulty, need, or distress." To help you understand the use of this word we have prepared a little drama of a maiden—schoolteacher—in distress.

As our scene opens we behold a school teacher on summer vacation, who goes walking along the shore of a bay where the tide rises very high. However, the water is now some distance from our heroine as she finds a rock, which seems made to order as a perch upon which she can peruse—read, in other words—an exciting new book entitled, "The Use and Benefits of More Homework in Modern Education."

She is so fascinated with this stimulating book she fails to notice the tide coming in. Time goes by and our fair heroine is surrounded by water, which rises until . . .

TEACHER *(The water reaches one foot. She pulls it up and looks down. She is so startled to discover she is surrounded that she drops the book. She tries to catch it but it sinks out of sight.)*

NARRATOR. She loses her precious book on homework. What a tragedy! But she has another problem she can't solve by herself. The tide is still coming in and she can't swim a stroke. What would her dear children say if they knew their beloved teacher was in such a terrible fix?

TEACHER *(She has scrambled to her feet and looked all around in vain.)* Help! Help! Help! Oh, help me, somebody! Anybody! Please help me! *(Continues to call intermittently while the narrator speaks and also looks down at the rising tide, lifts her feet, then pulls up her skirt as the water continues to rise.)*

NARRATOR. Will no one hear her frantic cries for aid? Does the tide rise to claim her as its helpless victim? What will her poor scholars do without her? Ah! Someone has heard her. Yes, a poor, but honest—they're always honest if they're poor—fisherman has heard her cries and puts out to rescue her in his trusty boat. Never fret, dear children, he will save her. *(The fisherman rows up to the rock in the imaginary boat.)*

TEACHER *(As he comes alongside the rock.)* Oh, I knew if I kept calling some *suc-cor* would come.

FISHERMAN. Well, lady, if that's the way you feel about it, you can stay where you are. *(Turns the boat around* and *rows off. The teacher rings her hands.)*

(CURTAIN)

* * * *

COMRADE JUSTICE

(For 6 males or females, or both)

Six actors, who may be men or women, or both, appear in this skit. There is a mean-looking Comrade Judge, suitably seated at his bench, if practicable, two tough-looking policemen (or policewomen), and three sad-looking prisoners. The prisoners are standing to one side with one policeman, while the other policeman approaches the Judge.

POLICE. We have three candidates for the Concentration Camp, Comrade Judge.

JUDGE. Good! Our fee has just been raised to two cabbages and one parsnip per prisoner per year. Let's see, a ten-year sentence would be . . .

POLICE *(Quickly.)* Twenty cabbages and ten parsnips.

JUDGE *(Suspiciously.)* You too smart, Comrade Policeman. Maybe you American spy.

POLICE. No, no, Comrade Judge. Just fond of cabbages.

JUDGE. Ha! I get all the cabbages. You get parsnips.

POLICE. Shucks!

JUDGE. Bring on first prisoner.

POLICE *(Does so.)* Comrade Judge, this guilty enemy of the People's Government came to work late.

JUDGE. So! You hold up production of the People's Factory!

1ST PRISONER. Only ten minutes late, Comrade Judge. Trolley broke down.

POLICE. Silence!

JUDGE. Twenty cabbages . . . I mean, ten years in Concentration Camp. One year for each minute you late. Bring on next prisoner.

POLICE *(Does so.)* Judge . . . I mean, Comrade Judge, this guilty enemy of the People's Government came to work fifteen minutes early.

JUDGE. So! You sneak in early to spy and sabotage People's Glorious Factory.

2ND PRISONER. No, no, Comrade Judge. I only want to produce more . . .

POLICE. Silence! *(To the Judge.)* Does he get fifteen parsnips?

JUDGE. Yes! Fifteen pars . . . I mean, fifteen years in Comrade Concentration Camp. One year for each minute you sneak in early to spy. Bring on the next prisoner.

POLICE *(Returns the second prisoner and brings the third prisoner before the Judge.)* Comrade Judge, this guilty enemy of the People's Government came to work . . . *(Pauses, looks around, and speaks in a very tense voice) . . . right on time.*

JUDGE *(Horrified.)* Is that so? *(The third prisoner nods his head dumbly. The Judge is very angry.)* Take him out and shoot him. *(Rises and points at the prisoner.)* You! You! You have an *American watch. (All gaze in horror as the prisoner shrinks back.)*

* * * *

HAM ACTOR

(For 2 males)

The ham actor meets a friend on the street. The actor approaches with his head in the air.

BILL. Hi, Joe, you old baboon! *(He slaps the actor on the back as he passes.)*

ACTOR. I beg your pardon, sir! *(Turning around.)*

BILL. Don't "Sir" me, you old goat.

ACTOR. Why, it's Bill Jones, my old friend. You'll have to forgive me; I'm simply hounded to death by autograph seekers. I'm such a celebrity, you know. You saw my last play, of course.

BILL. Part of it.

ACTOR. That's too bad. You must have missed the beginning.

BILL. Oh, I saw the beginning. That's why I didn't see the ending.

ACTOR *(Puzzled.)* I don't understand.

BILL. Well, you know that scene when you were ill and the native girl says, "Me Lily Blossom. Me good girl. Me stay?"

ACTOR. Yes, indeed! Very touching!

BILL. Well, that's when I said, "Me Billy Brown. Me bad boy. Me go."

ACTOR *(With a forced laugh.)* You will have your little joke. But surely you didn't miss my deathbed scene. Why, when I said, "Farewell, my Little Lily Blossom," there was not a sound—not a breath in the house.

BILL. You mean everybody had left!

ACTOR *(Glares at him.)* You try my patience. *(Then tragically.)* And I'm not a well man!

BILL *(Appears penitent.)* I'm sorry to hear that, Joe. Anything serious?

ACTOR *(Hamming it up.)* I fear so. You know, when you give your all to your art, as I do, it does something to you. My very life is being poured out on the altar of fame.

BILL. Oh, it can't be that bad.

ACTOR. Ah, yes! *(His hand to his forehead.)* I am not long for this world.

BILL. Oh, come now. Why not take some sugar?

ACTOR. Sugar! What ever for?

BILL. Didn't you ever hear of a sugar-cured ham?

GOING HOME FROM THE DANCE

(For 1 male and 1 female)

Any skit, stunt or what-have-you involving a boy and a girl making love, sitting together or kissing can hardly miss, whether they are actually boy and girl, or both boys, or both girls. And so . . .

On a moonlit night a boy is taking a girl home from a dance. Let's have a nice, big moon hung conspicuously, and we need a car. This latter can be chairs, boxes, etc. The moon can be of cardboard, or green cheese, if you have a large green cheese handy. The emcee can set the scene, using actual names of actors and referring to some affair known to the audience.

The boy starts to get in first, from the right side, but catches himself and ushers the girl in. He then climbs in over her to get to the driver's seat. He explains the door doesn't open on the left side. The boy starts the car, notices he hasn't closed the door (the girl hasn't either), so he leans over her to do so, almost pushing her out of the car. He apologizes and drives a bit, stealing glances at her and sighing. Finally he gets up courage to speak.

HE. You're beautiful!

SHE. Thank you.

HE *(With another sigh.)* You have such beautiful golden hair.

SHE. Thank you.

HE *(Don't forget you are driving a car. He looks at the girl in a real calf-like manner.)* And those beautiful blue eyes. They're beautiful!

SHE. Thank you.

HE *(Starts to put his arm around the girl, loses his nerve and withdraws it; drives a bit, sighs a bit, and then . . .)* Your teeth, they are like pearls, so white, and beautiful.

SHE. Thank you.

HE *(Again makes an indecisive motion with his right arm.)* And your lips, they're so red—like raspber . . . like rubies.

SHE. Thank you. *(He starts to move closer to her. The car swerves and he hastily moves back behind the wheel, concentrating on driving a bit. Then he sighs once more, opens and shuts his mouth. He is really in a bad way. She speaks softly.)* Can you drive with one hand?

HE *(Comes alive.)* Sure! *(Starts to take his right arm off the wheel.)*

SHE *(Quickly.)* Then wipe your nose. It's running.

* * * *

JUST MADE IT

(For 4 males and 1 female)

Woman driver, her young son, and three motorcycle policemen mostly ad lib this one. A stagehand sets out signs "GAS" and "MEN" at proper time.

A woman driver, with a young son, pretends to be going down the road at a good clip. Makes like a car motor. Boy comments on speed, which is now about 60 miles per hour. Then he says, "Gee, Mommy, you better slow down; here comes a motorcycle cop."

Instead she goes faster and gets up to 70. The mother, the boy and the policeman move about the stage, the policeman bent over the handlebars. The boy tells mommy there is another motorcycle cop behind them, as he swings onto the stage.

Mommy steps it up to 80. The boy says, "Gee, Mommy, you're doing 80 and now there's three cops after us." (There are, too.)

The stagehand sets out signs "GAS" and "MEN" across the stage from the approaching mommy and son. Mommy spots the signs, whispers to her son, and swings over to "GAS" sign and stops with a screech of brakes. The boy opens the car door, jumps out and races over to the sign "MEN," opening the door and dashing in.

At the same time the boy is getting out of the car, the three motorcycle policemen swing up beside mommy and start getting out their pads and pencils. When the boy goes through the door (imaginary), mommy turns to the policemen and says sweetly, "I'll bet you men thought he wouldn't make it."

The policemen look at one another and toss the pads in the air.

* * * *

THE HEAVY CHIFFONIER

(For 2 males and 1 female)

In this skit two boys dressed as moving men pretend to carry a heavy chiffonier up three flights of stairs to the fourth floor. Each flight of stairs involves a sharp turn. The movers never mention what they are carrying until the end of the skit.

From the very beginning it is obvious they have a tough moving job as they maneuver to make the original lift, changing holds several times and checking with each other to be sure they are both set before lifting. They may make such remarks as, "Are you all set, Bill?" "Hold it, Joe!" etc. Finally, after considerable effort, the load is lifted and the climb begins.

Each flight is negotiated with great difficulty because of low ceilings, sharp turns, the heavy load and such. Several times the chiffonier almost topples on the rear man; they stop to balance it on the step in order to get fresh grips, they stumble and grunt, and shout warnings.

At each landing they set the chiffonier down carefully and gasp for breath, loosening clothing and mopping their brows with handkerchiefs (bandannas are excellent). If desired, the men may have on several sweaters or jackets, one being peeled off at each landing. Reluctantly, but manfully, they return to their labors to negotiate the next flight of stairs. By the time they reach the fourth landing, they are at the point of collapse, hanging on to each other, after setting down the chiffonier, in order to stay on their feet.

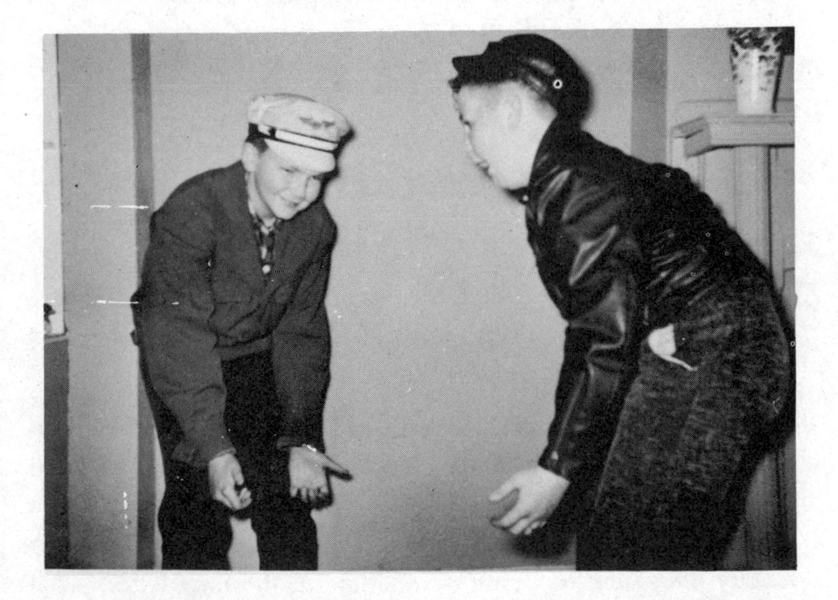

"A smile might help — but I don't know how," comments Ronnie James as he and Charley Watkins lift the heavy chiffonier.

Puffing and staggering, they face the problem of knocking on the door.

JOE. Knock on the door, Bill.

BILL. I can't get my arm up.

JOE. I'll help you. *(With Joe pushing Bill's arm up, both doing a stagger dance, Bill succeeds in knocking on the door. The two men stand bent at the waist and knees, swaying slightly, as the door opens.)*

HOUSEWIFE. Yes?

BILL. Where do you want this chiffonier, ma'am?

HOUSEWIFE *(Looking around.)* What chiffonier?

BILL *(Looks around.)* The chiffonier right he . . . *(In amazement.)* Great Scott, Joe, we forgot the chiffonier!

* * * *

HOT CAKES

(For 7 optional players)

We need a Narrator, a Waitress (or Counterman) and five customers. The only prop required is a piece of cardboard on which the word "Syn-o-nym" is printed.

NARRATOR. It is our pleasure to bring you one of our famous dramatized Vocabulary Lessons. Now, kindly bend your ears this way as we learn the word "Syn-o-nym" *(Holds up the card)*, which means: "a word having the same, or nearly the same, meaning as another in the language," such as, "joyful, glad, elated," or "a word or expression accepted as another name for something."

Now to illustrate this, we request your cooperation in using your imagination to picture a lunch counter with a row of stools before it and our lovely young waitress behind it. You don't have to imagine the waitress. *(Indicates the lunch counter. The waitress takes a place behind it. The four customers enter together and pretend to take seats on stools, stepping over them and squatting slightly as though seated. The waitress hands them menus and sets out glasses of water, which the customers study and drink respectively. A fifth customer enters and takes a place beside the other four. The waitress gives him, or her, a menu and a glass of water.)*

WAITRESS *(To the four.)* Are you ready to order now?

No. 1. Hot cakes.

No. 2. Pan cakes.

No. 3. Griddle cakes.

No. 4. Wheat cakes.

No. 5 *(Has been listening and assuming a puzzled look.)* They're all synonyms, aren't they?

WAITRESS. No, sir. If you want cinnamon, I can give you a bun.

WHERE'S GRANDPAP?

(For 2 males and 1 female)

A barefoot mountain boy in tattered overalls or dungarees and shirt is stretched out, one leg bent upward with the heel of his other foot resting on the bent knee. A pie pan with a hole cut in the bottom is held in his toes and the boy is trying to shoot peas from a pea shooter through the hole. Peas should not be aimed in the direction of the audience. After some time his Mammy comes out:

MAMMY. Well, if you ain't the mostest good-for-nothin' youngun I ever seen!

CLEM. Shucks, Mammy, you always say sich nice things about me. Supper ready?

MAMMY. Pert near. Where's Grandpap?

CLEM. Don't rightly know, but he went thataway. *(Shoots with the pea shooter to indicate the direction.)*

MAMMY. Well, you best go fetch him.

CLEM. Yes, Mammy. *(Mammy goes in. Clem gets up and starts looking for Grandpap, calling as he looks.)* Grandpap! Oh, Grandpap! *(He wanders around the stage, now and then firing a pea through the hole in the plate.)* Grandpap! G-Grand-pap! *(All the time Grandpap has been standing on one side of the stage in the bushes, which can be a large card-board box with "Bushes" marked on it in large letters. Clem finally sees Grandpap a little way off.)* Grandpap, be that ye?

GRANDPAP. Yup!

CLEM. Well, it's a-gitten dark, Grandpap.

GRANDPAP. Yup!

CLEM. Supper's pert near done.

GRANDPAP. Yup!

CLEM. Ain't ye hungry?

GRANDPAP. Yup!

CLEM. Well, air ye comin'?

GRANDPAP. Nope!

CLEM. Air ye mad 'bout sumpin'?

GRANDPAP. Nope!

CLEM. Then why ain't ye comin' home?

GRANDPAP. Can't!

CLEM. Why can't ye?

GRANDPAP. Standin' in a b'ar trap.

* * * *

LOVE THAT TRACTOR

(For 7 males and 1 female)

The characters are: Comrade Girl, Comrade Boy and Comrade Tractor, consisting of one Comrade Engine, four Comrade Wheels and one Comrade Seat. The Comrade Girl is standing near the Comrade Tractor. Wheels are boys sitting with knees drawn up under their chins, arms clasped around their legs, head bowed. Engine is a boy on hands and knees, head forward. Seat is a boy on hands and knees, head backward. This means that the legs of the engine and the seat are four abreast, so that anyone getting in the tractor must be careful where he places his feet. Comrade Boy enters.

BOY *(Spies the girl and the tractor.)* Wow! Is that something! *(Hurries over toward the girl, who is very pretty and pushes by her to admire the tractor. Neither the girl nor the tractor parts think much of this.)* This is the most beautiful Comrade Tractor I have ever seen. *(Steps gingerly over the tangle of legs and hitches up his pants before sitting down. The seat looks around disapprovingly. The boy sits and the seat sinks somewhat, but struggles back up again under the load.)* Just think! Some stupid boys fall in love with girls, but I am a true Comrade Boy and I love finer things, like tractors. In Comrade Tractor I shall ride triumphantly forth to my glorious Comrade Destiny. *(Makes like examining the tractor's instruments and testing the wheel.)*

ENGINE *(To the right front wheel.)* For that girl I'd be a *fan* and *belt* this boy out. What say I spark a little revolution?

RFW. Suits me. I'm revolutionary minded right down to the ground. *(To the right rear wheel.)* Who are you for? Comrade Girl or Comrade Boy?

RRW. Comrade Girl, of course. Don't you think I get

Now the Tractor is Happy

With the Comrade Girl (Johnny LaMonte) on seat (Ray Hack), engine (Johnny McGuckin), right front wheel (Jimmy Trainor), right rear wheel (Howard Dunlap), left rear wheel (Tony Devine, but try and see him), and left front wheel (Bob Hack) eager to take off and leave the sprawled Comrade Boy (Jim Mealey).

around? *(To the seat.)* How are you situated? Are you with us?

SEAT. You bet your spokes I am. Giving this flat tire . . . *(Jerks a thumb toward the boy.)* . . . the air will be a load off my mind. *(His rear end sinks a little but struggles back. Speaks to the left rear wheel.)* Can we count on you?

LRW. Don't worry! This is one time I won't be left behind. *(To the left front wheel.)* When Comrade Engine sparks, Comrade Boy gets the old heave-ho.

LFW. Good! I'm plenty tired of him.

BOY *(Starts the tractor which throbs into life. The engine backs toward the boy, who leans back on the seat, which rears up. The right wheels seize the boy and thrust him to the left. The left wheels grab him and yank him from the tractor, the seat and engine assisting with a foot apiece to the seat of the boy's pants. Since the tractor faces the audience the boy sprawls on the far side from the girl. Tractor parts give the girl the eye and the nod. The girl gets in and sits down while the wheels and engine watch admiringly.)*

GIRL *(Starts the tractor which purrs contentedly into action.)* Love that Tractor! *(The tractor parts smile, wink at the audience, etc.)*

BOY *(In disgust.)* I should have known it was an American tractor.

* * * *

NOTE: *American idea can be emphasized by the engine wearing a red shirt, the seat a white shirt and the wheels blue dungarees.*

THE DUMB SENTRY

(For 3 males)

General Nuisance and Major Difficulty are approaching the sentry post of Private Dimwit. The Private, of course, needs something that at least faintly resembles a gun.

SENTRY. Halt! Who goes there? *(They halt across the stage from the sentry.)*

MAJOR. General Nuisance and Major Difficulty.

SENTRY. Give the password!

MAJOR. Lassie Come Home.

SENTRY. You know it . . . *(Jerks the gun toward the major.)* . . . but how about the other guy? *(Jerks the gun toward the general.)*

GENERAL. Yes, Lassie Come Home.

SENTRY. There's no "Yes" to it—just "Lassie Come Home."

MAJOR *(Much annoyed.)* We know it.

SENTRY. Advance to be recognized. *(They start forward.)* Halt! Who goes there? *(They halt about halfway across the stage.)*

MAJOR *(Angry.)* We told you once—General Nuisance and Major Difficulty.

SENTRY. Give the password.

MAJOR *(Real angry.)* Lassie Come Home, hang it all!

SENTRY. There's no "Hang it all" to it, just—"Lassie Come Home."

GENERAL *(Explodes.)* We know it!

MAJOR. What's this all about anyhow?

GENERAL. How many times do we have to go through the same thing?

SENTRY *(Calmly.)* Three.

MAJOR *(Shouts.)* Three!

SENTRY. Yes, sir. My orders are to halt you three times and then shoot. So I'm going to halt you just once more. *(Snappy.)* Advance!

MAJOR *(Turning.)* Let's get out of here! The man's crazy!

GENERAL *(Takes his arm.)* Wait! The General must lead the way. *(Runs off with the major after him.)*

SENTRY *(Shouts.)* Hey! You can't do that! *(Rests the butt of his gun on the ground and scratches his head.)* Now what do I do? They didn't wait for the third "Halt."

* * * *

THE GREEK MERCHANT AND THE LIONS

(For 7 males)

Actors include the Greek Merchant, the Roman Emperor, two Roman Guards, and three Hungry Lions. A generous dose of imagination can take care of most of the costuming as well as the scenery.

NARRATOR. If you will just imagine you are seeing things hard enough, you will observe before you the Emperor's Palace in the Rome of the Caesars. A little later you can imagine that I am one of three Hungry Lions, but right now a Greek Merchant is being escorted before the Emperor. *(The Emperor stands looking emperorish as the guards bring in the Greek Merchant.)*

GUARDS. Hail, Caesar!

EMPEROR. Hail, me! What crime has this pagan committed?

GUARD. He has been making over 1000 per cent profit in his dealings with your loyal Roman citizens.

EMPEROR. Egad! How is this?

GREEK. Can I help it if you Romans are so stupid?

EMPEROR. What insolence! Throw him to the lions!

GREEK. But, Your Majesty, I don't think those lions can catch me.

EMPEROR. Well, you'll give them something to chew over. Take him away! *(The guards drag the luckless merchant off.)*

NARRATOR. And now we are in the great arena where the luckless Greek Merchant is being thrust out to face the Hungry Lions. Pardon me, while I hasten to be on time for my dinner. *(Exits. The guards push the Greek forward, and the lions come roaring out. The first lion charges up to the Greek, who holds up his hand as a "Stop" signal. The lion stops. The Greek whispers in his ear and the lion slinks off. The same thing happens with the second lion; also the third. You can toss in a fourth lion if you wish. Lions can roar around while waiting their turn to charge up.)*

EMPEROR. What gives! *(To a guard.)* Fetch that Greek here so I can find out what's cooking. *(The guard brings the Greek to the Emperor.)* Tell me, what are you whispering to those lions?

GREEK. Do I get my freedom if I tell you?

EMPEROR. You do. Now, what is your power over lions?

GREEK. It's really very simple. I merely said to each lion, "Now remember, after dinner you'll be expected to say a few words."

THE HANDY MAN

(For 1 male, 1 female and 1 optional)

If done indoors, two large cartons can be placed one on top of the other on the back end of a sturdy table. A clock face is drawn on the top carton. Two doors, opening in the middle, are in the bottom carton (these doors can be flaps of carton). A small boy or girl, playing the part of Cuckoo, crouches in the bottom carton, where he can push the doors open and move out to the forward part of the table in order to "Cuckoo." If outdoors, or not wishing to bother much with props, a narrator can describe the situation and request the audience to use their imagination.

In addition to "Cuckoo," the skit calls for a Husband and Wife. The husband will need some tools. The Husband and Wife approach the Clock.

WIFE. Tom, you'll have to get someone to fix this cuckoo clock. It simply doesn't work right.

TOM. What's the matter with it?

WIFE. Well, it's just twelve o'clock. Listen?

CUCKOO *(Comes out.)* Cuckoo, Cuckoo, Cuckoo, Cuckoo, Cuckoo, Cuckoo, Cuckoo, Cuckoo, Cuckoo, Cuckoo, Cuckoo, Cuckoo, Cuckoo—Whoops! *(Scratches his head and counts on his fingers.)* Sorry, scratch that last "Cuckoo." *(Goes in.)*

WIFE. See what I mean?

TOM. Yeah. I'll fix it as soon as I get my tools.

WIFE. No, no! Let's get a watchmaker who knows what he's doing.

TOM *(Gets tools.)* I know what I'm doing. I'll have that clock fixed in a jiffy. *(Goes to work on the clock from behind, hammering, twisting, prying and whatnot in an exaggerated fashion. "Cuckoo" can yell "Help" or "Ouch" a cou-*

ple of times. The wife stands in front looking worried or can give helpful advice. Tom finishes and wipes his hands with

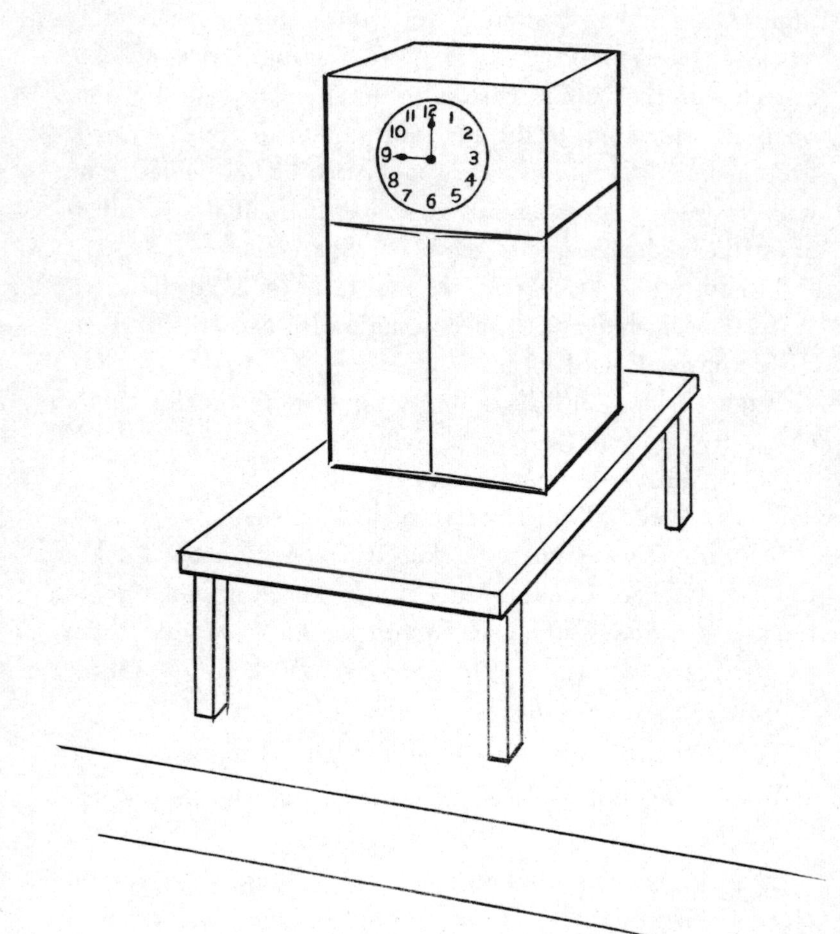

satisfaction. He speaks to his wife.) Now, it's as good as new.

WIFE *(Dubiously.)* We'll see! It's one o'clock.

CUCKOO *(Backs out, looks up at the clock face, shakes his head, peeks around at Tom and wife.)* Could somebody please tell me what time it is?

* * * *

TOO MUCH MARY JANE

(For 1 male and 2 females)

A love seat, the Boy Friend, his Girl Friend, and her little sister, Mary Jane, will do nicely. The love seat can be improvised by throwing some covering over a couple of chairs, or a log if at a campfire.

The scene opens with the Boy Friend and his Girl Friend seated alone with each other on the love seat.

BOY. Has the kid really gone to bed?

GIRL. I guess so. *(Sighs.)* That Mary Jane takes a lot of persuasion. No wonder the folks like to get out once in awhile.

BOY. Anyhow, we're alone at last so what are we waiting for?

GIRL *(Briskly.)* On your mark! *(They straighten up, ready to go into a clinch.)*

BOY. Get set! *(Their arms go up.)*

BOTH. Go! *(Just as they go into a clinch they see that*

Mary Jane has returned and is standing watching them. They come out of the clinch.)

GIRL. Mary Jane, I thought you were in bed.

MARY JANE. I'm not sleepy.

BOY. Here's a quarter. Now go to bed. *(Hands her a quarter which she takes and leaves.)*

GIRL. Goodnight! *(Turns for a clinch.)*

BOY. I hope! *(Takes the girl in his arms. They're just going into the clinch when they see Mary Jane coming back. They break the clinch but before either can speak, she does.)*

MARY JANE. Here's half a dollar. Let me watch.

BOY. Grrr! *(Jumps up and starts for Mary Jane who runs out.)*

"Let me watch," says Mary Jane (Judy James) to her sister's boy friend (Bob Clarson) as her sister (Caroline James) looks on in disapproval.

"WHY, DADDY?"

(For 2 males, 1 optional)

This skit is written for a Narrator, Daddy and Junior. However, it can just as well be Mother and Janie, or Daddy and Janie, or Mother and Junior. The scene opens with Daddy seated comfortably, reading the newspaper.

NARRATOR. Socrates got quite a reputation just by going around asking people questions. Evidently he didn't have any competition from the Small Fry in those days, but today, believe me, any four-year-old could make Socrates look like an amateur, as we'll show you.

JUNIOR *(Runs in and climbs up on Daddy's lap, messing up his paper in the process. An older boy dressed to resemble a four-year-old should go over big.)* Daddy!

DADDY *(Resignedly.)* Yes, Junior.

JUNIOR. Why can't I fly like a bird? *(Flaps his hands like a bird.)*

DADDY. Because you're not a bird. You're a little boy. You see, son, each form of life—that is, every animal and bird . . .

JUNIOR *(Quickly.)* And fish?

DADDY. Yes—"and fish" is different. Each has its own way of doing things. Fish have fins, and birds have wings, and monkeys have tails, and little boys have hands.

JUNIOR *(Thoughtfully.)* Oh!

DADDY. So now you understand why you can't have wings?

JUNIOR. Yes, Daddy, I understand that. But Daddy!

DADDY. Yes, Junior.

JUNIOR. Why can't I have a tail like a monkey? *(Starts making like a monkey, crawling over Daddy, and Daddy registers hopelessness.)*

NO DEAL!

By JOHNNY McGUCKIN

(For 1 male, 4 to 6 optional)

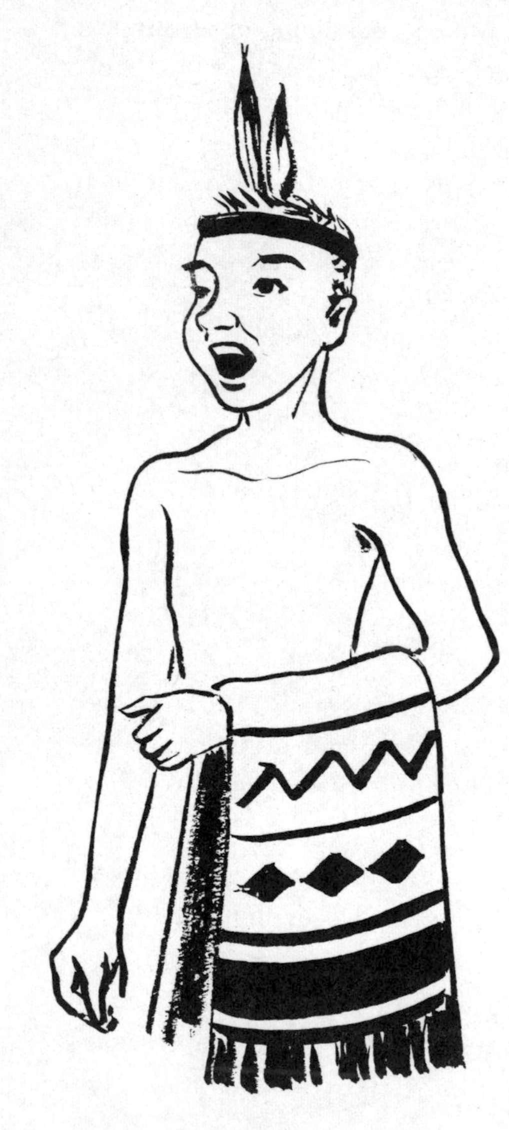

Characters: One well-padded Indian, three to five tourists, one bystander. The scene opens with an Indian standing with a blanket over his arm with a "For Sale" sign on it. Tourists approach.

TOURIST No. 1. Say, Chief, I'll give you $5.00 for that blanket.

CHIEF. No deal!

TOURIST No. 2. I'll give you $10.00 for it.

CHIEF. No deal! *(Tourists gather around and bid—$12, $15, $18, $20, $22 and finally . . .)*

TOURIST No. 1. Chief, I'll give you $24.00 for that blanket.

CHIEF. No deal! Ugh! *(Tourists move off as a bystander approaches the Chief.)*

BYSTANDER. Say, Chief, why wouldn't you sell that blanket to any of those tourists?

CHIEF. What do you expectum—deals like Manhattan Island every day?

* * * *

SMITH BROTHERS COUGH DROPS

(For 1 male, 6 or more optional)

A "pitch" man with a display of Smith Brothers Cough Drops is addressing a group of curious passersby (group can be half dozen or so). He is talking in a hoarse whisper. "Ladies and gentlemen, please come closer. I want to tell you about one of the greatest boons ever evolved by medical science for the relief of suffering humanity. Yes, ladies and gentlemen, in this small box (holds up a box) which I hold before you, for the small price of one nickel, five cents, only one-twentieth of a dollar you get the benefit of millions of dollars of research; you get the fruit of years of effort; the distilled essence of the wisdom of some of the world's greatest doctors. Yes, ladies and gentlemen, Smith Brothers Cough Drops are a truly amazing product of medical science. Smith Brothers Cough Drops are good for colds and coughs, sore throat, laryngitis, bronchitis, tonsillitis, asthma, hoarseness . . ."

VOICE FROM THE REAR OF THE CROWD. "Well, why don't you take one yourself?"

PITCH MAN. "All right, ladies and gentlemen, I will take one of these wonderful, marvelous, amazing Smith Brothers Cough Drops. *(Does so. A slight pause as he sucks on the cough drop; then he speaks in a clear, vigorous, normal voice.)* Now then, ladies and gentlemen, step right up and get your Smith Brothers Cough Drops. Only five cents a box."

SWEET REVENGE!

(For 3 or more males)

A statue occupies the center stage. Can be a general on horseback, the horse being another boy holding the general in piggy-back style or two boys covered by dark material and using a large paper bag as a horse's head, or a padded and covered sawhorse. Or the statue can be a soldier or a pioneer in an heroic stance on a box pedestal. The statue must have a pistol or rifle. A mad scientist, carrying a bottle and a paper cup, approaches with a reporter.

M. S. You shall see whether I am mad or the greatest genius of all time. In this bottle I have the fruit of my life's work—the one and only Inanimate Animator. With this I can give life to anything. And when I say anything I mean *anything*. Write that in your newspaper.

REPORTER. You mean to say you can instill life in . . . *(Sees the statue.)* . . . the general there?

M. S. Yes! One drink of my Inanimate Animator and even that thing of cold, lifeless stone will become a warm-hearted human being, endowed with love and tenderness.

REPORTER. This I have to see.

M. S. And you shall. *(Takes the bottle and pours a drink into the cup.)* Here, hold the bottle. *(Sternly.)* Don't drop it. *(Approaches the statue.)* Here, sir, drink this.

STATUE. Don't be ridiculous. Everybody knows a statue can't drink.

M. S. *(Very excited.)* Drink, I say, or I shall become violent.

STATUE *(Aside.)* Guess I better humor him. *(To the scientist.)* Very well, then, if you insist. *(Takes the cup.)*

M. S. I do insist. Drink it all. *(With a wild look in his eyes.)* Now we shall see what we shall see.

REPORTER. I'll buy that.

STATUE. What can I lose? *(Drinks and makes a face.)*

M. S. *(Wildly.)* Drink! Drink! Drink! *(The Statue drinks and shudders slightly. The M. S. throws his arms wide and fairly shrieks.)* Drink it all! Drink, I say! *(The Statue drinks, shudders violently and a wild expression comes over his face. He throws down the cup. The M. S. speaks triumphantly.)* You see!

REPORTER *(Amazed.)* You've done it. He's alive!

STATUE. You bet your life I am. *(Flexes his arms and swells his chest with a savage sternness to his face.)* And now—now I shall have revenge. At last, revenge!

M. S. *(Alarmed.)* No! No! I did not give you life for that!

STATUE. But you gave me life. Ha! Ha! Sweet Revenge! *(Raises the gun.)*

REPORTER *(Excited.)* Revenge on who? Who has wronged you so?

STATUE *(Dismounting from the horse or the pedestal with the gun ready for use.)* I'm going to get me a *million pigeons!*

* * * *

SUSIE

(For 3 males and 4 females)

This skit calls for three boys and four girls, Susie being younger and smaller than the other girls, who consider her a pest. Our scene opens after school with Peg, Clara and Janice talking. All have school books, etc.

PEG. I hope that Susie doesn't show up before the boys get here. She's a pest!

CLARA. I'll say! And does she do the dumb things! Why, when our English teacher told us if we repeated a word ten times it was ours, Susie started saying, "David, David, David, David . . ." *(Girls laugh.)*

JANICE. That's nothing! In the library today she wanted to take out *Scouting For Boys. (More laughter.)*

PEG. She's nuts about cooking. Says her mother says the way to a man's heart is through his stomach. Well, I told her you don't have to worry about food when you've got what I've got. *(Struts her stuff. Others do likewise.)*

CLARA *(Excited.)* Here come the boys!

JANICE *(Dismay.)* And here comes that Susie.

SUSIE. Hi! Any boys in sight?

PEG. Yes, three, and there's three of us. So beat it!

SUSIE. I will if you pay me off. I've got a quarter and I need a dollar, so it will cost you twenty-five cents apiece.

CLARA. You little gold digger!

JANICE. Let's pay her quick. Here's my quarter, and it's all I got. *(Gives Susie twenty-five cents.)*

PEG. Here's mine, and that cleans me out. *(Gives Susie twenty-five cents.)*

CLARA. Likewise. *(Gives Susie twenty-five cents.)*

JANICE *(Pushing Susie.)* Get going.

JACK *(As the boys come up.)* Hi, girls! Any dough? I'm flat.

JIM. Ditto, and I'm hungry.

JOE. I'm busted and starved. *(The girls look at one another in dismay.)*

SUSIE *(Comes back.)* I've got a dollar. *(Holds out a hand showing four quarters.)* Will that do for the four of us?

JACK. Baby doll! You're a life saver! *(Kisses her on the left cheek and takes her school books.)*

JIM. You little sweetheart! *(Kisses her on the right cheek and takes her gym sneakers.)*

JOE. Honey chile! I love you! *(Kisses her on the lips and takes a small bag she is carrying. The boys exit with Susie while the girls register extreme annoyance.)*

* * * *

SUSIE WONDERS

(For 4 females or 4 males or 4 optional)

This skit calls for four girls; however, either boys or boys and girls will do just as well. We open on Peg, Clara and Janice talking about Susie.

PEG. I'm telling you that Susie is really dumb. Today the teacher asked her to use "stupefy" in a sentence, and Susie said, "My little cousin has a playhouse in her yard, but the door is so small I have to stoop if I don't want to bump my head." *(The girls laugh.)* Then the teacher started to tell her what "stupefy" means. She started to say it meant to "dull the faculties." *(Starts to laugh.)* And so Susie said, "You mean that's why our faculty's so dull?" *(The girls laugh.)*

CLARA. No wonder she was kept after school!

PEG. I'll say. Teacher was really burned up.

JANICE. Shh! Here she comes now.

SUSIE *(Approaches.)* Hi! Say, could I ask you girls to explain something to me?

PEG. Sure, Susie!

CLARA. We're always glad to help those who are not as smart as we are.

JANICE. What is it you want to know?

SUSIE. Well, I was wondering what "officiate" means.

PEG. That's easy. It means to take charge of.

CLARA. I'd say it meant to preside at some affair, like a master of ceremonies.

JANICE. Or to carry out the duties of some position, like an officer of a club.

SUSIE. Well, I was wondering, because I heard today of a man who died of a fish-he-ate. *(She laughs and runs off while the girls register chagrin and shake their fists.)*

* * * *

TALL, DARK AND HANDSOME

(For 1 male, 2 females, or 3 females)

The characters consist of Lady, Fortune Teller and Servant. For props you need one light-colored balloon with a weight attached to hold it snugly on top of a small dish in which the weight can be placed, so as to give a "crystal ball" appearance; one candle in a candle stick; a book; a table and two chairs. Fortune Teller and Servant may have some sort of improvised costumes.

We begin with Lady approaching an imaginary door and ringing a bell. The Servant goes to the door.

SERVANT *(Opens the door; very solemn.)* You wish to see Madame Sherossa Mygosha?

LADY *(Nervously.)* Yes, yes; I wish to have my future told.

SERVANT. Come with me. *(Conducts the Lady to where Madame sits behind the table, a crystal ball before her, a lighted candle to one side before an open book. The table is at an angle to the audience. The Servant bows.)* Madame Sherossa Mygosha! *(Withdraws.)*

MADAME. Come in, my dear. Please be seated. *(Indicates a chair on the other side of the table.)*

LADY *(Takes the chair.)* You can tell my future?

MADAME. What will be, I see. If you will gaze into the globe of mystery, I will tell you your fate. *(Pause.)* Ah! I see my lady has dreams of romance. Ah, yes! Someone is coming into your life. Someone who will woo and win you. *(Passes a hand before her eyes.)* Now I see more clearly. I see a tall, dark-haired man at your side; a gentleman of culture and breeding . . .

LADY *(Excited.)* Good looking?

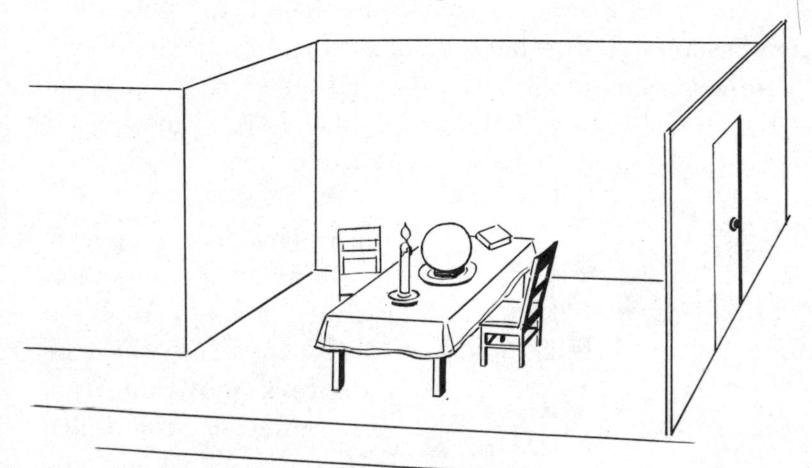

MADAME. Ah, yes! He is very handsome and debonair, and he is . . .

LADY. Rich?

MADAME. Very rich. *(Moves the candle closer to the balloon as though to see more clearly.)* Ah! He is the president of a very large company. He has a palatial home in Florida, another in Maine, another . . .

LADY *(Quite excited.)* Yes, yes, but tell me one more thing.

MADAME. And what is that?

LADY. What happens to my husband and five kids? *(Madame moves the candle so that it explodes the balloon.)*

THE BURNING SCHOOLHOUSE

(For 7 players)

This skit is written for boys but can be done just as well by girls, or boys and girls, for that matter. The characters are an old man and six boys (more or less).

The old man *(Uses a cane.)* is slowly wending his way across the stage when a boy comes running on from one side, yelling, "Fire! Fire! The schoolhouse is on fire!" Boys come running from all directions, yelling, "Fire! Fire! The schoolhouse is burning down!" The first boy runs off on the opposite side of the stage, followed by other boys as they arrive on the stage. Some can come from different parts of the audience, all yelling and excited.

The first boy re-appears before all of the boys have run off. He is carrying a filled paper cup which he takes back across the stage in the direction from which he first came. A second boy, also with a paper cup, follows him, and then a third. About the time the fourth boy comes on with a cup, the first boy is running back with an empty cup, saying, "Hurry! Hurry! It's burning faster!"

This continues, so that one or two boys are crossing the stage in each direction, urging each other to greater speed, spilling some of the contents and cautioning each other to be more careful, i.e. "Steady there, you're spilling it." "Make it faster." "She's really burning now." "Hurry, hurry!"

The old man tries to keep out of the way of the hurrying boys, watching the whole business with growing astonishment. Finally he stops the first boy, who is making about his third trip.

OLD MAN. Look, sonny, you boys will never put out that fire with those little cups of water.

BOY. Water! Are you crazy? This is *kerosene! (Breaks loose from the Old Man and hurries off.)*

(CURTAIN)

* * * *

ALOYSIUS BIGMOUTH

(For 3 males, 4 to 9 optional)

This skit calls for one politician, Aloysius Bigmouth, a master of ceremonies, and an audience of five to ten. The scene opens on the audience, seated in chairs, facing the emcee standing and Bigmouth, seated to his rear and a little to one side. The snorer is one of the audience.

MC. And now, ladies and gentlemen, it gives me great pleasure to introduce to you a man who needs no introduction, a man known and admired by all of us, one of our outstanding citizens. Ladies and gentlemen, I give you . . . *(Hesitates, glances hastily at a card in his hand.)* . . . Mr. Aloysius Bigmouth. *(The audience claps faintly.)*

BM. *(Gets up to face the audience, bowing slightly. The emcee takes his seat. Bigmouth speaks in ham oratorical manner.)* Ladies and gentlemen, I come before you tonight as one who has always stood four-square for the people and against the public. *(The man in front rests his head on his hand and soon begins to snore.)* My record is an open book. *(Snore.)* And I am proud of my support of that great party of which I have always been a loyal member. *(Snore. Bigmouth looks annoyed.)* I point with pride to the glorious achievements of that great party, my party and your party, and I view with alarm the low antics and skulduggery of the opposition. *(Loud snore. Bigmouth much annoyed.)* In times such as these we must be vigilant, wide awake, alert. *(Very loud snore. Bigmouth pauses, raises his hand and speaks confidentially.)* My friends, let me depart from my prepared address one moment to illustrate for you what I mean when I say we must be wide awake. *(Lowers his voice.)* Everyone of you who wishes to be known as an intelligent, alert, patriotic citizen, kindly raise your right hand. *(All hands go up except the man sleeping who snores. Bigmouth raises his voice as he proceeds, emphasizing each word.)* Now then, anyone who doesn't care if he is just a stupid, dumb jackass, *(Shouts) Stand up!*

SNORER *(Leaps to his feet amid laughter, looks around confused, then looks at Bigmouth.)* Well, Mr. Bigmouth, I don't know what you're voting on, but it looks to me like the two of us are the only ones for it.

* * * *

SCHOOL DAYS

(For 2 males, 4 females, 3 to 7 optional)

Eight to twelve boys and girls as students and one teacher make up the cast. The only props needed are chairs and a small table to serve as the teacher's desk; also school books. The students' chairs are arranged so as to face the audience at an angle, the teacher's desk being sideways. The skit begins in front of the curtain with most of the students gathered in a group, singing:

School days, school days,
How we all love school days;
Readin' 'n' writin' 'n' 'rithmetic,
Sometimes I wish I would just get sick . . .

(The group pauses to look sick, drooping their heads, rubbing their stomachs and such. They brighten up as a boy and girl come on holding hands. The boy and girl stop at center in front of the group, turning to face toward the audience, but looking at each other.)

GROUP *(Sings.)*

You were the cutie for whom I'd go,
I was your clumsy, bigfoot beau.

(Pauses as the boy in scuffling feet steps on the girl's foot.)

MARY ANN. Ouch!

JOE *(Quickly.)* Gee, Mary Ann, I'm sorry.

MARY ANN. Oh, that's all right. *(Takes Joe's notebook; also pencil he has tucked behind one ear and writes in his book while Joe looks happy and sighs. The group crane their necks to see.)*

GROUP *(Sings.)*

And you wrote in my book,
"I love you, Joe,"
When we were a couple of kids.

(The school bell rings and the curtain goes up. Students take chairs. One girl is crying.)

TEACHER *(Seated at the desk.)* Why are you crying, Emmy Lou? *(Emmy Lou cries harder. To Peter.)* Peter, why is your sister crying?

PETER. Aw, she's crying 'cause I wouldn't give her none of my cake.

TEACHER. Didn't she have any of her own?

PETER. Yeah, and she cried while I ate that, too. *(Laughter.)*

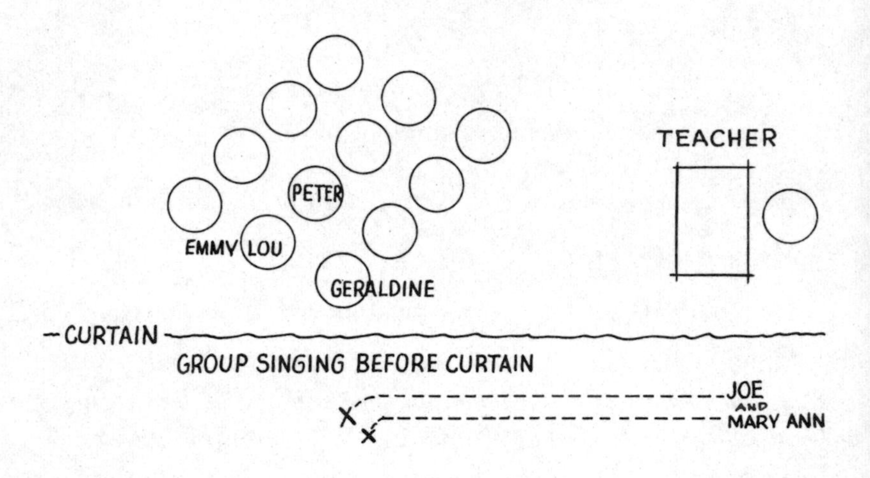

TEACHER *(Sharply.)* Peter, you will remain after school. *(Claps her hands smartly for attention.)* Now, children, as a part of our opening exercises, I will let someone choose a favorite hymn, which we . . . but suppose we have someone select the hymn first. Let—me—see. Geraldine, suppose you tell us your favorite hymn.

GERALDINE *(Hangs her head.)* Do I have to tell?

TEACHER *(Impatient.)* Why, of course, just tell us your favorite hymn. You have one, haven't you?

GERALDINE *(Wriggling.)* Uh, huh!

TEACHER. Then give us the name of your favorite hymn.

GERALDINE *(Raises her head bravely.)* It's Johnny Wright.

* * * *

NOTE: *Instead of "Johnny Wright" the name of some boy in the audience may be used, care being taken to select a boy whose attentions to the girls is well known, and who will not be unduly embarrassed.*

Section Three

STUNTS AND GAMES

Suggestions for the Leader

The stunts and games described in this section are designed for audience participation with varying amounts of advance preparation required. Actually there are about ninety different events described under the thirty-six titles given. Some are especially good for indoor programs, others for campfires, but most of them may be used under many different circumstances and with a wide range of age groups. Excellent entertainment material for shows, parties and campfires, these stunts and games can be invaluable aids in making any affair a big success.

Several general rules or reminders are suggested here with the thought they may prove helpful to you:

1. For most occasions, one or two audience participation events are sufficient, unless you are specializing on this type of show or party.

2. Make careful preparations and then check to see that everything needed has been secured and is readily available.

3. Practice anything about which there is some question or uncertainty. The Master of Ceremonies, or Leader, should be able to demonstrate or explain any event and then answer questions from a sure knowledge of how it works. This can only come from doing it himself or watching others go through it.

4. Try to anticipate any possibility of personal injury, however slight, or damage to clothing or property, and then take suitable precautions. Nothing is suggested here that can lead to trouble if ordinary common sense and good judgment are used. Some events can be messy though, which means appropriate measures should be taken to protect clothing and

property and/or clean up afterward.

5. Think about your directions ahead of time so as to give them clearly and as concisely as possible, but do not be afraid to repeat anything for added emphasis. It is particularly important that rules be made clear to participants, audience and judges.

6. Keep everything in good taste with due consideration for the feelings of all involved. If we cannot have a good time without embarrassing or humiliating someone else we should quit trying to put on programs.

7. In line with the above, contestants, especially "victims," should never be chosen because someone does not like them or wants to see them "fixed good." Only good sports should be used as "goats."

8. Prizes should usually be nonsense items that will add to the fun. Use your imagination here.

The Master of Ceremonies should overflow with enthusiasm but not to the extent of being artificial. Appropriate jokes and stories are often helpful to "set the stage" for some of these stunts, or to fill in during preparation periods. Keep things moving, everyone on their toes, and . . .

Good Luck!

BABY BOTTLE CONTEST

With baby bonnets, bottles, lollipops, and a rattle, this is sure-fire with any audience this side of the grave. It uses up to twelve contestants.

This is an audience participation stunt that affords considerable amusement whether the contestants be children or adults.

Properties

6 baby bottles (nipples should have holes enlarged with scissors. However, all holes should be just about same size.)
6 baby bonnets (real or made of crepe paper)
1 baby rattle
6 or 12 lollipops
6 chairs
Soda for baby bottles

The Master of Ceremonies asks for six volunteers from the audience for a special contest (type of contest should not be known in advance by the audience). If contestants are adults or teenagers, they are seated in chairs on the platform, facing the audience. If children, they are asked to stand beside chairs.

The emcee then announces that for this contest six "parents" and their offspring are required. The offspring are already on stage, but six parents are still needed. "More volunteers, please." The "parents" are then requested to sit in the chairs and hold their "offspring" on their laps, or (if said "offspring" are too big for this; i.e. adults or teenagers), to stand behind the chairs in which their offspring are seated.

When all the contestants are properly arranged and waiting, the emcee states that he may have neglected to say that these offspring are very young. "As a matter of fact . . ." At this point an assistant comes on with the six baby bonnets, which the emcee requests the parents to put on their "babies."

After this chore has been completed and silence restored, the emcee remarks that "giving baby his bottle" is one of the things every parent must be able to do and "this evening we will see which is the most efficient parent-baby team when it comes to taking the bottle."

"Nice Baby, Drink Your Milk"

Den Chiefs and Cubs of Pack 30 — Scout Jimmy Hines and Cub George Kinsley, Scout Ronnie James and Cub Jimmy Healy, Scout Jimmy Trainor and Cub Craig Smith and Explorer Howard Dunlap with Cub Bobby Kerr.

Assistant comes in with tray containing six baby bottles filled with soda (orange, etc.) and fitted with special nipples with larger holes as explained above. The larger holes are to speed up the contest. Bottles are given to parents while the emcee explains that they have been carefully sterilized and filled with a very special "milk" recommended for these particular babies.

Parents hold the bottles until the signal "Go" is given, at which time they give bottles to their babies, and the race is on. Care should be taken to see that the audience has a clear view of the bottles as they are being drained. With the larger holes, this is done very quickly, if the babies are any good at all.

The winner is duly cheered and presented with a pretty baby rattle, and all the babies are given lollipops. The parents may also be given lollipops.

Don't forget to collect the bottles and bonnets, as this is a stunt that can be repeated.

* * * *

STEADY AS YOU GO

Good test of nerves and brains, requiring only twelve paper cups for six contestants, and six chairs.

You must be prepared for wet weather if you use this one, so let's not do it over a Persian rug.

Approximately six contestants are lined up facing the audience and some ten feet behind as many chairs, between them and the spectators. The chairs should be turned sideways so as to give everyone a good view.

Each contestant extends his arms, bent at the elbows, with the backs of the hands up and as level as possible. Six assistants, one beside each contestant, place paper cups of water on the backs of these outstretched hands, each contestant receiving a cup on each hand. The cups are placed between the wrist and the first row of knuckles.

At the signal, the contestants must take the cups of water to their respective chairs, the first one placing both cups on his chair without a mishap being the winner. Before giving the signal the emcee should pass down the front of the line and assure himself that all cups of water are properly placed and balanced by the assistants, who then hold them in place until the command "Get ready," when they remove all assistance except one index finger, standing sideways and to the left of the contestants. (There should be sufficient room between the contestants to prevent crowding.)

At the command, "Get set," the contestants are left in sole possession of the cups as the assistants carefully remove their index fingers and place their arms at their sides. As soon as he sees that all is clear, the emcee gives the command "Go"

and the race is on. Nothing should be said about how the cups are carried to the chairs, so that if someone is smart enough to lift each cup in turn from the back of his hands and carry them in a more secure manner, more power to him. Someone else may try to get hold of one with his teeth.

Others will try to navigate the ten feet, balancing the cups as placed on the back of their hands, a tricky job indeed, and one which, even if negotiated successfully, still leaves them with the problem of getting the cups off after they reach their chairs.

But the audience always has such a good time watching the struggles of good-natured contestants.

* * * *

HOW DO YOU DO?

Balloons, paper cups and all-day suckers can provide some amusement and confusion here; four to six participants.

Two or three pairs of contestants compete for a prize, each pair performing separately against time. They draw straws for the order of performance.

At a signal in each case, the two members of the pair approach each other, both carrying a cup of water in the right hand, bouncing a balloon in the air with the left hand and sucking on an all-day sucker or taffy. When close enough to shake hands, they must say, "How do you do, this beautiful morning?" and shake hands with right hands.

They cannot speak until taffy has been removed from the mouth and, obviously, cannot shake hands until the cup of water is removed from their right hands. One way or another things are liable to get confused.

Probably the best method is to bounce the balloon high (it

must be kept in the air) and remove the taffy with the left hand. Bounce the balloon high again and transfer the cup of water to the left hand. Bounce the balloon high the third time and shake hands while saying, "How do you do, this beautiful morning?" finishing in time to bounce the balloon once more. Actions are then reversed to get back to their original condition. When both are finished, time is taken.

Disqualification or time penalties may be imposed for any mishaps. A campfire variation might be the carrying of a lighted candle in the right hand. In such a case it is always possible the balloon may get too close and—"Poof"—no balloon.

* * * *

PASS THE BALL

Two rubber balls, oranges or potatoes and enough chairs will furnish a bit of exercise for two teams of about four to eight each.

A surprisingly difficult stunt is passing a small rubber ball from one person to another by sitting in chairs and using the feet or, more precisely, the front of the lower shins for the passing. A ball is placed just above the turned-up feet of the first team member who extends his legs, tightly pressed together, to receive it.

He must then pass it to the next member of the team, no mean feat, as he swings his extended legs above the one receiving the ball and tries to let the ball slip between his legs easily so as not to roll off. If boys and girls are playing, they should alternate.

Every time a ball rolls off, the team must start over. However, the ball is started at a different end of the line each time. Six or more may participate on each team, and both teams should be lined up in chairs facing the audience.

Oranges may be used if they are hard enough so as not to break when dropped, or rounded potatoes about the same size as oranges are all right provided they are just about exactly the same size and shape. Otherwise one team may set up a howl.

One thing is certain—where a team keeps dropping the ball, they are going to get very tired legs, but quick. It's fun, though.

If more than 3 or 4 are on a team the chairs would be closer together and exchange made with legs extended forward in each case, the one with the ball swinging his legs just a bit sideways for the "drop."

THE MOVING FINGER

An index finger and a spirit of fun is all you need to get various people into the act, but you may need some other props for penalties.

For campfires, parties and other occasions where spontaneous audience participation is desired, the Moving Finger may be employed as a novel means for supplying entertainment.

The one providing "The Finger" (that is, the emcee for this stunt) announces in a very dramatic manner, "And now we come to "The Moving Finger."

The group (or at least part of them who have been coached in advance) will say "Ooooh!" in such a manner as to indicate that this announcement is one of frightening implications.

Then the leader says, "Remember, when the Moving Finger points at You, (Finger is pointed at several in the group who shrink back, moan, cover their faces with their hands, etc.) you must speak up, sing up, or . . ."

Group (or those coached in advance) "You'll be sorry!"

Leader: "That's right. You must tell a joke, recite a funny verse, sing a bit of something, or perform in some way. Because if you don't respond soon enough or well enough to secure laughter or applause, you'll . . ."

Group: "Be sorry!"

The leader then proceeds with the game by saying, "Ready, everybody! All right, here we go! The Finger is beginning to move. It is swinging around the circle (group, etc.) and it is pointing at . . ." (Brings the finger to point at one person whose name he can mention or not as he wishes, so long as there is no doubt as to who is meant.)

The person pointed at must promptly get up and do his bit of entertainment. It is best to point the first several times at persons who are "in the know" or who can be counted on to come up with a variety of jokes, funny verses, songs, etc., so that others will get the idea better and have more of a chance to "get set" for their turn.

In the beginning the leader and group will probably be tolerant of some rather feeble efforts at entertainment, but as the game progresses the group may tend to groan, or turn thumbs down on some joke, etc. Sooner or later someone will not be able to think of anything to say or do, or get the razzberry. Or, a victim may be secretly chosen in advance because of his willingness and ability to be a good victim.

However it happens, the whole group will groan as it becomes evident that a "You'll Be Sorry" victim has been secured. Various penalties may be used, including the doing of different stunts.

One penalty that will prove popular is to have a large square of cardboard or canvas in which a hole has been cut for the head. The victim, on hands and knees or bent over, or seated in a chair, puts his head through the hole. Extra protection for clothing may be provided by paper or cloth fitting around the neck. The victim may also wear a bathing cap or a pirate-style headpiece to cover the hair.

When the victim is all set, someone can hit him with soft custard or pudding in a paper cup, etc. This can be thrown (slapstick comedy style) or pushed into his face. Quite often the victim may try to eat some of this pudding with his tongue, which adds to the fun.

Washing facilities should be on hand and the mess promptly cleaned up. It is wise to try out anything like this in advance to make sure there is no danger of anyone's getting hurt or his clothing soiled. Properly controlled this can be highly entertaining for the victim and the audience alike.

A rubber bulb filled with water may be used with the executioner standing a prescribed distance away and getting "three shots" or "five shots."

More than one victim may be chosen in the same game. However, it is not a good idea to drag The Moving Finger out too long. It is not intended to fill up a major portion of the program; merely as a variety number to get everyone into the act.

* * * *

SWAPPING CLOTHES

Principal props are large cartons or other makeshift "dressing rooms" for one or more couples who do the swapping.

As once (at least) used on television, this stunt involved an exchange of clothes by a man and his wife, each being placed in a large cardboard carton, with a lid, with just enough room to remove their clothes (except underwear) in a cramped position, push the same through the hole in the side of the box and take exchange clothing from their mates.

Only one article of clothing could be safely exchanged at a time and each had to be sure the other got the article he extended, since he would really have a problem if anything fell onto the floor.

As an entertainment stunt, one couple could do this, or

several couples could race. If cartons large enough for the purpose are not available, similarly shaped "dressing rooms" can be improvised with the aid of chairs, card tables, blankets, poles, canvas, etc. It is important that these dressing rooms be dark, cramped and reasonably secure against collapse.

Ordinarily, the exchange would be confined to such items as shirts, pants, dresses, belts, ties, sweaters and so forth. Charm bracelets, hair ribbons and such may be used in order to equalize the number of items the couples must exchange. It goes without saying (but I'm saying it) that the couples should be of relative size and wearing clothes they don't mind putting through such an exchange game.

As soon as a couple is ready they emerge for audience inspection, the best dressed couple winning, unless there is not much to choose from, in which case time may count. The results should be hilarious.

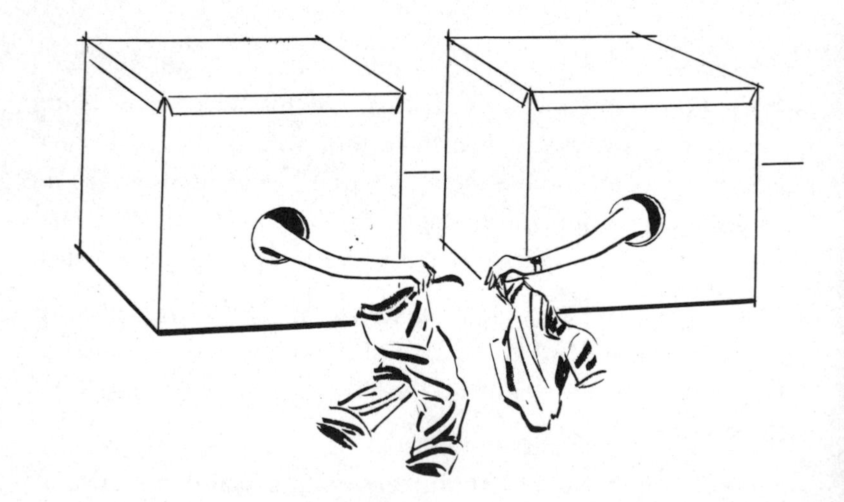

BOMBARDIER

Half a dozen couples for this, with empty ice cream cones, scoops and softly-mashed potatoes. Also protective and clean-up items.

This is another race for couples, although they both may be of the same sex if an all-male or all-female group. If boys and girls, the boys are the "goats," or targets.

Targets lie flat on their backs on the floor, holding empty ice cream cones between their teeth. Partners stand erect (and we do mean "erect") beside them and try to drop a scoop or a large tablespoonful of softly mashed potatoes into cones for a direct hit.

First, second and third places are determined by order in which direct hits are scored, each miss carrying a time penalty, perhaps ten seconds.

A towel or other protection should be given to each target as a covering over the chest and shoulders, and arrangements made to avoid or clean up the mess promptly.

This stunt is not recommended where a large audience will not be able to get a good view of the proceedings, but is a good laugh-getter where hits and misses can be clearly seen.

* * * *

SEATS FOR ALL

A tricky stunt for fifteen or more youthful participants; no props needed.

This is a tricky little piece of business which may be staged as a rehearsed stunt or surprise audience participation affair, depending upon the occasion and wishes of those putting on the program. It is not recommended for adults or for participants in dress clothes, nor for girls unless wearing slacks.

A group of about 15 to 30, or even more, are lined up in single file. It is important that a large boy should not be immediately in front of a much smaller boy, or a fat boy in front of a much slighter lad. The boys are marched around in a steadily shrinking circle until each boy is approximately two inches in front of the boy behind. The distance varies somewhat depending upon the number of participants and the size of the boys. Then, at the command "Sit" everyone sits down at the same time, each in the lap of the boy behind, steadying one another, if desired, by placing their hands on the trunk or the arms of the boy in front.

The feet and legs should be kept parallel and fairly close together. A first attempt will frequently result in a pile-up. However, it can be done the very first time by a well-coached and disciplined group.

Not only can the entire group sit down, but they can maintain their seats while singing a song, giving a cheer, or executing various limited actions, such as blowing noses, taking candy or gum out and sharing it, drinking from canteens, etc. A collapse may be precipitated by swaying while singing, or by one or more boys shifting their positions. Or, the group may successfully rise as a unit and march off.

A narrator may set the stage for this stunt and explain the actions as they take place.

For example, he may begin by telling the audience that on a recent hike Troop 30 ran into wet weather as the result of which the ground was quite muddy. After hiking for some time the boys were tired, but could find no place to sit down. However, since Troop 30 always comes up with a solution to every problem, even if it's the wrong solution, the boys arranged themselves in single file and made a circle. After satisfying themselves that each one had a seat-to-be behind him, the command "Sit" was given and all sat down. (If they collapse, the narrator ad-libs something to the effect that you know how these collapsible chairs are always collapsing at the wrong time. Anyhow, after brushing off the mud, they try again.)

Much relieved to find themselves comfortably seated, the scouts proceeded to mop their brows, blow their noses, comb their hair and share candy and gum just as though they were always in the habit of *each boy holding the entire scout troop in his lap.* In other words, each boy was holding over 2000 pounds of boy scouts in his lap.

They decided to sing a song. *(Scouts do so.)*

Having rested themselves, the Senior Patrol Leader gave the command, "Scouts, stand up" and the Troop was on its way. (Of course, if they fall down instead, some more ad-libbing is in order.)

Another variation would be for a question and answer relay to go around the circle, each boy tapping the shoulder of the boy in front, who turns his head to listen. The first question might be, "How much farther is it?" with the Senior Patrol Leader being immediately behind the scout who starts the question, so that it goes all around the circle, with the answer going back again. The answer might be, "Ten miles" with each scout registering consternation until, when the word has reached the original questioner, all collapse.

Or, the leader may start to give the answer to the boy behind him, and then say, "I'm going to take a short cut," and tap the boy in front of him who started it, saying "ten miles," at which all collapse.

Or, he may pass the word "Not far" all the way around, with the next question being "How far is that?" and so forth.

Just one more, and then it's up to you. One boy may ask, "Have you any candy?" This question goes around to the boy behind him, who produces a bag of candy, first taking one, and then handing it to the boy behind with, "Sure, help yourself." This goes around to the boy who originally asked the question, there being just enough pieces for everyone but him. He says (after finding the bag empty), "Hey! This bag is empty!" until it gets around to the scout who started it, who is right behind him and who inspects the bag carefully, shaking it upside down, and then saying, "That's funny!" The boy in front of him looks around and explodes, *"Tain't funny!"* and stands up, with an inevitable result.

Seats For All Is Right

Twenty-six scouts and explorers of Troop 30 sit down together, each holding well over a ton of boys in his lap. It just goes to show how resourceful scouts can be.

WHAT DID DELAWARE?

This song game literally takes in everybody and requires no props; a wonderful way to pep up an audience.

This song game is an old favorite. However, I do not ever recall seeing it in print and have learned from experience that the possibilities are greater than most groups realize. Therefore, both for those who have played it and those who have not, the following explanation and suggested verses are given.

The group is divided in half with a leader for each half, one side singing the questions and the other the answers. As each question is asked or answered, the leader of the other side whispers the next question or answer to his group, moving rapidly along the front to do so. Members of his team may also make suggestions, but the leader gives the word.

The song-game traditionally begins with:

Oh, what did Dela wear, boys,
Oh, what did Delaware?
Oh, what did Dela wear, boys,
Oh, what did Delaware?
Oh, what did Dela wear, boys,
Oh, what did Delaware?
I ask you again, as a personal friend,
Oh, what did Dela wear?

The answer, of course, is "She wore her New Jersey, boys," etc. The first two lines should always be repeated three times as above in order to give the other side a fair opportunity to get set.

The questions and answers continue until one side, or the other, is stumped. No question or answer may be used more than once, and every question and answer must be "plausible," although we sometimes stretch this plausibility mighty thin. Naturally there can be no general agreement on some questions and answers. However, the following suit me.

What did Idaho (hoe)?
She hoed her Maryland.

How did Flora die (Florida)
She died in Missouri. (misery)

What did Massa chew? (Massachusetts)
He chewed a Connecticut.

Where has Ore gon(e)?
He's seeing Okla hom(e).

What did Tennes see?
He saw what Arkan saw.

What made Pennsyl vain? (Pennsylvania)
He shot an Indian. (Indiana)

How did Wiscon sin?
He drank some West Vir gin. (ia)

or

He stole a New Brass Key (Nebraska)

What did Missis sip? (Mississippi)
She sipped a Minne sota. (soda)

What did Ala bam (Alabama)
He bammed an Illi nois(e).

What did Io weigh? (Iowa)
He weighed a Washing ton.

Where did Mary land? (As a question does not duplicate answer)
She landed in New York.

How did Connecti cut?
He used an Arkan saw. (Different from above answer)

Why did Georgi(e) "Ah!"? (Georgia)
He saw Louisie Anne. (Louisiana)

Who did Ohi owe? (Ohio)
He owed Colora dough. (Colorado)

If you want to get more farfetched:

What did Ari zone? (Arizona)
He zoned his New Hampshire.

What did Miche gain? (Michigan)
He gained a new Brass Key. (Nebraska)
or
He gained some Vira gin. (Virginia)

Sometimes the following answer is used in desperation, but can, as stated above, be used only once:

I don't know but I'll ALaska. (ask her)

The important thing is not to let it die on the vine, but to keep it going at a good pace, which is usually not difficult with a youthful audience.

TOMMY-TOMMY

Another nothing-needed stunt for universal participation with some appearing up front; a wonderful filler-in.

As a program warmer-upper, especially while waiting for everybody to assemble, Tommy-Tommy is perfect.

The leader explains that this is a test of observation which will definitely prove that most people do not watch carefully enough. He then says he will execute a few simple actions and say a few words, and that probably most, if not all, of those watching him will not be able to duplicate his actions and words—unless they already know the stunt.

The leader then says, "Tommy, Tommy, Tommy, Tommy, Whoops! Tommy," at the same time touching the tip of each finger and thumb of his left hand with the index finger of his right, beginning with the little finger and saying "Whoops!" while sliding right index finger down left index finger and up thumb (see drawing). The left hand is held about shoulder height for this purpose, with the palm turned inward. As soon as he has said the final "Tommy" the leader lowers his hands in front of him and interlocks the fingers (folds hands) at waist level; or, if sitting down, in his lap.

Volunteers are then selected to come forward—one at a time—to face the audience and try it. Almost invariably they will not have noticed the folding of the hands, and, when told they are wrong, will think, along with the rest of the audience, they did not get the Tommy-Tommy quite right. Thus, the leader will be urged to repeat it again and again, with different persons excitedly shouting, "Now, I've got it," "Let me try it," etc.

It may be necessary to over-emphasize the interlocking of the fingers in order to call attention to it since it is desirable that at least a few "get it right" before a halt is called. The fact that one and then more of the audience have figured it out causes the others to redouble their efforts. With a small group the final awakening may come with a rush, but a larger group could go on indefinitely, which is not good. Therefore, the leader may explain it, but it is generally better to simply discontinue the experiment and let the ones now "in the know" show their more obtuse companions or, if only a few know it and keep it to themselves, it can be used again and again.

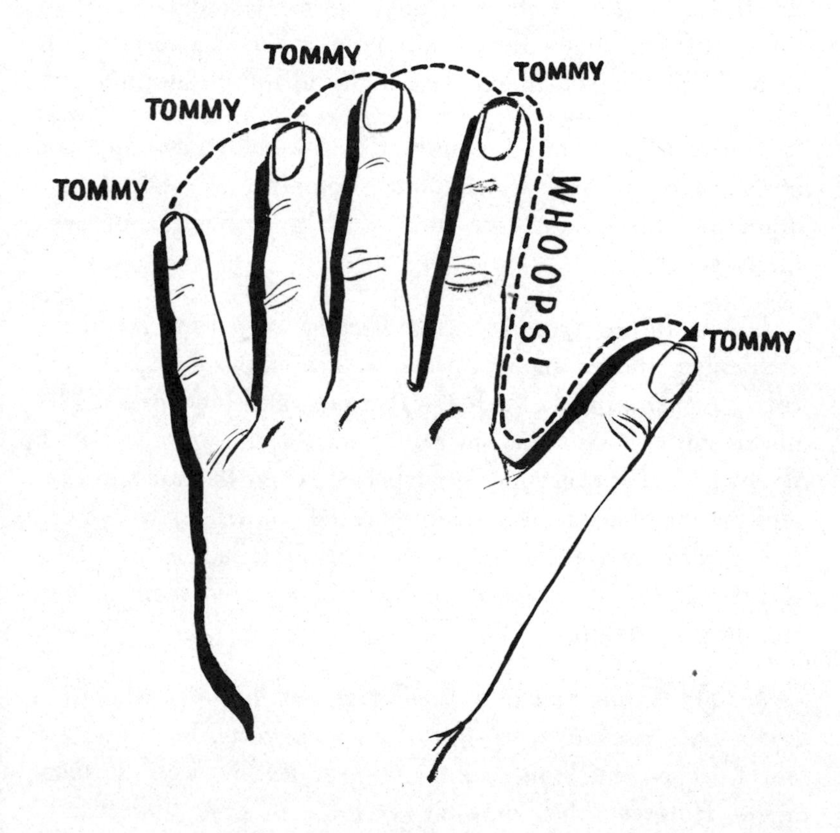

SHIRT RACE

Half a dozen or so can get in on this, and only need the shirts they have on their backs; a trick challenge event.

One "who knows" challenges others to a "shirt race," that is, "to see who can take his shirt off, put it on again and button it up" first. This may be a general challenge, which involves the risk of being taken up by someone who knows the trick, or who is sharp enough to see through it (rather unlikely). Or, the challenge may be directed to a certain part of the audience considered less likely to upset the applecart.

The shirt race may be limited to the challenger and one other, or up to half a dozen may compete, as desired. Another possibility is a time limit, such as a minute, or even thirty seconds.

Unless forced to move faster because of a time limit, the challenger moves more leisurely than the others, feeling fairly secure in the knowledge that men and boys practically never button a shirt up, but rather start at the top and button it down. Thus, everyone is surprised when the race is over and the announcement is made that the challenger won, until it is explained that the others were disqualified because they did not follow the instructions, which required them to button their shirts up, not "down."

A light dawns and everyone laughs at the ones who were taken in. I used to work this stunt with vests, but these are not worn so much these days, especially by boys or teenagers. However, they may be available in some audiences

HOW TO GET IT DOWN

A pole, a cup of water and a chair or table are sufficient to put your "victim" on the spot for the others to laugh at; but he can fool them—sometimes.

Where you have a ceiling not too high and a floor that will not be hurt by a little water, it is fun to get some unwary person to fetch a cup of water down from the ceiling without spilling any water.

For this you need a paper cup of water, a pole (a broom or mop will do) and a straight chair. A prize may be offered to someone performing successfully.

In any event, a volunteer is secured and told that he is to be the subject of an experiment to test his sense of balance, coordination and general ability to handle himself in a difficult situation. He may also be told that he will be rewarded with a prize if he succeeds.

The emcee, or an assistant, then climbs up on a chair or, if necessary, a table, and places a cup of water against the ceiling, the volunteer having been given a pole which he places against the bottom of the cup in order to hold it against the ceiling. The assistant then gets down and removes the said chair or table. However, a chair is placed just about at the limit of the subject's reach.

The subject's problem is to get the chair, or table, pull it over, get up on it and work his hands up the pole until he gets the cup of water. This is possible although he may have a time of it if he really has to stretch for the chair. Among other dangers, he may put so much pressure against the cup that the pole will go through the bottom, whereas a little wobbling of the pole will prove disastrous.

If you wish to frame the victim good, it is only necessary to select someone enough shorter than the person who placed

the cup against the ceiling so that he cannot possibly reach it. About the best he can do is suddenly remove the pole and try to catch the cup before it turns over, possible but not very likely.

This is a lot of fun for the audience. However, the victim should be someone who does not mind being the "goat" and care must be taken to ensure that no accident worse than a cup of spilled water takes place.

A prize may be awarded for a successful job, as promised, or the victim may be presented with the cup of water "since he worked so hard for it." It may then be necessary for the emcee to duck fast.

* * * *

LIVE TARGET

Requirements for this depend upon your weapons and ammunition, but you definitely need at least one live target (or at least his head) and a large piece of canvas, or poncho with a hole in it—for the head.

---

1. Throwing something at somebody's head stuck through a hole in a piece of canvas seems to have great appeal and to provide considerable entertainment, to say the least. Following are several ways this can be done with safety and so as to provide plenty of fun. In each case a snug-fitting pair of safety goggles are recommended although I have seen the sponge throw done without any such protection even though some husky teenagers were doing the throwing. As a matter of fact, they used a wet wash rag in lieu of sponges, which carried better and tended to unfold. However, the sponges are much better.

The distance from the throwers to the target must be determined by the missiles being used and the strength and ability of those throwing. Generally speaking the spot where the missile actually leaves the thrower's hand should not be closer than ten feet and it may be wiser to lengthen this. The only way to be sure is try it. The sponges should be thoroughly soaked in advance so as to eliminate any rough or hard part, and may be re-soaked if necessary. On the other hand the sponges should not be dripping wet, but should be given a little squeeze to remove excess water.

A leader should be in charge and throws made only on his signal, which should prevent any rapid-fire throwing, each throw being anticipated by the one who is playing target. The secret of his success in not getting hit is a close watch of the sponge (it should be large enough to be clearly seen) and a slow movement of the head to one side. It is really surprising how difficult it is to hit a clever target. Properly handled this can be quite safe without goggles, but not the following variations.

2. Using water or soda as ammunition, pistol marksmen may try to hit the target's face (he might also want to wear a bathing cap), while the person playing target tries to avoid getting hit, or, if he wishes to catch the "shot" with his mouth. If he wants to try catching the shots when he thinks he can, the weapon (water pistol or rubber bulb) should be sterilized in hot water in advance and tested to make sure any liquid used will come out clean. Naturally only good water will be used. If the target is not going to try to intercept any shots, only water should be used, the soda being used only to add interest for the target if he is thirsty. It is important that the shots be timed by the leader who should keep them short, not more than a couple of seconds, depending, as usual, on distance and the marksmanship of the participants. The leader may use some form of sustained noise, preferably resembling a gun, to denote the duration of the shot, giving the signals, "Ready, aim, zzzztttt!" If a marksman is slow starting, his shot may be finished by the time he starts.

3. If you really want to get messy, soft puddings in soft

paper cups may be thrown, or (more expensive ammunition) you may use containers of whipped cream under pressure. The distance for the latter will be shorter than any of the others.

Whatever you use, try it and be sure you know what is involved. Another problem is how to arrange the target and throwers or marksmen so as to afford the audience a good view of what is happening. They certainly do not want the throwers right between their view and the target. These problems can easily be worked out, however, and you can go a long way before you will find audience participation stunts that will be enjoyed any more enthusiastically than live targets.

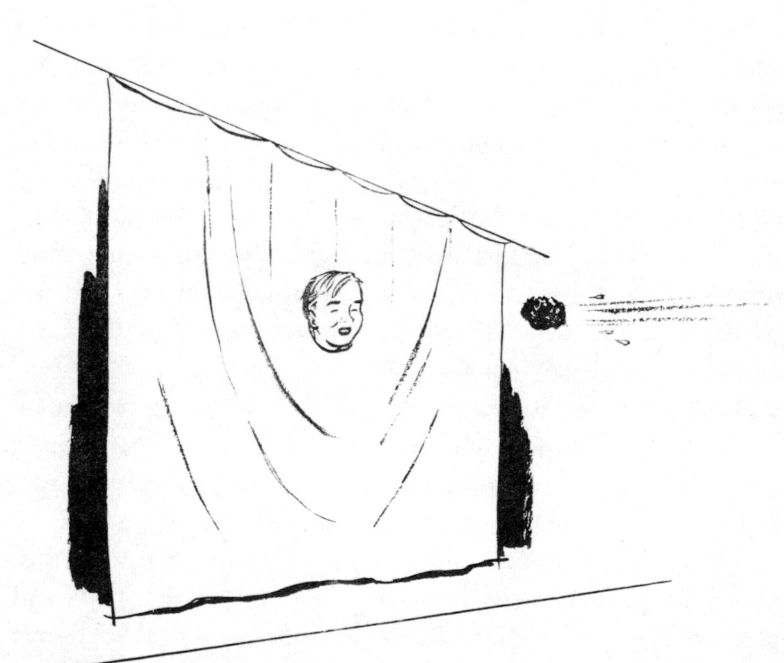

WRONG CUPS

A dozen unbreakable or expendable cups and saucers and as many contestants take part, with a dozen spoons added, if you prefer.

Three couples and a dozen unbreakable, expendable or paper cups and saucers can provide an exciting and amusing race to watch. Spoons may also be included as explained later. Six of the cups and saucers should be decidedly different from the others, different colors being the simplest solution. Each girl is given a cup and saucer of one color (say, blue) for each hand, the boys getting two each of the others (say, yellow). The emcee then explains that:

"It is now after dinner and the men have retired to the library and the ladies to the sitting room. The men all want coffee and the ladies all want tea. Because the maid is a contestant on a television show, they have to wait on themselves. There being six couples, three men and three ladies volunteer to fetch for the six. Not using their heads too well, each takes two cups, one in each hand, and they are all ready to go their different ways, when someone discovers that the men have picked up the tea and the ladies the coffee. Still not using their heads, they try to exchange in the hallway where they cannot set anything down, least of all on the floor as the cats will get into them."

Thus we have a race, each boy-girl team trying to win by successfully swapping cups and saucers without dropping them. It can be made tougher by putting water in the cups. Dropped cups and saucers may either disqualify a couple, or a penalty may be added to the elapsed time. Spilled water may also involve a penalty. The first couple to finish and turn to face the audience side by side wins, other things being equal.

Needless to say, the stunt can be done quickly and smoothly by a couple, each of whom simply place their right-hand cup and saucer on top of their left, take their partner's doubled-up cups and saucers and lift the top one off.

Many, however, will do it in some harder way, including holding a saucer with their teeth, or even attempting to balance one on their head. This is even more likely to happen if spoons are placed in the cups, making it impossible to set one on top of another. An alert couple will not find this any problem, though, each removing the left-hand spoon with the teeth, setting the right cup on top, taking the partner's cups and saucers, placing the spoon back in the partner's cup with his teeth after he has removed the top cup.

Most people are apt to get confused somewhere along the way, what with all the excitement, placing the spoon in the saucer, or trying to, placing their partner's spoon in their own cup (there must be a complete exchange), etc.

Anyhow, it is a lot of fun.

* * * *

THE MINISTER'S COMING

Some real entertainment can be furnished if you go to the trouble of making necessary preparations and planning it well; read about it to see what you need.

This stunt may be varied somewhat according to circumstances and the group using it. However, it generally involves three to six "small boys" and their "mothers." The "mothers" may be larger boys, men or genuine mothers. The "small boys" may be rather large. As a rule it is not too practicable to use girls at all unless the boys are actually small and the girls older teen-agers.

The small boys are selected in advance and taken offstage (out of sight) to be made ready, which means they must be "dirtied up," whether by the use of chocolate candy smeared on the face, burnt cork on the hands and face, or real, honest-to-goodness dirt. Their hair is mussed, their clothing disarranged and so forth. The boys will be instructed to come when called and submit resignedly when a mother takes hold of a handy ear, but to protest vigorously about being cleaned up because "the minister's coming" and to be unco-operative. However, there is no active resistance. In other words, the boys protest but permit themselves to be washed, pushed, combed and so on.

Next the emcee selects as many mothers as there are small boys, whether strictly by volunteers or by calling on individuals who he thinks will go all out to make it a good show. If these mothers are male, they should be given dresses and aprons so as to look the part. Each mother is given a name and told the name of her son. For example, Mrs. Brown and Willie, Mrs. Jones and Johnny, Mrs. Smith and Jimmy. They do not know which boy is theirs by sight nor do the boys know who their mothers are, except by name.

The emcee then explains that, as everybody knows, it is next to impossible to keep small boys clean, and that this was just as true a few years back when the coming of the minister was more of a social event, perhaps, than it is now. Just for fun we are going to have a little race to see which of our mothers is most efficient in getting her son ready for the minister's visit.

Wash basins and pitchers of water are brought on stage, also pails for discarded water, small tables or chairs, towels, wash cloths, soap, combs, clean shirts and ties. All of these are arranged in separate set-ups across the front of the stage and a mother assigned to each.

Prizes are offered for the "best" mothers who succeed in

getting their sons washed (including ears), dried, hair combed, nails cleaned, clean shirt and tie on. Speed will count only if needed to decide a close match. The final instruction to the mothers is that they must not speak to their sons after they have seized them by a handy ear which they will do as soon as he comes in each case.

At the signal the mothers run to a designated line on the stage, open imaginary doors and call their sons by name. The sons will enter as a group, all saying, "Yes, Mother" and going to the mothers who call the names they have been given. It is quite possible that in the haste and confusion, some sons and mothers will get mismatched, but more of this later.

Each mother will take one of her son's ears and march him to the wash set-up assigned to her, and proceed in the most approved manner of mothers cleaning up complaining offspring for the minister's visit. When the job is done each son is duly inspected; judges will also take notes during the clean-up. One or more winners may be announced, going by the neatest and cleanest-looking sons. If it is hard to choose, the judges may consider any tidying up of wash set-ups, method of procedure and speed of operation.

Almost as an after thought the emcee will check to make sure each mother has her own son. For example, he may say, "Well, it looks like Mrs. Brown won first prize for the fine job she did on her Willie. (He then turns to the boy and says:) "You are Willie Brown, are you not?"

If the boy isn't, he will say so, and others will too. In such an event, everyone will be taken by surprise and it becomes necessary to check the others, since there must be at least one other mother and son mismatched. The mother, of course, is disqualified since no matter "how dirty a boy gets, his own mother should know him."

Even though the winner has the right son it will not hurt to check all the others because any mismatches will be funny. If every mother has her own son the emcee may say, "Well, folks, you can see that a mother always knows her own boy no matter how dirty he may get, and loves him too." Mothers may duly "love" sons if they wish.

Any prizes should be nonsense items so it should not matter if a winner turns out to be disqualified. As a matter of fact, you may want to arrange a couple of mismatches just for the laughs.

However it is done, this stunt is thoroughly enjoyed by the audience and should be good fun for the participants, too. A final touch may be gained by giving the boys chocolate for being so good, only to see their faces immediately becoming smeared around the mouth.

* * * *

FUNNEL TRICK

Primarily a boys' campfire stunt involving a funnel, a quarter and a "victim" and, oh yes, a pitcher of water. Plus some dry clothes.

This is an old campfire favorite of boy scout troops and other boys' organizations.

It is announced that a prize will be given to anyone who can balance a quarter on his forehead and, by bringing his head forward drop said quarter into a funnel, the small spout of which is inserted inside the waistband of the trousers of the one trying it. (This is strictly for warm-weather campfires where the campers will often be wearing shorts or dungarees.)

The leader can then demonstrate and it is a good idea for

him to miss the first try and then do it the second. It really is not hard to do with a reasonably large funnel, it merely being a matter of keeping the chin in close to the chest when tipping the head.

One or more others "in the know" can then try it, getting it one or two times but missing out by the third. By this time, excitement is running high and a victim (always select a good sport) is selected from the volunteers. It is desirable that he "make it" once or twice amid cheers. The third time the quarter is balanced somebody who has been discreetly screened before the fateful moment, slips up and starts pouring water into the funnel from a pitcher.

If the victim misses, several "in the know" should plead for "another chance," and the water is promptly brought forward.

A reverse twist on this stunt is to send a younger camper from the scene on some pretext, or anyone who may be presumed not to know it, after which the stunt may be performed as above. While the group is still enjoying it, the leader reminds them that "so-and-so" is not here so we can work it again on him.

The one who left, however, has gone to prepare himself with a water bottle strapped to his thigh inside his trousers (he must not wear shorts). A rubber tube from this water bottle runs up the front of his pants to just below the belt where the end is held upright by means of a safety pin down several inches. Two safety pins may be needed. The device should be tested in advance in order to make sure it will work right. For instance, that the pins don't block the tube.

When this supposed victim returns he is told about so-

and-so doing the funnel trick and winning a prize and, because he was absent he will be given a chance. The stunt is then demonstrated and the "victim" laughs at doing anything so easy. He is so sure he can do it that the audience is eager for his "surprise." Naturally they cheer him lustily when he does it the first two times and are gloating when they see the water advancing.

Imagine their surprise when the water does not wet his pants and he drops the quarter the third time into the funnel of water. As soon as he does so, the water pourer stops pouring and looks puzzled. The victim fishes out the quarter, which may block the spout, lets the remaining water go down, and then pulls out the spout and hands the funnel calmly to the water pourer.

He can then say, "I told you there was nothing to it" and exits.

Care must be taken to insert the funnel spout snugly into the tube lest the water back up and wet the "victim" who is not supposed to be a victim. The leader can do this by making a business of inserting the funnel firmly in place, while the "victim" pulls in his stomach and assists. Also, the water must not be poured too fast since the tube can only carry a limited amount at a time.

A fast one can be pulled on the fellow with the water bottle if the leader fails to insert the funnel spout snugly into the tube and the water pourer pours too fast. This happened once with us and the indignation expressed by the pretended victim who became a real victim brought down the house.

One more variation where a number are wise to the trick

is to trap the leader in the first place as he explains it.

However it is handled, it should be possible for any victim to make a quick change nearby and return to the campfire at which time he should be cheered handsomely for being such a good sport.

WILLIAM TELL — MODERN STYLE

Four soft (real soft) and one hard baseballs, a container for same and a paper cup will supply your two participants with all they need to do their stuff.

For this stunt you need about four rag baseballs, that is imitation baseballs filled with rags or cotton so that one can be hit in the face with such a ball without any danger. An old "hard" baseball should also be covered to resemble the stuffed ones. All of these balls are then placed in a cardboard tube, box or bag with the hard ball in position to come out first. The only other prop needed is a paper cup or similar target.

The emcee selects two "volunteers" who may be father and son, mother and daughter, mother and son, or any combination you wish. He then explains that everyone is familiar with the story of William Tell who was sentenced to shoot an apple off his son's head by the tyrant who then ruled Switzerland. What we want to know is, are modern parents just as sure with a baseball as William Tell was with bow and arrow. After all, America is the land of baseball.

Accordingly, the "child" is placed in position, sideways to the audience with a paper cup inverted on his head. Our modern William Tell is placed about ten to fifteen feet away, depending upon his known ability or lack of same at throwing a baseball accurately.

The emcee then tells the audience that while he has

full confidence in our modern parent's ability, and he knows this confidence is shared by his son (daughter), just for an extra precaution he has ordered some special baseballs stuffed with rags (cotton) which are so soft they could not hurt anyone. In other words, he wrote the manufacturer that he wanted "soft," not "hard" baseballs.

He then starts to take baseballs from a container, fumbling the hard ball, which comes first, so that it drops on the floor with a thud. This should bring quite a reaction from everyone. The emcee should look dumbfounded and confused, recovering to say, "Well, I guess the manufacturer misunderstood; he must have thought I meant "hard," not "soft" baseballs. Oh well, as long as "so-and-so" throws straight, nobody has anything to worry about. You're not worried, are you (addressing the victim)?

Whatever the child may say, the catcher (who has been assigned to stand beyond the victim), should look worried and move to one side. It may be necessary to reassure folks before any balls are actually thrown. The hard ball is definitely eliminated from any possibility of being thrown. The parent gets four throws to knock off the cup, no credit being given if it falls off because victim ducks or flinches.

If you get a victim with good facial reactions this can be especially funny.

ONE WIDE RIVER TO CROSS

Two mental alertness testers that are easily staged with almost no advance preparations; a variable number of participants.

Two old mental alertness puzzles may be dramatized on stage as good entertainment.

1. First there is the fox, goose and bag of corn problem the farmer faced when he got to the river and found the boat would carry only him and one of the other three at a time. If he left the fox and goose together while he took the corn over, the fox would eat the goose, and if the goose and corn were ever alone on one bank, the goose would do you know what. It would be a good plan to improvise a boat, denote the shore lines and actually move from one to the other. The boat in its simplest form could be two poles between which the passengers moved from one side to the other, holding said poles in their hands.

To add to the fun and the eagerness of the audience to try their hand at it, the goose could have a paper of candy corn to eat if given the chance, said corn being supplied to the "bag of corn" at the beginning of the stunt. Likewise, the goose could carry something for the fox, perhaps a cookie. If the fox does not get the goose, or the goose the corn before the end of the stunt, the ones playing goose and bag of corn may eat them. No balks or re-takes are permissible. The farmer must always put his passenger into the boat first and once he has indicated that one of them is to enter, that's it; he must go through with it. This is important, because exclamations will arise as soon as he indicates which passenger is to go.

This stunt is rather easy to figure out, so it is better for young children. If the first farmer fails, get four more participants and try it again, until some farmer succeeds.

2. A little more difficult is the cannibal and missionary problem. In this case three missionaries and three cannibals must cross a river in a boat which will not carry more than three of them at one time. Only one missionary knows how to row so that he must always be in the boat. The problem is to keep the missionaries balanced numerically with the cannibals at all times, or else to have the missionaries outnumber the cannibals, because if there are more cannibals than missionaries in any one place, it is too bad for the latter.

There are three possible places for the missionaries to get eaten: on either bank or in the boat. When the boat is one side or the other those in the boat are considered as being in the same place as those on that bank. Needless to say, the boat cannot be held a little way off from the bank while somebody jumps in or out, nor can anyone swim, or be towed. Again, something should be used as a boat, and as soon as the missionary who rows (he chooses his passengers) gives any indication that someone is to enter the boat, that's it. He gets in and the rower must proceed as best he can.

I can think of at least two ways this can be done, one of which is given below:

1. Missionary rower takes one cannibal over.

2. Rower takes the second missionary (he himself is the first) and the second cannibal over, leaves the second missionary and brings the second cannibal back with him.

3. Rower again takes the second cannibal over with the third missionary, leaving both.

4. Rower returns to get the third cannibal.

In this stunt, the missionaries might be given something

to eat, which the cannibals claim if they "eat" the missionaries, and which the missionaries keep if not eaten. If one group comes to grief, choose another and try it again. You will have plenty of volunteers.

* * * *

HUNGRY PEOPLE

Seven different feeding and eating events for a general good time. Read all about them to see what you must do and get.

Marshmallows

Everyone is familiar with the two types of marshmallow races, the one being that of eating up a string to get the marshmallow suspended from it. The important thing is to see that each marshmallow is hanging down the same distance when the race starts. The winner should remove the string at once when the marshmallow is pulled into his mouth. Trying to eat it with a mouthful of string may not turn out so good. The other race is where two opponents each have one end of the string in their mouths at the start of the race with the marshmallow halfway between them. No hands are allowed in either race.

Hot Dogs

A much funnier and fairly difficult stunt is biting the hot dog. For this the old hard straw hats are ideal but if these are not available, a tight-fitting cardboard affair along the same lines may be used. Across the top of these straw hats or cardboard replicas, small dowel sticks are fastened, running from front to back, the forward end extending six to ten inches beyond the forward end of the hat. These sticks must be firmly held in place. If a cardboard crown is used (top is not really essential), the crown must be sturdy enough not to collapse under the following stress and strain.

From the forward end of these sticks, hot dogs, tied about the middle in each case, are suspended by means of cords, which again may be six to ten inches long, depending on how high the stick is above the head and how long the face is. The hot dog should be hanging safely out of reach and slightly below the mouth. The trick is to bite off each end of the hot dog by moving the head so as to cause the dog to sway back and forth.

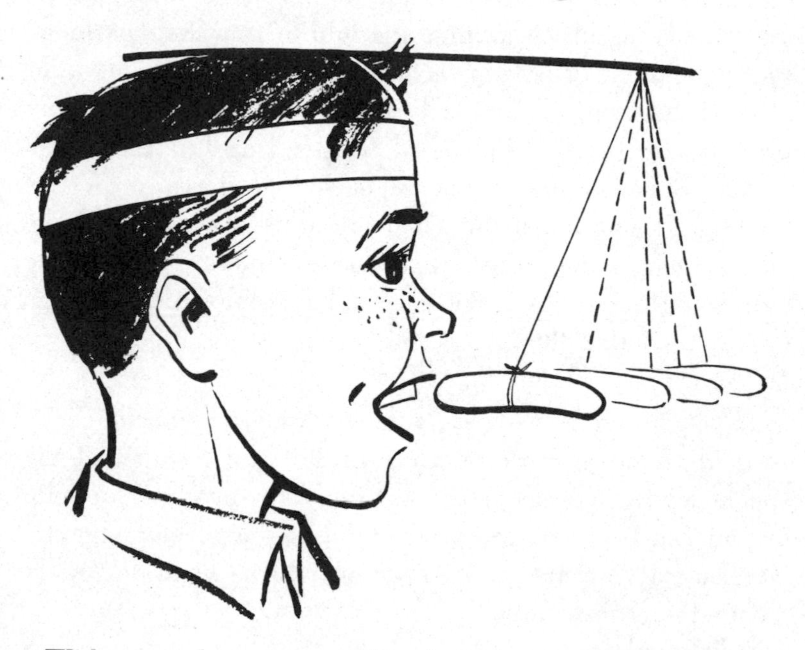

With several contestants lined up in a row, snapping at hot dogs swaying in the breeze, you can be sure of a hilarious time of it. By all means try it out before the program to make certain it is not too easy but still possible.

Puddings

Then you can always use couples to feed each other or, more customary, for one to feed the other. Using large aprons for protection and blindfolded (heavy blindfolds to protect the eyes) a couple can try to feed each other simultaneously with something like puddings, using paper spoons. The first couple to give each other at least five spoonfuls successfully wins. Things should be good and messy by that time, so be ready with wash cloths, water, towels and mops.

Bananas

One member of a couple team may try to feed the other a banana with blindfolds on both. In this case several couples are mixed up, turned around and told to find their partners, the one with the banana in each case seeking his mate in order to start the feeding. Naturally they will call each other but are still apt to get mismatched if operating fairly close together. Bananas should not be peeled until ready to start feeding. Losing a banana to the floor is just too bad. The first banana eaten wins for the side, unless eaten by the wrong partner. Let's make sure nobody falls off the stage or anything like that.

Jello

If you prefer to see what you are doing, one partner may feed his mate jello or pudding by holding the end of the spoon between his teeth and getting five spoonfuls of jello or pudding from the dish on the table to the partner's mouth. Neither may use his hands. There should be separate supply dishes for each couple.

Salted Peanuts

Two partners standing on lines several feet apart may take turns tossing salted peanuts, jelly beans and such, that couple winning where each one first catches five tossed edibles.

You can easily dream up more of these but always remember to guard against choking or foreign matter in the eyes. It is more fun to be safe.

CLAPS A-B-C-D

If your audience has hands, you are all set. Your only problem is to get them banged together in time.

A well-known warmer-upper clap which is supposed to be done by a group in perfect time goes 1-2-3-4, 1-2, 1-2; 1-2-3-4, 1-2, 1-2; 1-2-3-4; 1-2-3-4; 1. All too often there are two or three who add an extra clap or who are a bit behind so that the final big clap is marred. There are usually groans from the group and the leader usually asks them to try it again and "get it right."

Not so well known are some follow-up claps to the above, which is classified as "Clap A."

Clap B goes exactly the same until the end, when, instead of a final big clap everyone is supposed to miss, their hands fanning by each other, so that there is nothing but silence. Or rather there is supposed to be silence, but generally a few "goof" and clap in error. So, again another try must be made.

If the group is really on the ball, Clap C may be tried next, which goes exactly the same as Clap B but after the miss, everyone should swing their hands back together and get the final clap on the second try. It really is amusing how such simple variations confuse.

Clap D ends with two misses and the final clap. After that you are on your own with all the trick variations you want. After all, there are 22 more letters in the alphabet.

DIFFICULT IF NOT IMPOSSIBLE

Five tricky little stunts with props needed running from none to a trifle more than that.

---

1. Our first entry here is the old one of rubbing your stomach with a circular motion while patting your head straight up and down at the same time with the other hand. It can be done with close concentration. In the meantime it is very funny to watch several people trying it.

2. A very deceptive one is that of one person placing one hand on the top of his head with the palm down, and another trying to lift it off using both hands. Unless the one lifting is considerably stronger than the one holding his hand on his head it is well nigh impossible to pry it loose. Plenty of volunteers are usually surprised at their failure to do this.

3. For those with plenty of puff you can stick a postage stamp on the end of their nose and tell them to blow it off. This should be a contest with half a dozen participants in a row. The stamps should be affixed firmly along the bridge of the nose with the forward end of the stamp at the tip of the nose. If this proves too easy you can set the stamps back a bit. All should be exactly the same, of course, and should not be fastened down at the sides of the nose.

4. Another tricky and difficult one for couples is to have one hold a pencil between his upturned upper lip and nose and pass it to his partner who must take it the same way

without the use of hands. Several couples should be lined up sideways to the audience for this bit of facial muscle control.

5. One which I believe to be absolutely impossible, but which many will have to prove for themselves is that of folding a piece of paper in half nine times. The paper should have straight edges and four right angles so that the edges may always be folded evenly. It matters not how small or large the paper is nor how thin it is. If it is folded in half each time, you will not be able to do it nine times.

* * * *

BALLOON RACES

Balloons and contestants will fill the bill; four races to choose from, but No. 3 requires ice tongs.

---

1. Balloons are always fun, and one of the simplest races is to simply line up several contestants, give each a balloon, and at the signal have them blow the balloons up until they bust, the winner being to first to bust his balloon.

2. A more humorous version is to provide the contestants with chairs and tell them to bust the balloons by sitting on them. In this case they should stand erect in front of their chairs, hold the balloons in front of them with both hands and then, on "Go," release the balloon, blow at a designated neighbor's balloon (contestants are paired), grab their own balloon, place it on a chair and bust it by sitting on it. It is not permissible to hold the balloon on the chair, hands being in the lap when "sit" is made. Watch this carefully so that no chair gets moved from under anyone, whether by accident or ill-considered design.

3. Another possibility is a race between couples carrying a balloon between them with ice tongs. The balloons should be

of the heavier variety but even so the chances are not any too good if they have to go very far.

4. Then of course there is the mad scramble where each person has a balloon tied to each ankle and the object of the game is to bust everyone else's balloon without getting your own busted. It is important that these balloons be on strings that trail at least a couple of inches or so as otherwise ankles may get worked over by feet coming too close. Two sides may be used on this one which adds to the fun because, in the general confusion, participants are likely to step on balloons of their own side.

* * * *

ROPES AND HANDKERCHIEFS

Which tells you exactly what is needed for each, plus a few people who think they can do it.

A few four-foot lengths of light rope (clothesline will do nicely) can lead to an amusing and confusing situation if several couples are called forward to do their stuff, two ropes being needed for each couple. First one partner has one length of rope tied to each of his wrists (not too tight) after which he holds his hands horizontal and perhaps two feet apart. Then his partner has one end of the second rope tied to her right wrist, after which this rope is dropped down on the inside of the partner's rope and the lower end is then tied to her left wrist. The same procedure is followed with each couple.

The trick is for the partners to separate themselves without slipping their hands out of the ropes, untying the ropes or cutting them. All manner of acrobatics and pretzel antics ensue whereas the solution is very simple. The partner whose right hand was held above the horizontal rope, reaches down

1. Problem: How can two boys become separated?

2. Boy on right makes loop in his rope and starts to slip it under friend's rope where tied at his wrist.

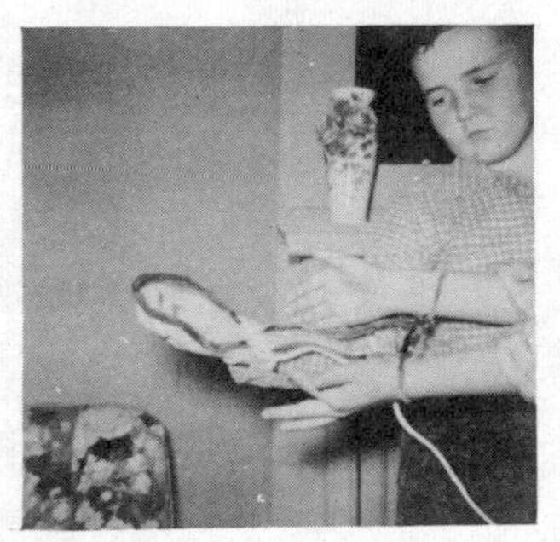

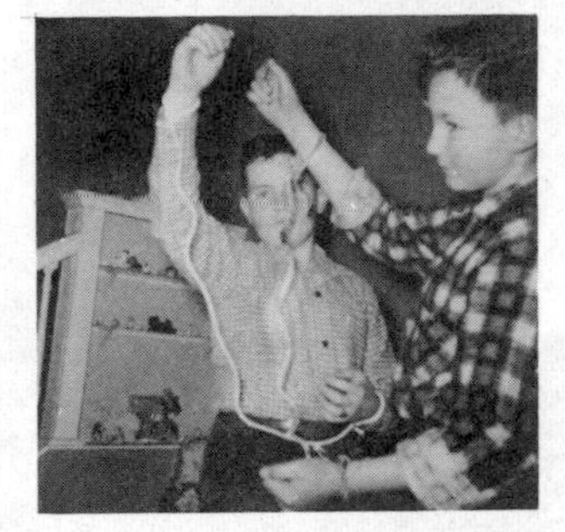

3. Loop has been slipped under rope where tied at wrist and is now ready to go over friend's hand.

4. Loop is then brought back under friend's rope at back of wrist and two boys are separated.

inside her partner's rope, takes a loop of her own rope and slips it over her partner's right hand, working from the inside and going under her partner's rope, which should have enough leeway to permit this. Then they simply step apart as per drawing.

A large handkerchief or triangular bandage can be used for another very simple but seemingly impossible trick. Several volunteers who come forward are told to fold their arms, take one end of the handkerchief in each hand and tie a simple overhand knot without letting go of either end. This not only seems impossible but is, if you take the handkerchief in each hand before folding your arms. However, if you fold your arms first, it may be a bit awkward to get hold of each end of the handkerchief, but when you do you merely unfold your arms again and there's your knot as per picture.

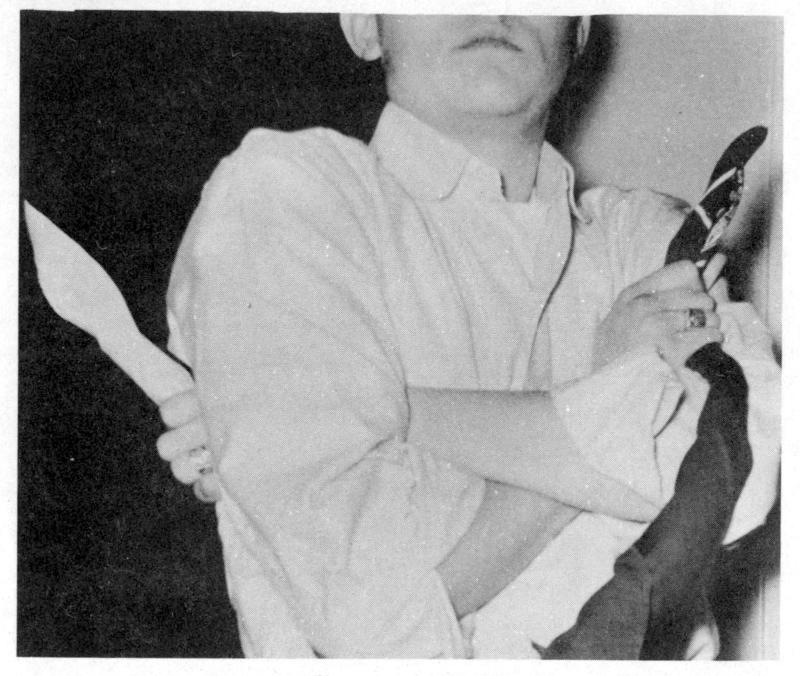

It's All In How You Do It

Pick up a kerchief, fold your arms and then try to tie an overhand knot without letting go of either end, and you just can't do it. BUT, fold your arms first, and then pick up both ends of kerchief, and PRESTO, just unfold your arms and there's your knot.

MOTHER'S LITTLE HELPERS

An assortment of kitchen capers to really mess things up. Study the directions to see what is needed to do what must be done.

Don't Cry

This one you may wish to start and then go on with something else while waiting for the onions to take effect. Anyhow, you get several contestants lined up with some onions to peel and slice, the hardy soul who keeps back the tears the longest, winning. Make sure the onions are close up by using some such device as a plank table which comes about chest level. The prize to the winner might be all the rest of the onions. The loser might get a crying towel.

Boy Scout Stuff

Biscuit baked on a stick by twisting the dough around the stick is an old boy scout cooking device that is very good when done right and highly messy and amusing to watch if not "just right." As an entertainment feature with volunteer "boy scouts passing their cooking test" it can be a lot of fun and might go well with the above since by the time the biscuit bakers have been issued their materials and have started messing things up, the onion peelers should be coming to grief.

The sticks should be something like two feet long and an inch thick with the bark peeled off where the dough is to be wrapped in spiral form about the same thickness as biscuits placed in a pan. Since much of this dough is likely to find its way to the floor, newspapers or something to intercept the dough should be put down. The cooking fires may be large candles, firmly held in holders.

The boy scouts are given prepared biscuit flour, milk, mixing bowls, measuring cups, spoons, boards for rolling the dough, aprons, and "grease" for the sticks. You will also need clean-up materials later. The contestants are then told that all they have to do is follow directions (which may be read from the package or written or typed on slips of paper) in mixing the dough, grease their sticks, wrap the dough around the peeled part and bake over their fires. It may be explained that it is merely necessary to slightly brown a small part of the twist to win. On the other hand, at a campfire, this may be an early event on the program and performed to one side with small fires, so that the contestants have an opportunity to really finish the job, if they can.

Besides making a gosh-awful mess of themselves (beware of good clothes) these biscuit bakers are going to have their twists falling off, perhaps putting out the candle, and generally have some time of it. Thus non-boy scout audiences can be assured that some of the things scouts must learn to do are not quite as easy as starting a fire by rubbing two boy scouts together.

Succotash Scramble

Bowls, glasses and succotash are needed as well as competing teams of three each; also an observer for each team to help the chief judge (leader) of the stunt. It is desirable that the center man of each team have something on which to rest his bowl of succotash (chair, small table, stool, etc.) The other two members of the team, on each side of him, have glasses that are ringed with black crayon about an inch or so up from the bottom.

It is then explained that we have gotten succotash for dinner, but unfortunately some of the diners only like lima beans while the others only want corn. Thus it becomes necessary to sort out the succotash, lima beans going to the sorter's left to be placed in his glass and corn to the sorter's right for his glass. The observers will make sure no mistakes are made, stray beans or kernels being sent back to the bowl.

The sorter hands out corn and beans as fast as he can separate them, with all participants, including observers lined up in a row facing the audience so as to give a good view to everyone. Sometimes the observers may have to partially block off someone as they do their checking, but this should not be necessary most of the time. The team which first gets both glasses filled to the marked line wins. Observers check to see that glasses are filled level. However, they should not push down on contents at any time, it merely being necessary to shake or wobble the glass a little to even things up. Chief judge confirms the winner when the observer calls to him.

Spaghetti Madness

Again we use teams of three, plus bowls, spaghetti and a stick about a foot or so long for each side man, the center man having the bowl and spaghetti therein. In this case, there have been so many arguments among the boarders at this boarding house that the spaghetti was not evenly divided, it has been determined to count the spaghetti. Therefore, the center man will separate the strings and hang them by turns on the two sticks held horizontal by the two side men of each team. To win he must have a specified number of strands hanging from each stick. The length of these strands may also be stipulated, short pieces not counting, but the stipulated length should be a minimum that most of the strands exceed so that it is merely necessary to measure a strand in dispute.

Only the sorter may touch the spaghetti, the side men merely holding the sticks steady and shouting warnings if some strands start to slide off, which they will do if too lop-sided.

A variation that will require close observation is to give the sorter a fork and a spoon with which to separate single strands and hold them up, one at a time, for a single assistant to eat, the assistant catching one end with his mouth and sucking it in, the one eating a certain number of strands first winning. In this case observers may quickly call out "too short" if they feel a piece of spaghetti is not long enough, but no measuring is possible.

* * * *

GOT A MATCH?

Balloons, matches, candles and confused people should make this highly interesting, to say the least.

For this we need a "Daddy" and four children, the five participants actually being almost any age except that "Daddy" and one of the children must be male.

Daddy is given four balloons of fair size, not the little penny doodads, and they must be the typical balloon shape rather than sausages and such. Daddy is to carry these across the stage to get the strings for them and then he will give one to each child. However, he is stopped four times, once by each child and asked to do something. He must not let any balloon touch the floor, set any down anywhere or ask anyone else to hold them. He must keep them himself at all times. He is also given a box of safety matches to put in his pocket.

Child No. 1 says, "Daddy, will you tie my necktie?" and

Daddy must somehow do this while hanging onto all the balloons.

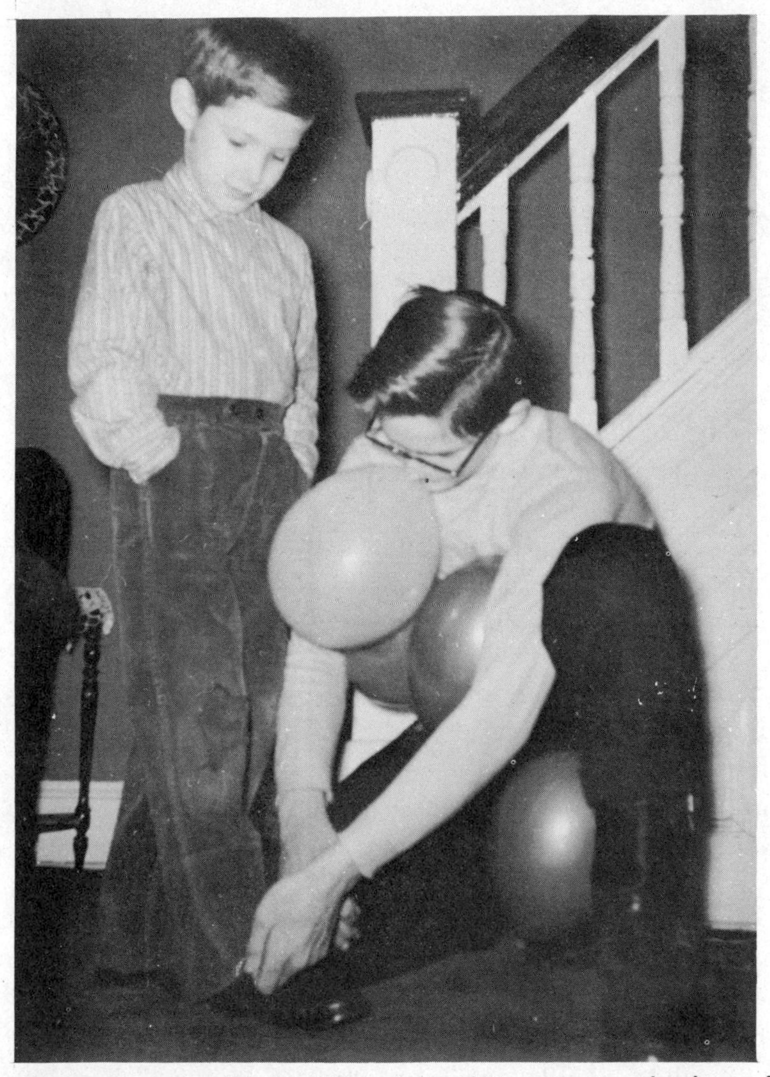

Dave Dahl, as "Daddy" in "Got A Match?" stunt, ties shoelace of son, Frank Dahl, while holding four balloons. Dave and Frank are actually Uncle and Nephew.

No. 2 says, "Daddy, will you cut out my paper doll for me?" handing Daddy scissors and a doll to be cut out. This should be a fairly simple doll design. If Daddy drops the scissors or doll, he must pick them up. If he loses a balloon, he is flunked out as a Daddy and somebody else can try it.

No. 3 says, "Daddy, will you tie my shoelace?" This really puts Daddy on the spot, but it can be done if he is careful.

No. 4 comes up with a candle in a holder and says, "Daddy, will you light my candle?" Daddy must fish out the matches and light the candle, which the child carefully holds close enough to heat up the balloons, moving the candle, accidentally like, so as to heat as many as he can; a couple may be out of his reach between Daddy's legs. In this case he can linger to ask Daddy when they will get their balloons, and taking advantage of any chance to heat more as Daddy fetches them up again.

By this time, one or more balloons should be exploding from the heated air inside and in the confusion, Child No. 4 may be able to heat up others as he accompanies Daddy to get the strings. He still may be able to explode others as Daddy ties the strings on, if he now has any left.

All the children should be bawling by this time as they realize their balloons have gone "boom." If Daddy succeeds in getting any safely through the "works" the children should set up a big howl as to who gets them, or it. If he gets them all through, Child No. 4 should be spanked by the emcee. Obviously the children should be tipped off in advance, Child No. 4 being a very special brat.

BETWEEN FRIENDS

If the old three-legged race seems out of date, here are some novel ways that two can run a race as partners.

Whether as a straight race or relay there are a number of ways two boys, or two girls, or boy and girl, can race as a pair with something held between them—*no hands allowed.* For example:

1. A ping-pong ball between:
   (a) Foreheads;
   (b) Cheeks (either with both faces in same direction or opposite which would necessitate one of the pair walking backward or with the body twisted and eyes to rear);
   (c) Ears (as above).

2. A marshmallow between noses or lips.
3. An ice cube between foreheads or cheeks (for the rugged types).

4. A balloon between heads or shoulders (both facing forward).
5. Bean bag, a folded newspaper, etc., between the feet.
6. A book (not too good a one) balanced on both heads.
7. Stale roll or something similar balanced on two spoons, held between the teeth of each partner.

In every case a fumble means return and start over if this is practicable, otherwise disqualification.

* * * *

STRAWS IN THE WIND

Drinking straws and tissue paper are all you need for some of these with not much more for the others.

Drinking straws can be used for various relay races that are amusing to watch:

1. Inch-square pieces of tissue paper can be passed from one to another by means of straws, the one who is to receive the paper drawing in on the straw and the one passing it breathing out. In the excitement it is easy to get this simple process crossed up. A very short run (or walk) may be used, each member of the team, after receiving the paper on the end of his straw, going around a chair several feet in front of the team, and then passing the paper to the next in line. If a paper flutters to the floor, the one losing it should get down and pick it up by placing the end of the straw on it and inhaling.

2. A *snow storm* may be staged with two or more snow-flake gatherers competing against each other, first in catching the snowflakes in the air, and then in picking them up off the ground. For this purpose the inch-square pieces of tissue

paper are tossed into the air very much like a peanut scramble, there being maybe a dozen tosses of a few each time.

The snowflake gatherers try to get their straws under the descending flakes and thus catch them in the air, passing on any caught to a partner who stands waiting to take the flakes on the end of his straw and deposit them in a small receptacle he holds for this purpose. This receptacle can be a small bag, box, etc., into which papers must be transferred without the use of hands (in fact he should be holding the receptacle with one hand and the straw with the other.) If he loses the paper (after its transfer to him) he must pick it up with the straw.

The chances of anyone actually getting any of the papers in the air are not too good, but it's lots of fun to watch them try. When all the snowflakes have bit the dust, the snowflake gatherers can turn their attention to picking them up off the floor — with their straws. This they can do but getting them up and to their partners and thence into the receptacles can be a struggle.

Two points are awarded for each snowflake caught in the air (if any) and one for each picked up off the floor.

3. A *bucket brigade* may be run with straws, with small glasses or dixie cups at one end of the stage (or floor) and cups or bowls of water at the other end, but the distance apart should not be too great. An assistant should be standing by

with a pitcher of water to refill supply bases when the runners spill too much en route.

At a signal, the first member of each team draws in on his straw from the water supply and carries it to a cup where he empties it, running back to touch off the next man. The first team to fill their cup wins.

It may be well to stipulate that when water is delivered to a glass or dixie cup, the mouth of the deliverer must not be above the glass or cup. In other words, the water must run down through the straw, not cascade down around it from a well-filled mouth.

4. A message may be written on a piece of paper (3x5 pad sheet will be plenty large) and then torn into a number of pieces — 5, 6, 7 or 8 perhaps — one for each member of the team. These bits of paper are then inserted in as many pieces

of drinking straw torn up for this purpose. The pieces of straw are piled together across the stage or floor from each team, and, at a signal, the players run up, one at a time, and bring back the pieces.

Bits of message are removed from their tiny containers and fitted together to be deciphered. Messages might read, "All get down on hands and knees and bark like dogs," or "Sit in a row on heels and meow like cats," etc. The first team successfully carrying out instructions on the message wins.

5. You may even have a *Pony Express* relay by passing the inch-square pieces of tissue paper from one piggy-back rider to the next. A dropped piece of paper will necessitate dismounting to recover it with a straw and remounting again, which takes a bit of doing, or should we say "breath control?"

Where practicable and you have enough relay teams, such a race can be run all around the audience. However, relays will be needed at frequent intervals. Most participants are not going to be able to hold their papers on the end of their straws very long.

6. A *tissue-paper tug-of-war* may be waged. The first two members of each team stand facing each other with the tissue between their two straws which are lined up end to end. The referee also holds the tissue until he gives the signal to start, whereupon each contestant starts shuffling his feet backward while pulling in on his straw. In this situation the tissue must go one way or the other, or down.

A contestant, seeing the tissue moving away on the end of his opponent's straw may pursue it, trying to take it away by placing his own straw against it and pulling in harder than his opponent. The one with the tissue may try to evade his opponent's move by swinging his straw sideways, but he must keep it on a horizontal plane — tipping up or down being taboo.

He must also back away by sliding his feet on the floor. The feet may not be lifted clear of the floor, the body must not be turned in any direction, and he may not ward off the opponent with his hands. The referee may impose a suitable penalty for violating these rules.

If the tissue flutters to the ground, both may go after it (bumping heads in the process being prohibited).

As soon as this mighty tug-of-war begins, the referee (or assistant) should begin to count slowly to ten. As soon as he reaches "10" the contest is over, and the next two members of opposing teams start a new contest where the first one ended. Thus, the tide of battle rages back and forth until all have had their turn, the winning team being decided by the final location of the tissue. They should be allowed to keep it as a trophy.

Or, they might be given something more interesting to use their straws on, such as sodas. They may need fresh straws, too. Sodas can be used as prizes for other races as well.

* * * *

MODERN ART

Paper, pencils, a dark room and a bunch of willing guinea pigs should produce some masterpieces, or anyhow, something.

The emcee, or leader, can announce that he has finally discovered how modern artists get those crazy pictures. They are not only so poor that they have to live in attics with nothing to eat but cheese and crackers, but, since their windows are never washed so that no light comes through them, and they can not pay their electric light bill, and the mice ate up their last candle, they must work in the dark.

If they could only sell a picture or two, they might be able to at least buy some more candles, but who in the world would pay money for such pictures?

To better appreciate the problems of these crazy artists and their poor pictures — that is, poor artists with crazy pictures, an art contest will be conducted under similar circumstances. Each contestant is given paper, a magazine or something to use as a drawing board, and a pencil. Also a paper napkin with crackers and cheese.

When all is set, the lights are turned out. (If it is broad daylight and the room has lots of windows, it would be better to try something else, or else blindfold all the contestants.)

Everyone is then told what to draw — a ship at sea, a cow in the meadow, two lovers on a park bench, or what have you. To add to the fun, they must take time out to nibble at their crackers and cheese. In fact, it may be stipulated that crackers and cheese must be consumed by the time the contest is over.

The total time for this contest should not be long — just a few minutes, and the leader should make suggestions and comment from time to time; including remarks such as, "It sure is cold in this attic. Just listen to that wind howling around the eaves" (someone is likely to howl at the suggestion, or the leader can arrange for said howling). Or he might suddenly shout, "Watch that the mouse doesn't get your cheese." Probably there will be plenty of remarks by the contestants as they struggle to draw in the dark and, in turn, find cheese and crackers or pencil and paper.

The leader will need a small flashlight to check the elapse of time, and should give several warnings as time runs out — two minutes, one minute, 30 seconds. When time is up, the lights are turned on, everyone signs his work of art; and they are arranged for viewing, judging and awarding of prizes.

Prizes can be candle stubs, mouse traps, packages of cheese and crackers, second-hand crayons, and so forth.

* * * *

IT TAKES A LEVEL HEAD, OR SHOULD WE SAY FLAT?

Two tests of nerves and muscular control, with the aid of some pie pans and a flock of marbles.

Contestants sit on the floor cross-legged with pie pans balanced on their heads. At a signal they start lifting marbles, one at a time, from bowls in front of them into the pie pans. The first one to get a dozen marbles into his pan wins, assuming the pan is still on his head.

One hand must always be in the bowl, which means he must wait until one hand gets down before starting the other up, if permitted or instructed to use hands alternately. The natural instinct when a pan begins to slip over one ear or something like that is to grab for it with the free hand, or both. This is forbidden.

However, if the contest proves too difficult, a fresh start may be made with both hands free, which means one can either work faster by starting the second hand up as fast as the first one comes down, or may have a spare hand poised to grab the plate when it slips. In no event should the contestants be permitted to simply hold the plate all the time or deposit any marbles in it while it is being held.

Before the contest starts one or two marble rounder-uppers may be appointed since it is very likely that some marbles will be rolling around. These rounder-uppers and the emcee will keep counting marbles in each contestant's pan and bowl to make sure each has enough to get his dozen in the pie pan to win, replenishing the dwindling supplies from a reserve stock as necessary.

All may be started with exactly twelve marbles in their bowls, or with one or more to spare. Inasmuch as players will forget how many they have overhead and counting them is hardly practicable for those under the pans, the emcee and rounder-uppers should keep the contestants advised of their respective situations, as well as the audience.

A variation of this contest is to place the pie pans with marbles already in them on the contestants' heads and tell them to walk among the audience, passing out marbles one at a time, until all have been distributed. If a pie pan bites the dust, marbles must be recovered, or replacements secured from a designated supply base, and the handing-out process continued. This involves a checker-upper for every marble passer-outer.

One hand should be kept in a pocket or behind the back during this contest. It is more fun for the audience to watch someone frantically try — and often fail — to save his pie pan with his working hand than to have a spare hand handy for this detail.

The winner of either of these contests may be given a sack of marbles.

* * * *

FAIR EXCHANGE

With several blankets and some small tags you are all set for hilarious confusion.

This is a good game for teams of younger boys especially. Two or three teams of five members each will work fine; the members of each team should be approximately the same size. Each team will be lined up, one behind the other, facing the audience. A blanket will be issued to every team with the information that it is for emergency use. These blankets can be placed to the rear of the teams.

The emcee explains that he will call an article of clothing and the first two members of each team will swap that article as fast as they can. The first couple finishing and passing inspection will win one point for their team. The first two members then go to the end of the line and, when the emcee calls the next article of clothing, members 3 and 4 swap same. This continues with 5 and 1, 2 and 3, and 4 and 5.

The emcee may call out "Shirt," "Shoes," "Sweater" (if both are wearing one), "Belt" and so on. After two or three swaps he may call out "Pants." It is then up to two members of each team to get their blanket and hold it up as an improvised dressing room, so that boys swapping pants are only seen from the chest up. This should be done for the fun of it even though the audience be all male.

With a mixed audience particularly, calling "Pants" will evoke considerable amusement and may cause some momentary confusion or even consternation among team members who may have forgotten their blanket or fail to make the necessary association of ideas. Some may have to be advised on this point while others will be as sharp as tacks. Accidental dropping of the blanket may do no harm and make a big hit. Naturally suitable discretion should be used, including due consideration for the feelings of participants.

Shorts and socks, of course, should not be swapped. However, undershirts may be exchanged under proper circumstances. This game goes best with cubs or scouts in uniform, or when boys are wearing "second-best" or play clothes. Team members should be dressed alike or as nearly so as possible. With cubs and scouts, there are also neckerchiefs and slides which may be swapped. Extra confusion may be added by saying, "Neckerchief slide and left shoe," "belt and right shoe," etc.

After five or more swaps, the clothing of team members will really be mixed up. Thus it may be wise to ask everyone if they are sure they can identify all their clothing before the game starts, issuing small tags with safety pins where needed.

There should be at least five and probably no more than ten swaps. If the emcee can keep from getting mixed up himself, he may insist that no two members can swap together more than once, which will work up to ten swaps with teams of five members each; i.e., 1 and 2, 3 and 4, 5 and 1, 2 and 3, 4 and 5, 1 and 3, 2 and 4, 3 and 5, 1 and 4, 2 and 5. The team with the most points is declared the winner. However, a further contest may be held to decide which team now looks the best.

Or, men and boys from the audience may come up to hold the blankets while a grand race is staged to see which team can get back into all their own clothing first. They will have to re-organize themselves anyhow.

* * * *

BALLOON GAMES AND RELAY RACES

A baker's dozen of balloon races and games described should provide plenty of entertainment and give you ideas for more.

---

1. Balloon Volley Ball is exciting to watch and need not take much space. All you need is several round balloons (one is enough if it doesn't break but . . .), 12 to 20 feet of light rope or heavy cord, 2 poles about six feet long, two pole holders (human variety), a referee and a score keeper.

The rope or cord is tied to the ends of the two poles which are held erect by the pole holders who stand in the front center and rear center of the stage, making two courts with a dividing line down the center from front to back. The balloon must be batted over the rope by the server without any assistance from his teammates. Where the server stands to do this is left to the discretion of the referee who can take the size of the players into consideration, but, as a rule, he will have to stand reasonably close to the net (rope). If the server fails to get it over the first try, he may try again. Two failures forfeits the balloon to the other side for the serve.

After the serve the game proceeds very much as in regular volley ball. The balloon may be batted as many times as necessary to get it over but the same player may not bat it more than once in succession.

For small boys or girls the pole holders can simply rest the poles on the floor beside themselves. However, the poles can also be held higher, if desired, without too much strain on the pole holders. Or, longer poles may be used.

The number of players on each side is variable, depending upon the size of the courts and players.

2. A variation of the above may be had by lowering the rope and blowing the balloon back and forth with the exception of the serve which is still done by batting.

3. A relay race may be played with two or three teams of six or eight members each, using the above described "net." If eight to a team, Nos. 1, 3, 5 and 7 of each team line up at one side of the stage with Nos. 2, 4, 6 and 8 opposite them on the other side.

Nos. 1 and 2 of each team have a balloon (different colors) and, on a signal, start toward each other bouncing the balloon by batting it in the air. A minimum height for the bounces may be established, such as a foot or two feet. Anyone failing to bounce the balloon sufficiently or permitting it to touch the floor must return to his starting point and begin again.

At the center rope, No. 1 bats his balloon over to No. 2, who bats his to No. 1, both returning with exchanged balloons for 3 and 4 to take, and so on until everyone has taken one balloon up and another back. To win, both sections of the team must be lined up as before the race with Nos. 1 and 2 holding their balloons.

4. A simpler form of the above race is simply to have No. 1 bat a balloon to the center rope, over it and on across the stage to No. 2, who takes it back to No. 3 and so forth. You only need half as many balloons this way and there is less chance of the balloons of the different teams getting mixed up. On the other hand, the confusion is great sport for the audience.

5. Instead of a center rope there can be as many boys as there are teams, standing with their legs spread apart. No. 1 then bats his balloon to this center boy, bats it hard up in the air past the center boy, and dives through the center boy's legs so as to be able to bat the balloon again before it touches the floor. He then continues across the stage to No. 2, and so it goes.

6. A relay race may be run with No. 1 keeping the balloon in the air by blowing it across the stage to No. 2, and so on, no center obstacle being required. In this case, particularly, the players are likely to cross the lanes of opposing teams in pursuit of wayward (or is it windward?) balloons, which is fine and dandy.

7. With each player supplied with a small balloon, at a signal the first player on each team blows his balloon up, grips it by the open end between his teeth so as to prevent the air escaping prematurely, crosses his arms behind his back,

leans forward and releases the balloon. Player No. 2 runs to take a position where the first balloon landed and repeats with his balloon, and so on. At the referee's direction, succeeding runners (or blowers) may start in their own lane in line with the landing spot of the previous balloon.

This race may be run with the winner being the team which thus covers the most ground, doubling back across the stage around the turning device as necessary, or the winner may be the first team to get the balloon across a finish line. If the latter method is used and all the players do not get a chance to launch their balloons before the race ends, a second race can be held, starting with the last man on each team and proceeding in reverse order.

If some contestant blows his balloon up too vigorously and it bursts, the next player must start from the spot he (the balloon buster) was standing when the balloon exploded. Long balloons (small size) are good for this race, but any type may be used as long as all are the same size and shape.

8. The race may be held with each player, in turn, holding a round balloon on his head with his right hand and his left ankle with his left hand, hopping on the right foot. If the balloon gets away, the hopper may release his foot while recapturing it, but he must return to the starting point and begin again. If the balloon bursts, his team just naturally loses.

This race can be run (hopped) with half of the team on each side of the stage, or the entire team on the same side, each hopper then hopping across the stage and returning. In this latter case he can be required to shift his hands and feet for the return trip.

9. Balloons may also be passed from one team member to the next between his legs or over his head, the last one on each team running to the front to start it on its next trip, until

all have started the balloon once and No. 1 is back at the head of the line. Obviously a bursted balloon is always a good possibility, with an accompanying disqualification.

10. By getting some cardboard cartons a bit larger than the balloons, and cutting out the tops and bottoms of them you will have some improvised baskets. Or you may devise something else for the baskets, but whatever it is, all should be exactly alike. Then you will need one basket holder per team, all of whom must hold baskets at the same height, perhaps shoulder level.

The team members then take turns, bouncing the balloon in the air, in racing up to their basket, maneuvering the balloon down through, catching it with a bounce before it hits the floor and bouncing it back to the next player, until all have made a basket.

The balloon may be bounced sideways when it comes through the basket, but it may not be pushed.

In their anxiety to keep the balloon from hitting the floor, the players tend to hit it too soon on its descent, thus forcing it back up into the basket. This can be excused, or, if you want to be tough about it, a player forcing any part of his balloon back up into the basket may be required to send it through again.

If your players are quite good you can make it tougher by lowering the baskets so that you make it harder to bounce the balloon from under the basket and back up into the air again without hitting the floor, which means the run must start over for that player.

11. For general confusion there is the nice little stunt of having a relay race with each player in turn bouncing a balloon in the air while bouncing a ball on the floor, up and around the turning marker, and back to the team.

12. A jumping jack race is run by holding a blown-up balloon between the legs to the turning marker and return. Balloon casualties may be high on this so it might be well to permit replacements to those who bring their bursted balloons to the "new balloon" man, who should be stationed behind the turning markers. The player getting a new balloon (they should be already blown up) runs back to his team and makes a fresh start. This also applies to runaway balloons.

13. A live bomb race is run as a piggy-back relay, each team having four sets of horses and riders. At a signal, the first rider mounts his horse and places a balloon between his chest and the horse's back where it must be cradled until the horse and rider have run around the turning marker and back to the team. The rider may use his chin to help keep the balloon in place but may not touch it with his hands which must be around in front of the horse's chest.

In fact, it is a good idea to forbid any rider from touching the balloon except to pick it up if dropped, in which case they must start over. Thus the race begins with the No. 1 man on each team holding the mouth of the balloon between his teeth until he is mounted when he must release it and depend upon his chest, arms and chin to hold it in place.

The balloon is passed from the first rider to the second by the No. 2 rider leaning over to get hold of the mouth of the balloon with his teeth and lifting it over to its resting place between his chest and the horse's back. This race can be plenty exciting. Balloons should be fairly large and round. If the bomb goes off the horse and rider are blown up and that's that so far as their team is concerned.

(Now it is your turn to dream up some more games and races with balloons. If you have some good ones, why not let me know about them?)

FIND THE BOMB

A bit of dramatized nonsense can be used as the prelude to a serious safety program or simply as is.

Before the arrival of those who will participate, a clock is hidden somewhere so that it cannot be seen and just barely heard when close by and listening intently. It should not be placed in a location where someone may hear it before you are ready.

At the proper moment and in a theatrical manner (but not so as to really mislead anyone) the emcee receives word and advises those concerned that a bomb has been planted in the room or area. He may blame a rival group for the dastardly deed.

Everyone is instructed to go around in absolute silence, listening, and when anyone thinks he has the bomb spotted he must signal the bomb disposal unit to handle it. No one else should attempt to touch the bomb or dig it out of its hiding place, lest all be blown to somewhere or other. There should be much holding of fingers to lips, shushing and tiptoeing.

The bomb disposal unit, looking very grim and businesslike, enters and stands by for a signal to go into action. The members of this unit should be equipped with various implements (more or less ridiculous) and a bucket of torn newspaper to serve as water.

When the bomb is discovered by someone, who signals this fact, rather excitedly, the bomb unit rushes over, the crowd (fast collecting) is held back by the police (designate several for this duty) and the bomb disposal unit makes a big effort of getting the bomb out of its hiding place, using implements of one kind or another that have little relation to the job at hand. They pretend to disarm it and then immerse it in a bucket of water.

There are all sorts of possibilities for clowning. An alarm may be set and then released to go off during handling, causing great consternation among the disposal unit crew who almost drop it. After its immersion and when members of the bomb disposal crew straighten up with a sigh of satisfaction and relief, a blown-up paper bag may be exploded nearby (but out of sight) and the crew pretend to drop dead.

A bit of nonsense like this can serve as a good introduction to a serious talk on safety, including what to do when bullets, blasting caps, etc., are found, and what not to do. A fireman, policeman, or other expert, carefully chosen for this purpose, may be invited to give an appropriate talk and demonstration for the group.

* * * *

WHAT'S IT TASTE LIKE?

This will require some ingenuity and trouble to prepare but it offers tasty possibilities.

Several contestants are blindfolded, arranged in a row facing the audience, and told to keep their mouths tightly closed until the signal "Taste" is given. The emcee may make a point of inspecting "mouths" to see if they are really shut tight, perhaps instructing one or more to open and close again since none must be left ajar.

An assistant then places a dab of something on the chin, the upper lip or to either side of the mouth, but within reach of the tongue and in the same place on each contestant. Beware of placing anything on the upper lip that may too easily flow down, thus giving the ones who get it first a head start on its identification.

When the signal "Taste" is given each contestant sticks out his tongue to where he felt the dab being placed and tries to identify its taste. If he thinks he knows, he calls out. The first one to call out the correct answer gets one point. Some "toughies" may be worth two or even three points. However, this should always be announced in advance. Anyone who calls out a wrong answer loses half a point (it looks like you need a wide awake scorer).

Various jellies, jams, marmalades may be used, honey, sugar, salt, flour, butter, milk, ice cream, puddings, chocolate, vinegar, potato (mashed), baked beans (in some cases contestants might be instructed to tip heads back while item is placed on upper lip), lemon, orange, cheeses, etc.

A final taste might be a large tablespoon of ice cream, each contestant having a spoon placed in his hand and his arm carefully arranged so that the spoon is pointed directly toward and about an inch from his mouth. Unless handled well, you will have some accidents. There may be some talk about castor oil or something else during this process. When all spoons are poised and right side up, the signal "Taste" is given. This should be funny as some boys try to down all the ice cream and call out at the same time. However, there is less danger of choking on ice cream than about anything I can think of. The winner must give correct flavor — not just ice cream.

The above can also be run as a relay race, each contestant getting about two tries, unless you only have three or four on a team which really would work better under the circumstances (less blindfolding). It seems like the winner should be rewarded with something he enjoys tasting — ice cream, candy, cake.

NECKING PARTY

Some oranges and a group of boys and girls and you are all set for a lot of fun.

For teams of boys and girls, passing oranges from neck to neck is sure to be a big success. If the first member of each team is a girl and the second a boy (the only sensible arrangement) an orange is tucked under the chin of No. 1 girl, to be held between the chin and chest.

At the signal "Go" she must pass this orange to the boy behind her while both hold their hands clasped behind their backs. This involves some twisting of heads and necking but it can be done all right and proves highly enjoyable for participants and observers alike. The oranges travel in this fashion to the end of the line where the last boy runs up (with the orange between the chin and chest) to return it to No. 1 girl, after which he goes back to the end of the line.

If an orange bites the dust, it must be picked up by hand and returned to the person who had it just before the two who dropped it between them. That is, if 2 and 3 drop it, it goes back to No. 1; if 1 and 2 drop it, a handy assistant must get it for transfer to No. 1.

As a second race, the line may be reversed with the last boy in front, and this time he places the orange between his shoulder and the side of the head. The girl behind removes it with her chin and chest and places it between the shoulder and the side of the head of the boy behind her. When it gets to the last girl, she quickly transfers it to a resting place between her shoulder and the side of her head, and the boy in front takes it with his chin and chest, and so back to the head of the line again, the orange ending up between the chin and chest of No. 1 boy.

Oh yes, the oranges should be nice and firm unless the contestants are wearing clothes that won't be harmed too much should all this necking bring a poor orange to the point of collapse.

SNATCH THE BACON

Five variations are offered for your selection, depending upon the occasion, participants and your desire for a change.

---

1. This old standby of boy scout troops and other groups is usually played with two sides of equal numbers facing each other from lines at least twelve feet apart, preferably a little farther. An old hat or something on that order is placed midway between the two lines. This is the "bacon."

The players of each side are numbered from 1 to 8 or whatever number of players there are on each side. The referee calls a number, perhaps "4," whereupon No. 4 on each side comes out to try to "snatch the bacon." If the player gets the bacon and back to his own line without being tagged by his opposite number, his side gets two points. If a successful "tag" is made, however, the tagger's side gets one point.

If either player tags the other or crowds him with his body before a snatch is made, the referee may award a point to the other side, the players retire, and another number is called.

Sometimes a circle is drawn around the bacon into which neither player can step, or even lean his body into or extend his arm over unless a snatch is actually started; violators forfeiting a point to the other side at the referee's discretion. Fake snatches may be permitted, if desired, with the opponent liable to a point penalty for the mistaken tag, or the rule may be that once an apparent "snatch" is started, the opponent may either tag, or snatch the bacon himself.

The numbering of players may be changed by either side in a secret huddle by calling "time out."

2. Instead of keeping points, all players may be on an individual basis and a piece of candy awarded for each successful snatch or tag. If this is done it is very important

for the referee (or assistant) to keep track of the numbers called so that no one may be slighted.

3. The bacon can be a balloon. Long ones or balloons of odd shapes are good for this, especially if a different kind of balloon is set out each time one busts. Anyone having a balloon burst in his hands, forfeits two points to the other side.

4. "Snatch the Tail" is another variation, played by having each player (if scouts or cubs) double his neckerchief over the back of his belt, with the ends hanging clear and one quite a bit longer than the other. Short ropes may also be used, or anything similar that can be had of the same size in a sufficient number for all. All "tails" should be without knots and of identical appearance. An inspection may be held before the game starts.

When a number is called the two opposing players with that number come out and try to snatch the other's tail. More or less wrestling or pushing for position may be permissible, provided the referee insists upon a "no holding" rule. In other words, quick pulls of opponent's arm to swing him around, etc., may be allowed but no continuous holding which would result in an automatic tag if the holder's tail were snatched. The referee will have to be forceful about ruling fouls and imposing point penalties.

If we have room enough to get our lines far enough apart to make it practicable, we permit a player's team members to snatch his opponent's tail if the said opponent gets close enough for them to do it. That is, if No. 5 of "A" team succeeds in maneuvering No. 5 of the "B" team close enough to the "A" line, with his back toward them, someone in "A" line can reach out and snatch the tail. It is important that no one be allowed to step over the line when this rule is used.

5. "Bust the Tail" is played with each member having a small balloon or blown-up paper bag attached to his belt in back by a small string. Every player has a rolled-up newspaper (not too heavy), and when his number is called, he goes out to try to bust his opponent's tail. If he does, he gets two points. However, if his opponent can bust his tail before he gets back to the safety of his own line, the opponent's team gets one point. In other words, the first bust is worth more than the second.

Here again, team members may be permitted to bust the tail of the opponent getting within reach (but all feet must stay behind the line at all times). On the other hand, if you do not have sufficient space between lines for a reasonable amount of maneuvering, it is better to restrict the tail busting to the two in center.

A couple of assistants are needed for this — to blow up and attach new tails as needed.

When it is time for this game to end, the referee may call out, "Every man for himself," whereupon everyone tries to bust everyone else's tail until there is nothing but pieces of balloon or paper bag and torn newspapers all over the place.

* * * *

BLIND MAN TOUCH IDENTIFICATION

Some blindfolds will do the trick. This is a good way to test powers of observation and whatnot.

Teams "A" and "B" face each other. One member of Team "B" is blindfolded. Then, at the command "Go" ABSOLUTE SILENCE DESCENDS ON BOTH TEAMS, TO BE MAINTAINED UNTIL THE IDENTIFICATION TIME IS UP. Team "A" is given thirty seconds to change positions, swap wearing apparel, etc., in an effort to disguise themselves.

At the end of 30 seconds, the command "Freeze" is given, whereupon Team "A" assumes an "At ease" position in a line facing Team "B". This means that every member of the team stands with their legs slightly apart and their hands behind the back, one hand holding the other at the wrist. They must not be permitted to continue adjusting clothing; a shirt half tucked in should stay that way.

The blindfolded member of Team "B" is led over to the first member of Team "A" on his left and advised that he is now on his own and can move down the line at his own discretion, attempting to identify each boy in turn. He is given a time limit in which he must cover the entire team or as much of it as he can. This time limit should not exceed an average of 30 seconds per boy; 20 seconds may be better.

He may feel a boy's head, face (but not eyes), exposed portions of body, clothing, jewelry and shoes, but may not unfasten or disturb any clothing, reach inside clothing or pockets, or attempt to investigate the teeth. If he thinks he knows who a boy is, he calls out the name and the judge notes it, giving him one point for a correct identification. Later on he may call out the same name if convinced he is right the second time.

The emcee should announce the passing of time so that the blindfolded boy will know whether he is progressing too slowly or quickly down the line. The emcee, moving down to the rear of Team "A" to protect their eyes especially, will make sure that members of Team "A" do not interfere with the blindfolded boy and that he does not violate the above rules. When the blindfolded boy has finished the line, or the time is up, his blindfold is removed and the points earned are announced.

A member of Team "A" is then blindfolded while Team "B" prepare for identification. A brief spell of talking should be permitted in between, or the boys may explode. During this time Team "A" reorganizes itself.

The teams may draw for the first identification and be given two opportunities to identify the other team, either choosing their blindfolded members or drawing lots for the job.

It is very interesting to observe the different ways boys (or girls) will go about trying to identify someone under these conditions. This is not recommended for mixed groups, however.

Section Four

DRAMATIZED SONGS

There is no better way to get "everybody into the act" than by the use of a dramatized song, especially when the song is well-known or easily learned, as are the nine described here. Dramatized songs can give a real lift to any show and make for a delightful change of pace. They are generally thoroughly enjoyed by both entertainers and actors.

However, it is well to keep in mind that with props at a minimum in most cases, and individual lines few or absent altogether the fun of singing the song may lull a director into thinking everything is under control without too much thought being given to careful timing of all actions with the singing. Dramatized songs should be practically dress rehearsed from the very beginning, since in this way a director can discover if some change in the singing is necessary in order to tie in with the acting. If this is discovered only after the chorus has the song well in hand it will be difficult to change things successfully.

Also, a group entering into the spirit of the song may lead to one or more members of the chorus improvising impromptu actions that a director may decide to include in the act. It is extremely important that the chorus appears to be having a good time singing.

Current popular songs may often be successfully pantomimed and audiences are most receptive to them. However, they come and go so quickly it would not be wise to include any in a book such as this. The songs I have included are either old favorites, the words of which are quite widely known, or my own parodies of well-known tunes. "Oh, Don't Give Me Homework No More," "You Are My Girl" and

"The Goodies and the Baddies" are of the latter group.

I have made some changes or additions to the usual words of "My Grandfather's Clock," "Ivan Skizavitsky Skivar," "Clementine," and "The Scout Company," and added echo lines to the music of "The Mermaid."

These should give you some good ideas of what can be done with others as well as affording a fine variety in themselves from which to choose for your program.

MY GRANDFATHER'S CLOCK

An old favorite that can be very entertaining, with four male and one female actors and a mixed chorus. Chief props are a bed and clock; the former being quite easy and latter not too difficult. Two or three beards and whatnot also required.

Cast includes Grandfather, Grandfather as a boy, Grandfather's spirit (in long white nightgown or sheet), his buxom bride, the Clock and the members of the chorus.

Grandfather and his spirit sport identical long, white beards. The boy is a barefoot, farm lad with a large white bandage on the big toe of one foot. A short beard is optional. As long as the bride is plenty big and looks something like a bride it doesn't matter too much what she wears.

The "Clock" stands on a box inside of a cardboard frame constructed to look like a grandfather's clock. Most of the back will have to be open so that the spirit of the clock can get in and out. The spirit of the clock wears a clockface frame which fits snugly under his chin, up the sides of his face and over the top of his head. This face has numbers around the rim. A pair of clock hands are held in position and moved occasionally by spirit's hand, which uses his nose as a center position for the clock hands.

Where the clock face would be, the spirit's face appears, and where the pendulum belongs, the cardboard is cut away and another piece of cardboard is held in place several inches behind the outer frame. This can be done by using small dowels or short pencils, poked through the four corners of this insert and the cardboard frame. The pendulum is suspended from a fifth dowel in the top center of this insert, the pendulum being continued up out of sight of the audience so that the spirit of the clock may move it back and forth. The pendulum can be of wood or heavy cardboard.

The spirit holds the clock hands with his right hand and moves the pendulum with his left. There is a hole in the side of the clock at a convenient height for the spirit's left hand to come out, and this hole should be large enough to permit necessary actions described below. The hole may be concealed by a piece of hinged cardboard inside the clock. A piece of coarse sandpaper may be fastened to the outside of the clock near this hole.

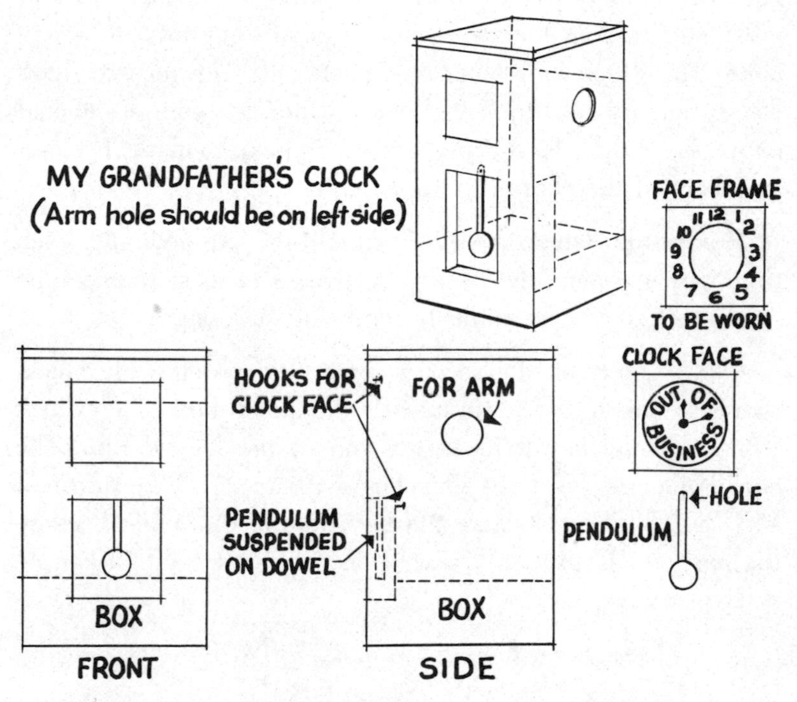

The "Out of Business" clock face may be hung out of sight inside the clock until needed. The spirit of clock wears a sheet, but this should not be in evidence when his arm comes out during the song. He should also have a polishing cloth handy, and a wooden match or two.

Grandfather needs a bed for the last verse, which can be

contrived with the aid of four straight chairs and a couple of planks, plus a few bed clothes which should hang to the floor.

* * *

The curtain opens on Grandfather's Clock in the center of the stage and the chorus lined up on either side and a little back of the clock. The "Clock" yawns on the third line, and the hand holding the clock hands partly supports a weary head. The Clock snores on the fourth line. The face straightens up hastily for the fifth line and then assumes a shocked expression when loud baby cries are heard (made by rear members of the chorus).

The words "stopp'd short" should be clipped and each time they are sung, the pendulum pauses in its swinging. The "tick, tocks" can be made by clucking the tongue.

A boy enters on the second verse, and watches the clock, swinging his head in time with the pendulum. The Clock winks and the boy exits at the end of the second line. The chorus pauses and the Clock begins to recite "The Barefoot Boy" by Whittier, to give the boy time to put a bandage on his big toe. He probably would only need to recite a couple of lines:

> Blessings on thee, little man,
> Barefoot boy, with cheek of tan!
> With thy turned-up pantaloons,
> And thy merry whistled tunes:

when the boy comes running back in crying, and hugs the clock. The chorus sings the third and fourth lines as the clock's hand comes out through the hole to pat the boy's head. The chorus pauses again for the following:

CLOCK. There, there, little grandfather, don't cry.

BOY *(Sobbing.)* I can't help it. I stubbed my toe, and my best kite is up in the apple tree, all busted, and my mother and father don't love me any more.

CLOCK. Why, of course, your mother and father love you.

BOY. No, they don't. They don't love me at all.

CLOCK. Now how can you say a thing like that?

BOY. Because it's true; I know it is.

CLOCK. But how do you know it?

BOY *(Sobbing louder.)* Because I tried them out on a daisy.

CLOCK. Now, now, little grandfather, don't cry. Daisies don't always know who loves who. Now you run along and make a new kite. *(The boy goes sniffling out. The Clock's arm comes through the hole to polish the woodwork where the boy was crying. Speaks to the audience.)* Salt tears are hard on my polish.

The chorus repeats the third and the fourth lines, using the word "Yes" instead of "And" at the beginning of the third line. Grandfather comes struggling in with his bride while the clock strikes 24. This is done by the chorus singing "Boom, boom, boom-boom," etc., to the tune of "Wedding March" until 18 booms are sung, by which time Grandfather's gallant attempt to carry his bride over the portal has ended in front of the clock, with the bride and Grandfather sprawled on the floor in a most ridiculous manner. The clock (that is, the chorus) adds six final booms with great haste. The clock looks duly shocked, can spread his hand before his face, close his eyes, etc. The chorus finishes the second verse and chorus with the bride, struggling to her feet, giving Grandfather the merry dickens as they both go out.

Grandfather enters at the beginning of the third verse, trying to light a corncob pipe, but the match goes out, and he cannot find another. The clock reaches an arm through the hole, strikes a match on sandpaper and lights the pipe for Grandfather. The chorus pauses at the end of the second line for this action to be completed, then continues as Grandfather pretends to wind the clock. The clock smiles sweetly on the fifth line as Grandfather finishes winding and leaves.

The curtains partially close at the beginning of the third chorus so that Grandfather's bed may be brought in on one side of the stage and placed just a little forward and to one side of the clock. Grandfather gets in bed and Grandfather's spirit gets down behind one side of the bed (away from the audience). The clock should always be in view. If the singing of the chorus is not sufficient time to get set for the last verse, the chorus may be repeated.

An alarm should ring when mentioned at the beginning of the last verse, as the curtains open wide. Several members of the chorus, representing both sexes, gather around the bed, but not so as to completely block the audience's view of Grandfather and his spirit.

The clock's pendulum stops on the seventh line, the sheet is pulled over Grandfather, and his spirit arises in back of the bed. The spirit moves over to the clock and beckons to the clock. The spirit of the clock nods its head, steps down off the box and places "Out of Business" clock face in position to be seen. The two spirits leave as the chorus finishes the song.

My Grandfather's Clock

In watching its pendulum swing to and fro,
Many hours had he spent while a boy;
And in childhood and manhood the clock seemed to
know
And to share both his grief and his joy;
For it struck twenty-four when he entered at the door
With a blooming and beautiful bride;
But it stopp'd short, never to go again,
When the old man died.

My grandfather said that of those he could hire,
Not a servant so faithful he found;
For it wasted no time and had but one desire,
At the close of the week to be wound;
And it kept in its place not a frown upon its face
And its hands never hung by its side;
But it stopp'd short, never to go again,
When the old man died.

It rang an alarm in the dead of the night,
An alarm that for years had been dumb;
We knew that his spirit was pluming for flight,
That his hour of departure had come;
Still the clock kept the time with a softly muffled
chime
As we silently stood by his side;
But it stopp'd short, never to go again,
When the old man died.

IVAN SKIZAVITSKY SKIVAR

Almost any group can handle this, although it is normally a male number, calling for three male actors and a supporting chorus. Costumes, a gun and a broom horse make up all the props needed.

This is a good song to burlesque, with an easy swinging tune for any group to sing. Only three actors are needed; the two antagonists and the Sultan, who rides in on a broom horse at the end, and it should be a mighty fancy steed with appropriate decorations.

All three should be garbed picturesquely, as befitting Turkish and Russian warriors of some years ago. Fancy scabbards should be worn. However, the weapons themselves should be imaginary or cardboard. The scabbards, too, may be cardboard. Ivan also needs a gun to shoulder which can be most any improvised makeshift.

Incidentally, according to my dictionary, a "chibouque" is a Turkish pipe, with a stiff stem, some four or five feet long, so if this gives you any ideas, go ahead with them, but I am not sure where you will go. Perhaps it would be better to settle for a sword-like weapon.

Generally speaking, Abdul and Ivan simply dramatize the action as the song is sung by the group, putting plenty of swagger and bluster into it.

The curtain opens on the group singing, and Abdul strides on stage at the end of the third line of the first verse. The chorus really shouts for Abdul at the end of the second verse, and he pulls out his weapon and charges forward as though to battle, charging right off stage.

Ivan then comes on to do his stuff, including making like Caruso. Ivan must not forget his "sneer" when he shoulders his gun in the fifth verse.

If Abdul and Ivan are up to it, they should sing their lines solo. Otherwise, they mouth the words in exaggerated fashion while the group sings.

Ivan (or group) should stress the word "Old" at the beginning of the fourth line of the eighth verse, as though sorry for poor old Abdul.

Regardless of whether or not Abdul sings his own lines, he ought to do his own shouting of "Allah-il-Allah! Akbar!" Abdul strikes down Ivan first and starts to turn away with a leer (a nasty look of triumph) when Ivan gets him.

The group pauses at the end of the eleventh verse while the following dialogue takes place:

SULTAN. So long, Abdul. It's been nice knowing you.

ABDUL. Be seeing you, Sultan. I hate to rush off, but that's the way the cookie crumbles."

Abdul flops down, while Ivan raises himself with an effort and as the group sings the last verse, lunges at the Sultan on the third line, and then falls back across Abdul, with the Sultan toppling onto the heap. And that's that.

Ivan Skizavitsky Skivar

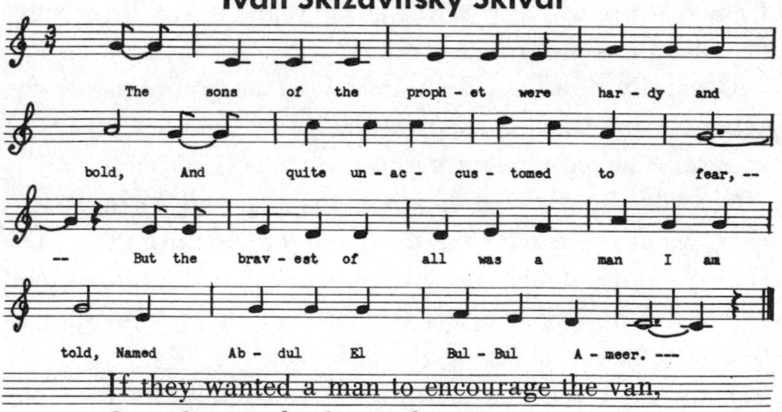

If they wanted a man to encourage the van,
Or to harass the foe in the rear;
Or to storm a redoubt, they would set up a shout,
For Abdul El Bul-Bul Ameer.

There were heroes in plenty and men known to fame,
Who fought in the ranks of the Czar;
But none of more fame than a man by the name
Of Ivan Skizavitsky Skivar.

He could sing like Caruso, both tenor and bass,
He could play on the Spanish guitar;
In fact, quite the cream of the Muscovite team
Was Ivan Skizavitsky Skivar.

One day this bold Muscovite shouldered his gun
And walked down the street with a sneer;
He was looking for fun when he happened to run
Upon Abdul El Bul-Bul Ameer.

"Young man," said Bul-Bul, "is existence so dull,
That you're anxious to end your career?
For, infidel, know you have trod on the toe
Of Abdul El Bul-Bul Ameer.

"So take your last look at the sunshine and brook,
And send your regrets to the Czar;
By which I imply that you are going to die,
Mister Ivan Skizavitsky Skivar."

Said the Russian, "My friend, and you are *not* my
friend,
Your talk is most wondrously queer,
For it's you, and not I, who is destined to die,
Old Abdul El Bul-Bul Ameer!"

Then the Bul-Bul, so bold, drew his trusty Chibouque,
Crying: "Allah-il-Allah! Akbar!"
And with unkindly intent he most suddenly went
For Ivan Skizavitsky Skivar.

But just as he thought he had finished his foe,
In fact, he indulged in a leer,
He felt himself struck by that subtle Calmuck,
Brave Ivan Skizavitsky Skivar.

When the Sultan rode up the disturbance to quell,
Or to give the victor a cheer,
He arrived just in time to take hasty farewell
Of Abdul El Bul-Bul Ameer.

And this is what happened, believe me, it's true,
I swear by that yon twinkling star,
The Sultan himself was struck down from his horse
By Ivan Skizavitsky Skivar.

OH, DON'T GIVE ME HOMEWORK NO MORE

To the tune of "My Bonnie Lies Over the Ocean," this is a sure hit with any youthful audience, and is easy to learn and produce.

This parody of "My Bonnie Lies Over the Ocean" can be sung very easily by almost any sized group and very little action is needed. School books should be in evidence and those singing the verses may dramatize them as they wish. It is suggested that different individuals or smaller sections of the group sing each verse, with everybody coming in on the chorus, with plenty of emphasis on the "don'ts."

Some extra fun may be had by adding a second "surprise" chorus after the fourth verse, provided a group of teachers (if done by a school group) or parents or other adults (who may be present elsewhere) can be coached in advance and will come in promptly with the following just as the kids finish the chorus after the fourth verse:

Oh, yes! Oh, yes!
You'll still get your homework. Too bad! So sad!
Oh, yes! Oh, yes!
You'll still get your homework. How sad!

Obviously, if this can really be a surprise, the group on the stage will react in a manner most interesting to watch. If the surprise element is not considered practicable, this extra ending may still be used by a group in the audience, with the group on the stage coached to look very sad.

It would not be difficult to get a youthful audience to join in on the choruses, if desired.

Oh, Don't Give Me Homework No More

(Tune: My Bonnie Lies Over the Ocean)

My Mother, she always loved homework,
My Father says he liked it fine,
But to me, it means nothing but headaches
That I'd like to erase from my mind.

Chorus: Oh don't, oh don't,
Oh don't give me homework no more, no more;
Oh don't, oh don't,
Oh don't give me homework no more.

Last night when I studied my spelling
I thought I had all the words right,
But what happened today I'm not telling,
Or you'll think that I'm not very bright.

Now 'rithmetic's not what I'm good at,
I can't subtract, multiply nor divide,
But Pa says if I don't do much better,
He'll add a big switch to my hide.

Now history and suchlike is old stuff
That happened a long time ago,
So why expect me to know all about it
When I wasn't there, don't you know.

YOU ARE MY GIRL

This is a musical comedy type production (to the tune of "Alouette") for a mixed teen-age group. A fair amount of rehearsal time essential to do it right, but no special costumes or props needed.

A group of teen-agers with a spirit of fun can have a good time with this. Actual movements on the stage will have to be worked out to suit the size of the group and the stage. However, the following suggestions may prove helpful.

The curtain opens on several double lines of boys and girls, there being enough space between each double line for doubling around as explained below. All face toward the audience as the first two lines are sung by the group. Then the boys and girls face each other for repartee. As the group sings "Oh!" which is held for four beats, the first couple in each column doubles back and swings around at the rear of the column; other couples moving forward, so that the second couple in the double lines are now in front.

The boys and girls face each other again for repartee, the second couple in each column doubling back to the rear as the third verse is sung. Thus the couples keep moving up and to the rear, hand in hand on the fourth verse, their arms around each other's waists on the fifth.

The repartee following the fifth verse should be as fast as the group can handle it without tripping over their own tongues. The plea of the boys, by contrast, should be slower than previously and more pathetic. Girls say "No!" emphatically, whereupon the boys sing, "Well, I'm gonna smack you now," and kiss the girls on the right cheek, moving back as the girls sing and then slap the boys on the right cheek.

When the boys say, "You are!" and start for the girls, raising their arms as though for an embrace, the girls escape by dodging to the boys' left, and running off stage. More or less confusion is all right. There is sufficient pause here for the girls to clear the stage before the boys begin to sing "Oh! I'm a feller . . ." etc.

As the boys sing, "I'm a feller who hasn't got a girl," the second time, dragging the music, the girls steal in quietly to the rear of the stage and then up in their respective columns until each girl is opposite the boy she was with before her exit. The boys are now standing with their heads hanging, completely dejected, until the girls sing, "You do so have a girl."

At first the boys can hardly believe it, but when reassured with "Yes, you have," they joyfully sing, "Lucky me!" and all couples start doubling back and forward in columns, arms around each other's waists until the end of the song.

You Are My Girl

(Tune: Alouette)

GROUP. I'm your feller, and you are my girl,
I'm your feller, and you are my girl.
BOYS. Tell me that you are my girl.
GIRLS. Sorry, I am not your girl.

BOYS. Yes, you are.

GIRLS. No, I'm not.

BOYS *(Spoken pleadingly.)* Aw, come on.

GIRLS *(Spoken relentingly.)* Well, all right.

GROUP *(Singing.)* Oh! I'm your feller, and you are my girl, Down the lane we will take a stroll.

BOYS. We'll go walking down the lane.

GIRLS. No, we'll not walk down the lane.

BOYS. Yes, we will.

GIRLS. No, we won't.

BOYS. Yes, you are.

GIRLS. No, I'm not.

BOYS *(Spoken pleadingly.)* Aw, come on.

GIRLS *(Spoken relentingly.)* Well, all right.

GROUP. Oh! . . .

I'm your feller, and you are my girl,
Down the lane, how I like to stroll.

BOYS. But it's more fun holding hands.

GIRLS. Sorry, no fair holding hands.

BOYS. Yes, it is.

GIRLS. No, it's not. *(Repeat as above.)*

GROUP. Oh! . . .

I'm your feller, and you are my girl,
Hand in hand, far down the lane we stroll.

BOYS. Now let's shift to arm in arm.

GIRLS. No, we'll not go arm in arm.

BOYS. Yes, we shall.

GIRLS. No, we shan't. *(Repeat as above.)*

GROUP. Oh! . . .

I'm your feller, and you are my girl,
Arm in arm, my head is in a whirl.

BOYS. Now I'd like a little kiss.

GIRLS. You'll not get a little kiss.

BOYS. Yes, I will.

GIRLS. No, you won't.

BOYS. Yes, we shall.

GIRLS. No, we shan't.

BOYS. Yes, it is.

GIRLS. No, it's not.

BOYS. Yes, we will.

GIRLS. No, we won't.

BOYS. Yes, you are.

GIRLS. No, I'm not.

BOYS *(Spoken pleadingly.)* Aw, come on.

GIRLS *(Spoken emphatically.)* I said, "No!"

BOYS *(Singing.)* Well, I'm gonna smack you now. *(Boys kiss the girls.)*

GIRLS *(Singing.)* And I'm gonna smack you too. *(Girls slap the boys.)*

BOYS *(Spoken reproachfully.)* Gee, you're mean.

GIRLS *(Spoken contritely.)* Oh, I'm sorry.

BOYS *(Happy smiles.)* You are! *(Start for the girls.)*

GIRLS *(Alarmed.)* No, I'm not! *(Exit hurriedly.)*

BOYS *(Singing.)* Oh! . . .

I'm a feller who hasn't got a girl,
I'm a feller who hasn't got a girl.

GIRLS *(Return, singing.)* You do so have got a girl.

BOYS. Have I really got a girl?

GIRLS. Yes, you have.

BOYS. Lucky me!

GROUP. Oh! . . .
I'm your feller, and you are my girl,
Arm in arm, my head is in a whirl.

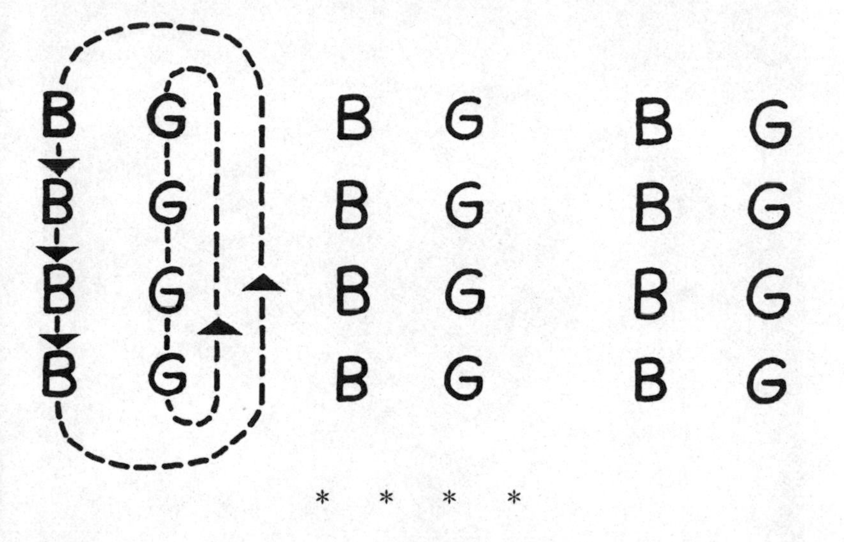

* * * *

THE MERMAID

An excellent number for boys, but also usable by girls. Sailor costumes and a mermaid outfit make this a colorful and enjoyable song on both sides of the footlights.

The Mermaid can be effectively done by a group of boys dressed as sailors. It is not necessary that all be dressed alike since they are merchant seamen. Nevertheless, a group of boys in white sailor pants and jumpers, or T-shirts, with white hats will make a good appearance.

The Captain, of course, should look the part, as should the Cook. The Captain may have a large spyglass (a black cardboard tube will do) or he may simply use his hands as though he had a glass.

The Mermaid should have a fish-like tail which begins at

the waist and continues to the fin beyond the feet. There should be some stiffening in the fin. A blond wig completes

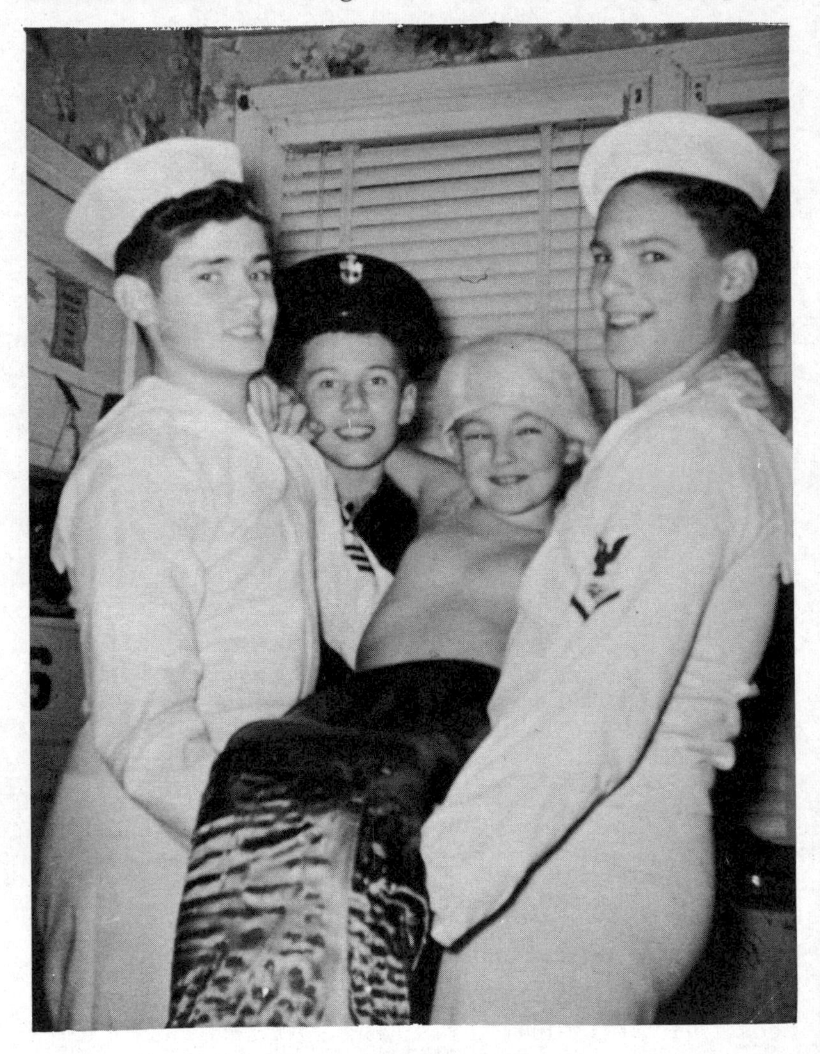

Anybody Want a Mermaid?
Sailors Howard Dunlap and Bob Clarson with an armful of live Mermaid (Ronnie James). Cap'n Bill Shunkwiler is sticking close by.

the costume, the boy being bare from the waist up. Needless to say, a younger, slighter boy is more suited to this part, unless it is decided to use a fat boy to burlesque the thing. A comb and a glass, and a small island or rock on which the mermaid may drape himself (herself) are required. The island may be a few boxes, table, etc., suitably disguised.

The curtain opens sufficiently to reveal the sailors in the center of the stage as they begin the first verse, opening the rest of the way to reveal the mermaid when spotted by the captain who has been scanning the horizon with his spyglass. The Captain should indicate considerable interest at this, as should the sailors as they swing into the chorus.

A "Leader" may solo the lines indicated in the chorus, or part of the group may sing these lines with the balance singing the echo lines. The third chorus should be sung at a faster tempo.

The Captain sings the last two lines of the second verse in a deep voice or attempted bass part; while the Cook, preferably fat and jolly (a pillow may help), sings the last two lines of the third verse.

The mermaid flirts with the sailors during the choruses and they, in turn, are much interested in her. During the fourth verse one sailor fades back and circles around to where the Mermaid is resting to one side of the sailors and, as they swing into the final chorus, picks up the Mermaid and carries her to the center of the sailors, where she throws kisses at the audience, having left her comb and glass on the island.

Just as the chorus ends, the Mermaid may kiss the sailor, if desired, and he may pretend to almost drop her from the effects of this potent kiss. The sailors close by move as though to catch her if he does, as the curtain closes.

The curtain may re-open, as though in error, to show the other boys laughing at the sailor holding the Mermaid, who has a wry look on his face while the Mermaid is holding a wig in one hand and wiping his mouth with the other. If the Mermaid has used lipstick, it will show on the sailor's face. The curtain is hastily closed once more.

GROUP. 'Twas Friday morn when we set sail,
And we were not far from the land,
When the Captain spied a pretty mermaid
With a comb and a glass in her hand.
(Chorus)

LEADER. Oh, the ocean waves may roll,
GROUP. Let 'em roll.
LEADER. And the stormy winds may blow,
GROUP. Let 'em blow.

LEADER. While we old salts go skipping to the top,
And the landlubbers lie down . . .
GROUP. Below, below, below.
LEADER. And the landlubbers lie down . . .
GROUP. Below.
GROUP. Then up spoke the Captain of our gallant ship,
And a well spoken man was he:
CAPTAIN. I married me a wife in Salem town,
But tonight a widow she will be. *(Chorus)*
GROUP. Then up spoke the Cook of our gallant ship,
And a red hot cook was he:
COOK. I care much more for my kettles and my pots
Than I do for the bottom of the sea. *(Chorus)*
GROUP. Then three times around went our gallant ship,
And three times around went she;
Then three times around went our gallant ship,
And she sank to the bottom of the sea. *(Chorus)*

* * * *

CLEMENTINE

Easy to learn and sing; adaptable for most any group—boys, girls or both. Lead parts are confined to pantomime; props and costumes should not be much trouble.

Our actors for this song are The Miner (forty-niner), his daughter Clementine, Clementine's little sister and, if desired, a separate member of the chorus to act the part of Clementine's beau. Otherwise, the chorus generally can act as the beau, including being kissed, so far as practicable, by "little sister."

Scout groups may also have someone to apply artificial respiration in the last verse. Others may end the song on the next to the last verse, or, if they wish to demonstrate artificial respiration they can change the third word of the first line of the last verse to "all" instead of "scouts."

The Miner (forty-niner) and Clementine should be dressed in keeping with the Gold Rush Days of '49. Clementine needs some box-type shoes, which can be held in place over the feet by cords and the Miner needs a shovel or pick. Clementine will also need some ducklings (which can be made of heavy cardboard mounted on spools and strung together) and a sheet.

The curtain opens on the chorus at the beginning of the first verse, the Miner (forty-niner) appearing at the end of the first line, pretending to dig or swing a pick. Clementine enters at the end of the first verse. Clementine clumps out at the end of the second verse, re-appearing with ducklings at the beginning of the third. She stumbles (Chorus holds up small sticks or wooden matches) and pretends to fall into the water, goes under and comes up blowing bubbles. Her beau, or the whole chorus, looks confused, distressed and whatnot, but finally shrug their shoulders in resignation.

The fifth verse is sung dolefully while some members of the chorus carry Clementine out as best they may. If she is very heavy, and she should be, an express wagon might be used.

In the meantime, the Miner (forty-niner) has been working away, mopping his brow with a bandanna, etc., but now begins to "peak and pine." He could solo the third line of the sixth verse, "Guess I oughter jine my daughter," shuffling out on the following line.

Little sister enters running on the third line of the seventh verse and proceeds to hug and kiss and be hugged and kissed by her beau, or the chorus, continuing to the end of the chorus, when she happily takes her place as a member of the group. The song can very well end here.

If the artificial respiration (eighth) verse is used, two or three members of the chorus quickly lie down while the others apply artificial respiration until the end of the final chorus.

Some extra nonsense may be added by changing final "Clementine" at end of each chorus to "Frankenstein," "Turpentine," "Valentine," etc.

Clementine

Light she was and like a fairy,
And her shoes were number nine;
Herring boxes, without topses,
Sandals were for Clementine.

(Chorus)

Drove she ducklings to the water,
Ev'ry morning just at nine;
Hit her foot against a splinter,
Fell into the foaming brine.

Saw her lips above the water,
Blowing bubbles, mighty fine;
But, alas! I was no swimmer,
So I lost my Clementine.

(Chorus)

(Minor key)

In a corner of the churchyard,
Where the myrtle boughs entwine,
That's the place where she reposes;
Where they planted Clementine.

(Minor key)

Then the miner, forty-niner,
He began to peak and pine;
Thought he "oughter jine" his daughter,
Now he's with his Clementine.

(Chorus)

(Major key)

How I missed her, how I missed her,
How I missed my Clementine!
But I kissed her little sister,
And forgot my Clementine.

(Chorus)

Now you Scouts should learn the moral
Of this little tale of mine;
Artificial respiration
Would have saved my Clementine.

(Chorus)

* * * *

THE GOODIES AND THE BADDIES

Nothing like a Western, and this is a pantomime production to the tune of "Oh, Susanna," which everybody knows. With dungarees and some brooms as a starter you are well on the way with this.

Everyone knows the tune of *Oh, Susanna* and a group can quickly learn this parody, singing as a chorus in rear center or at one side of the stage, while the action is carried on by another group in improvised cowboy costumes (dungarees and whatnot) and with guns and broom horses. The person playing the part of the cow can wear a paper bag cow head, or something like a headband with two pointed drinking cups on each side. A liberal dose of imagination takes care of the scenery.

The action simply follows the song, the Baddies riding in and surrounding the cow, which moo's and tries to get away. The cowboy rides in and the Baddies shoot him. The Baddies can then maneuver around off stage or around behind the chorus, as the Goodies ride in, dismount from their broom horses, and then raise their fists in a threatening manner when they discover their man has been shot.

The Baddies reappear for the chase, and there should be plenty of shooting and prancing around. The Baddies get ahead and supposedly set up an ambush; the Goodies dismount and start working around them, until they finally have them trapped. Needless to say all this action must be done in a relatively small space so that the actual maneuvering will have to be worked out to suit the size of the stage and the number of actors.

The Goodies should outnumber the Baddies; whether any get shot being a matter to decide. However, some Baddies get shot at the end and there should be at least two or three left to surrender. They are rounded up by the Goodies on the last chorus.

The Goodies and the Baddies

(Tune: Oh, Susanna!)

The Baddies are a'rustlin'—
They just got another cow;
They shouldn't oughta do it,
For the Law, it don't allow.
A cowboy tries to stop 'em;
But they fill him full o' lead.
He tumbles from his pony,
And we fear he's sorta dead.

Chorus: Oh, those Baddies!
Whatever shall we do?
Oh, will the Goodies capture them?
The Goodies brave and true.

The Goodies come a'ridin'—
And they find their fallen friend;
They swear they'll get those Baddies,
That their rustling days must end.
The Goodies mount their horses,
They're hot on the Baddies' trail;
But when the Baddies see 'em,
The lead flies as thick as hail.

(Repeat chorus)

The Baddies try an ambush,
But the Goodies will not bite;
So now they're all a-gettin' set
For one gosh-awful fight.
The Goodies get around 'em and
Their six-guns blaze away;
The Baddies beg for mercy,
At the closing of the day.

Chorus: Oh, those Baddies!
They've rustled their last cow;
So Kiddies always do what's right,
We're a-tellin' you right now.

* * * *

THE SCOUT COMPANY

A unique show opener for Boy Scout troops, requiring more rehearsal time and more props and staging than most of the others, but well worth the trouble.

I have used this song as an effective opening for a Boy Scout entertainment program, the entire troop participating.

The stage is set up to suggest a scout camp and for the most part you can use your own ideas as to displaying scout camping equipment, rustic washstands, etc., and woodland decorations. The props called for by the action described below are:

(1) A screen of some sort in the rear center of stage, which may be decorated as desired.

(2) One small tent (may be pup tent) which must be turned slightly to rear of the stage if not equipped with front flaps.

(3) Two washstand tripods, each lashed together and supporting a wash basin. A pail between them presumably holds water.

The tent is set up at one side of the stage and may be mounted on a wood frame, using nails as tent pegs. This can readily be done with a small tent. The tripods are on the same side of the stage to the front of the tent.

When the song begins two scouts are in the tent in sleeping bags or blankets, with pajamas over their scout pants and socks; their hair should be good and tousled. Two other scouts are off stage on the same side as the tent. One of these boys is bare to the waist and is wearing scout shorts, long stockings with garter tabs and shoes, sneakers or moccasins. He should have a well-developed physique. The other boy is wearing pajamas, with a sweat shirt or sweater pulled over his pajama coat, and sweat socks. He should have a big mop of hair wondrously well mussed up. Both have towels, washcloths and soap. The boy in shorts also has a comb.

Another scout is off stage on the other side from the tent. He is wearing his uniform, except a neckerchief, under civilian clothes. This means a loose pair of civilian pants, of course, and a lumberjack type shirt, scout shirt being unbuttoned at the top so as not to show. His neckerchief and slide are in a handy position behind the center screen, also a pair of civilian socks.

The curtain opens with a roll of the drum, if possible. Otherwise, a roll of the piano, and the balance of the troop, grouped in the center stage, start singing. Almost at once a scout in civilian clothes appears, one of the others spots him and goes over to him and appears to engage him in conversation. As the second verse begins, the scout in uniform points to the troop and the other boy nods his head, whereupon he is hurried around back of the screen for a quick change.

As he peels off his outer shirt and pants the other scout tosses them high in the air so that they appear above the screen before falling out of sight again. The shirt should go up first, then the civilian socks which were placed there ahead of time, and finally the pants. This action will have to be fast, because both scouts should reappear during the third verse.

If necessary, they can reappear with the boy who was in civvies, tucking in his scout shirt and the other scout fixing his neckerchief for him. The balance of the troop indicate friendship by smiling or slapping the "new scout" on the back. If the "new scout" doesn't quite get organized by the end of the third verse he should fade back to the side of the group away from the tent so as not to detract from the following action.

Reveille, or at least a few notes, can be sounded on the bugle at the beginning of the fourth verse. Or several of the group may lift their fists to their mouths as though playing the bugle. Two scouts in pajamas stick their heads out of the tent, crawling halfway out on their hands and knees. They duck back in almost at once, and should be out of sight as they work fast in order to reappear on the last verse.

As the fifth verse begins, the scout in shorts runs in, hangs a towel on one of the wash stands and begins to go through the motions of washing up with evident enjoyment. He should breathe deeply, swelling his chest, as he applies a supposedly wet washcloth to his chest, shoulders, etc. He washes his face and hands vigorously, and dries himself likewise. He then combs his hair quickly and hurries out to get his shirt and neckerchief.

The scout in pajamas mooches in after the scout in shorts. He appears to be half asleep as he gropes his way to the second stand, tries to hang the towel on it, but drops it on the floor, and then washes himself by dipping his fingertips in the basin and dabbing at his face with them, shuddering from contact with cold water. He gropes for the towel and finally sees it on the ground. He bolts offstage when the mess call blows.

In order to more adequately cover the above action, the troop can whistle or hum an extra verse after the fifth verse.

A bugle is most desirable for blowing the mess call offstage, but a good effect may be achieved by having one or two scouts place their fists to their mouths as above and singing the tune of the mess call with "Dah-dah-dah," etc. When this happens, the scout in shorts appears, walking briskly behind the screen; he may be putting his shirt on as he walks. The boys in the tent bolt out in different stages of dress, or undress. They should have gotten their pajamas off and shoes on, even if the latter are unlaced. Both hurry behind the screen, finishing their dressing as they go.

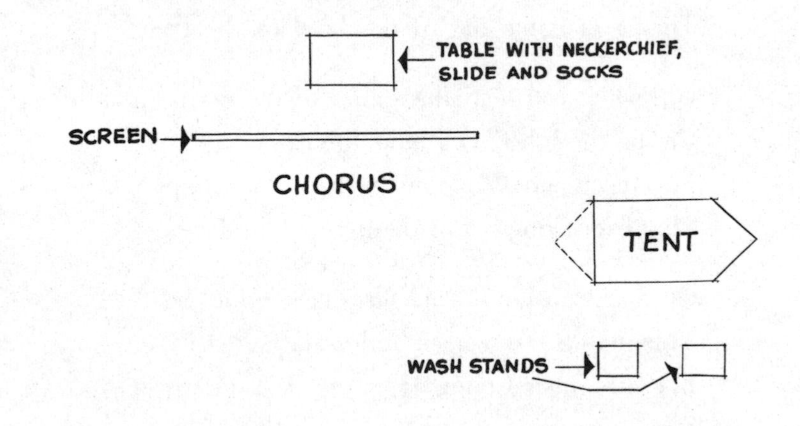

The Scout Company

Oh, when you get a line on a new recruit,
Make him a Scout in a khaki suit;
For the Scout Company is the best company
That ever came out of the land of the free.

For when you join the Scouts you are sure to find
You're among friends of the finest kind;
For the Scout Company is the best company
That ever came out of the land of the free.

Oh, when you hear the sound of the morning call,
Get on the job if you have to crawl;
For the Scout Company is the best company
That ever came out of the land of the free.

Oh, early in the morn you just have to get
Your hands, your neck and your face all wet;
For the Scout Company is the best company
That ever came out of the land of the free.

Oh, don't you be asleep when the mess call blows,
You'll find where it is if you follow your nose;
For the Scout Company is the best company
That ever came out of the land of the free.

From: THE BOY SCOUT SONG BOOK
C.C. Birchard & Co., Boston
(3rd & 5th verses added by Bob Smith)

* * * *

FOOLISH QUESTIONS

Easily sung by most any youth group, the eight lead parts may be classified as three male, one female and four optional. Props are nominal, costumes of no consequence.

Actors and props for this song are:

First Verse: Lover with a box of candy; girl.

Second Verse: Traveler with a suitcase; friend.

Third Verse: Shaver with a shaving brush, bowl and razor; questioner.

Fourth Verse: Victim; questioner.

All of these actors can be members of the chorus, simply picking up necessary props and moving to the front on cue. The action follows the song, of course, with proper characters handling solo parts in quotation marks.

In the first verse the girl should really grab the candy and the lover gets it back only after a struggle.

The friend should fetch the traveler a pretended hard crack on the back, and, after the traveler has sung his solo lines, the friend can walk off with him saying, "Gee, and I thought you were back," before the group sings the last line of the second chorus.

For the third verse, a boy hastily removes his shirt and

actually lathers up his face in the front center while pretending to look into the mirror. It will probably be necessary for the group to pause after the second line for the shaver to finish lathering up, singing the third line as he picks up the razor. When the shaver finishes his solo part, he should dab the questioner squarely in the mouth with a well-lathered brush. He then grabs up the bowl and flees with the questioner after him.

At the beginning of the fourth verse, someone from the group circles to one end of the stage and pretends to step through the elevator door into the shaft, falling by revolving slowly with his arms extended to either side and moving to the center of the stage, where he sprawls on cue. The questioner bends over to sing a question which the victim answers from the floor.

Foolish Questions

Or perhaps you've been away from home for several
days or weeks,
What will your friend first say to you, the first time
you he meets?
He'll rush right up behind you and he'll slap you on
the back,
And he'll nearly knock you over, as he hollers, "Are
you back?"

CHORUS: Foolish questions, you'll answer him in line,
"No, I'm traveling in Europe, I'm at Bingen on
the Rhine,

I'm traveling in Asia and I won't be home till May."
Now there's a foolish question that you hear 'most every day.

And always in the morning there's a fool around the place,
Who sees you take your shaving brush and lather up your face;
And as you give the razor a preliminary wave,
The fool is sure to ask you, "Say, are you going to shave?"

CHORUS: Foolish questions, you'll answer as I hope,
"No, I'm not prepared to shave, but I like the taste of soap,
And so I take my shaving brush and lather up this way."
Now there's a foolish question that you hear 'most every day.

And when the elevator boy forgets to close the doors,
And you go tumbling down the shaft, past twenty-seven floors;
And when you hit the bottom, and are lying there inert,
Some fool is sure to ask you, "Say, mister, are you hurt?"

CHORUS: Foolish questions, your dying words I know
Are, "I was in a hurry, and the darned thing was so slow;
So I thought I'd save a lot of time by coming down this way."
Now there's a foolish question that you hear 'most every day.

Section Five

GHOST STORIES

Suggestions for the Leader

There is nothing like a good ghost story as the climax for a campfire program or many an indoor party-type affair where the lights can be turned low for the thrilling of an audience from about 10 to 11 up into the teens.

Listeners in this age group particularly enjoy "Boo!" or "Sudden Scare" endings which, however, are not recommended for younger children or adults.

As a matter of fact, it is just as well to avoid telling ghost stories to children under ten (unless you are sure the story is appropriate for the group) or to older people or any adult audiences where such scare techniques would not be wise. On the other hand, a story with a "creepy" type ending will often satisfy a large age range, and it does not matter so much if some youngsters and oldsters are present. "Crooked Arrow and His Ghost Wolves," for example, while gripping enough to thrill most anyone, should, nevertheless, be acceptable for many types of audiences. I write from experience.

Humorous ghost stories may be excellent for adults, younger children or mixed audiences, but will not take the place of the real thing with youthful groups all set for a scare. Five of the stories included here are believed to be "the real thing," two with creepy endings, two with the "sudden scare" at the end, and one with a choice. One of the "sudden scare" stories also has a second, explanatory and somewhat humorous postscript, which may be used after the "scare laughter" has subsided.

The sixth story, "When a Little Girl Meets a Big Ghost," can be classified as a semi-humorous ghost story and will do fine for younger groups, such as cubs and brownies and also for audiences of wide age ranges. It should be told in a regularly lighted room.

He who tells ghost stories should know them well and go all out to set the proper mood for the occasion by insisting on:

1. Dim lighting (a dying campfire or dimly lighted room —complete darkness is *not* a good idea.)

2. Absolute silence and complete attention. Any tendencies to wisecrack must be promptly checked lest the story be spoiled for both the story teller and the audience. The right mood depends upon good rapport between narrator and listeners which must start at the very beginning of the story and grow with it.

3. His own best effort to tell it in a "ghost story" manner. He must get in the mood himself first, "feel it" and then tell it so as to build up a solemn acceptance of things unreal which increases to a tense, flesh-creeping excitement. If the story has a "Boo!" ending, the final build-up must be full of scary breathlessness, until all are "on the edges of their chairs" for the sudden "I GOT YOU!" A jump toward a section of the listeners is a recognized and very acceptable part of the act, being highly enjoyed by normal, healthy youth.

The creepy ending is usually followed by a dead silence and, when voices do begin to be heard, they are likely to be subdued in keeping with the effect that has been created. After a little pause the evening can be closed with a quiet song or other ending on a serious note. This scary sensation is also keenly relished by young listeners to ghost stories. It gives them such a satisfying sense of participation in something thrilling, that, whatever else may have transpired, the evening is a big success, and one that will be remembered and talked about.

I wonder if ghosts like to hear about people as much as we do about them. I am thinking especially of young ghosts.

THE HAUNTED HOUSE ON DARBY CREEK

Plenty of imagination, and possibly, a few little facts, result in a good, creepy-type ending story about a very real Boy Scout troop and the old stone house they used to call their "cabin."

Many years ago on the banks of Darby Creek not far from the City of Philadelphia lived an old man, who was known simply—as Old Bill.

For as long as anyone could remember Old Bill and his wife had been living there in the gray stone house on the side of the hill. So far as anyone knew they had no children, or any other relatives or friends. At least, no one ever came to see them, nor did they ever go away except for occasional trips to a nearby town to purchase a few supplies. When these infrequent trips took place, Old Bill hitched up an old horse to a very ancient buggy, and he and his wife drove slowly to town.

The old horse and buggy were kept with one cow and some chickens in a tumbled-down barn not far from the house. These, together with a garden and a few apple trees, which straggled along the creek, appeared to be the sole source of food and income for Old Bill and his wife, although it was rumored that the old man had gold buried somewhere about the place. It was also said that he sometimes took mysterious trips at night. Certain it was he did have the money he needed for supplies in spite of the fact he sold almost nothing from his tiny farm.

However, no one could be sure of anything except that they got along somehow and preferred to be left strictly alone. Since they never bothered any of their neighbors, their wish for privacy was respected. This was especially true because the piece of land they occupied along the side of the hill by the creek was an odd corner at the end of a simple dirt road which meant making a special trip to see them. And so Old Bill and his wife lived there all alone.

Until one day it occurred to some of the neighbors, a little farther up the creek, that they hadn't seen Old Bill's wife for some time. Fearing she might be ill and in need of assistance, several of the neighbors went over to inquire for her.

"She died last month," Old Bill explained, "and I buried her up on the hill." Then, after a little pause, he added, "I buried her at night; there was a full moon."

Not much else was said. Old Bill did not seem to want their sympathy and they could not think of anything else to say or do. It was not right, of course, this strange burial by night, but what could be done about it? So the neighbors went away, but more than one shuddered as he thought of Old Bill toiling up the hill alone, with the body of his wife, and then burying her there by moonlight—all alone.

For a time after that Old Bill lived completely alone—with his old horse, the cow and the chickens—in the old stone house on Darby Creek.

But then, one day, Old Bill hitched up the old horse to his ancient buggy and drove away. To the astonishment of the neighbors he was dressed as though for a wedding, and the mystery deepened when he drove right on through town, moving at a sedate pace to the West. No one could remember when Old Bill had ever gone farther away than this before. No one could imagine where he had gone.

When he didn't come back that day the neighbors went over to look after his cow, half suspecting Old Bill knew they would, even though he had not asked them to.

About two weeks later Old Bill returned in his ancient buggy, bringing with him a new wife, to live with him in the old stone house on Darby Creek. And for a time the two of them lived quietly together, as Old Bill and his first wife had before, visiting no one and having no visitors—simply living there all alone.

But it wasn't very long until the neighbors began to realize that all wasn't well with Old Bill and his new wife. Indeed, something was very wrong in the old stone house on Darby Creek. For the neighbors would hear weird laughter that sent the cold shivers up and down their spines. And sometimes they would see Old Bill's wife wandering aimlessly around at night, swinging a lantern and talking to herself, or laughing, as though at the moon. Perhaps they would meet her on the road, a wild look in her eyes and a lantern in her hand, even though it were broad daylight.

People talked, and after a time men came and took Old Bill's new wife away, to place her in an institution where she could receive proper care. The old man made no protest at this, nor did he show any emotion at this second loss of a wife. In fact, all he said was, "I guess it was too lonely for her."

And then, once again, Old Bill lived all alone in the old stone house on Darby Creek. He was growing feeble now, and the neighbors began to wonder what would become of him, as they saw him, from a distance, moving slowly about his garden, tending his cow and chickens.

Until there came a day when several of the neighbors were talking and it occurred to them that no one had seen Old Bill about for several days. Perhaps he was sick, or he might have fallen and hurt himself. They went over to the old stone house and knocked on the door. There was no answer, and the door was securely locked. They went around to the windows, but all on the first floor were tightly shuttered, and they could see nothing within.

They went down to the barn and found the old horse and cow half starved. The chickens had gotten out and scratched around and appeared to be all right. Much concerned, the neighbors had just started back for the house when they saw a turkey vulture appear high above the house and begin to circle around, high up there in the sky. Then another vulture came, and another, and the three of them swung there in slow circles, above the house.

One of the neighbors went for a ladder, and they climbed up to a second-story window, and forced their way in. They found Old Bill lying in his bed, where he had died—all alone.

They buried him on the hill, beside his wife.

Some time went by, and then a family came to live in the old stone house on Darby Creek. They said they had rented the place and would have a little farm along the top of the hill.

But this family did not stay very long. They said they could hear someone walking slowly across the floors at night —downstairs.

After awhile another family moved in, but they too, did not stay very long. They told the same story of someone, or something, walking across the floors at night—downstairs. Several more families came and went, each telling the same story. Until, finally, no one would live there, or even go near the house at night.

Folks said the Ghost of Old Bill haunted the place. Thus it became known as the "Haunted House on Darby Creek."

The years passed on and the house slowly fell apart. The roof fell in, the floors gave way, and the windows became great empty, staring holes. Only the sturdy stone walls remained. The barn rotted away, weeds grew where the garden had been, and the apple trees, long neglected, went to seed. It certainly seemed unlikely that anyone would ever live in the old house again.

But one day a troop of boy scouts on a hike stopped to cook their lunch near the old house and to swim in the cool waters of Darby Creek. Later they looked at the sturdy old walls and decided the place could be fixed up as a "Cabin" for overnight camping trips.

They located the owner of the property and told him about their plans. Since no one else wanted this odd corner of land and the owner had no use for it himself, he agreed to rent it to the scouts for one dollar a year—a much better bargain than the troop expected.

So Troop 30 of Philadelphia came into possession of the Haunted House on Darby Creek. The scouts scoffed at the neighbors' stories of the Ghost of Old Bill haunting the place, and were soon hard at work fixing it up.

They built new floors and a roof, put in windows and doors and constructed a porch. When they were done there was one large room downstairs and another upstairs, with a ladder to serve in place of stairs. A movable gangplank was built to reach from the second story window to the hillside, to serve as a back door.

With double deck cots installed upstairs and tables, benches, and stoves downstairs, the old house was ready for Troop 30's first overnight camping adventure. The scouts could hardly wait to show Old Bill they were not afraid of any old ghosts. Nor were they during the day, or even that evening, what with their bright, new gasoline lanterns, their flashlights and all the noise a healthy bunch of boys can make.

But it was a little different, after the lanterns were blown out, and all was still in the old house. The scouts lay there in the darkness listening to the murmur of the creek outside and straining their ears for any strange sounds—inside. Even the nearness of other scouts and the leaders did not take away that scary feeling that comes when you are completely in the dark—in a haunted house.

But all was as still as the grave, and—one by one—the tired boys dropped off to sleep in the Haunted House on Darby Creek.

It was sometime later when one boy woke up. He swallowed hard—in the darkness—as he heard, or thought he heard, something walking downstairs. His heart was pounding as he lay there—listening—to the sound of footsteps moving slowly across the floor downstairs.

Quietly he got up and woke the Assistant Scoutmaster who was sleeping near him. And as they listened together, they both heard something moving around down below. They woke the Scoutmaster and he, too, heard something moving around downstairs.

They stole quietly over to where a railing went around the hole in the floor where the ladder came up, and they carefully lifted the safety board which had been placed there to prevent anyone falling through during the night.

Looking down into the blackness below, they were startled to see something move across the faint path of moonlight shining through the side window. And they all distinctly heard the sound of footsteps as of someone—or something—slowly walking across the floor.

Ever so quietly, the Scoutmaster got his flashlight and soon a bright beam of light swept the darkened room below. There was nothing there. The footsteps ceased with the first flash of light.

The rest of the scouts were now waking up—all excited—and more flashlights were brought. The lanterns were lit and the boys swarmed down the ladder. The door was unbolted and pajama-clad scouts searched the ground all around the old house. But nothing unusual could be found, either within or without.

Puzzled and uneasy the scouts went back to bed. A watch was posted for the balance of the night, but nothing else was heard, except the breathing of the boys, the squeak of springs and the rustle of straw mattresses as the scouts dreamed of Old Bill, and turned restlessly in their sleep.

That was Troop 30's first meeting with the Ghost of Old Bill. It was not the last.

For as the years went by and the Scouts of Troop 30 continued to come there for overnight hikes, Old Bill was heard again and again by boys waking during the night. From time to time the safety board would be lifted at the head of the ladder and, if the moon was shining right, a dim shadow might be seen moving across the path of moonlight coming through the side window.

But nothing was ever seen or heard when flashlights were turned on. Nor was Old Bill ever known to come upstairs. It was agreed that he didn't like to climb the ladder, but suppose he should walk in from the hill up the gangplank and through the rear window?

Some boys didn't like to sleep near that rear window and some wanted to pull in the gangplank at night. But others pointed out that a ghost didn't need a gangplank and anyhow, it was only necessary to turn on your flashlights to be safe. That is why no scout in "30" ever went to sleep without checking the handy location of his flashlight. It became traditional in "30" to have an extra bulb and batteries in your pack and to test your light before you went to bed.

A Scout is brave, however, and the boys would not be scared away by the Ghost of Old Bill. Some even dared to go downstairs at night—alone.

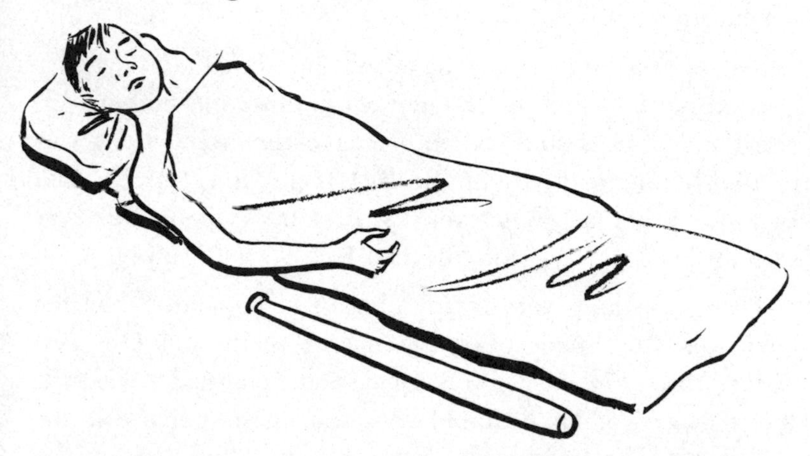

But it remained for Tom to defy Old Bill on his own terms. For Tom had ridiculed the whole story and, on a dare, slept one night downstairs—by himself.

But the next morning he was strangely subdued. He said something was walking around and he knew it wasn't any of the fellows trying to scare him, because he had searched the whole place before he turned in, and every window and door downstairs was barred and the safety board was in place when he turned on his flashlight. Still he heard footsteps right in the room with him.

It was evident Old Bill made no effort to bother Tom, however, and a feeling of friendship for the lonely old ghost began to grow in the boys of Troop 30. He became Troop 30's Ghost and was spoken of as one would speak of an old friend of the family.

Not long after that, on another overnight hike, a strange light was seen outside by one of the boys who woke during the night and looked out a front window. He roused the troop and, as the boys crowded to the windows, this light was seen to move around the front of the old house and then disappear up the hill.

Seizing flashlights and lanterns, the scouts and leaders hurried out to search the ground all around, but nothing unusual could be found. Some scouts claimed the light was carried by the mad wife of Old Bill, trying to get in, but that he wouldn't let her. Whatever it was, nothing like it was ever seen again. The boys said Old Bill had chased it away.

Then something very strange began to happen. When the boys went to summer camp, some of them said Old Bill walked through their camp at night. Some claimed to hear his footsteps and others declared they saw his dim figure in the moonlight. The story grew that the poor, lonely Old Ghost had become thoroughly attached to Troop 30 and went where they went—to guard the camp for them at night.

As time passed on a real estate development forced Troop 30 to abandon the old house and after a time it became as tumbled-down and neglected as when the Troop first discovered it. Now it's been years since they have gone camping on Darby Creek, but the boys still say Old Bill walks through their camp at night—wherever they may be.

Scouts in other troops that have camped where "30" has camped have claimed Old Bill was heard and seen in their camps, too.

It might well be. For the boys of "30" say Old Bill is a nice old ghost and they don't really mind having him visit them at night.

But still, when you wake up in the middle of the night, and the wind is whispering through the trees, you can feel awfully alone—as you lie there in the dark—with the Ghost of Old Bill walking slowly through the camp.

* * * *

THE VALLEY OF DEATH

Where the boys like to be handy for the girls to jump into their arms, this story will be most welcome to both boys and girls.

Roger Davison and Jack Williams were determined to take a canoe trip up the Dark River to the Valley of Death. Ever since they could remember they had heard stories about this mysterious hidden valley entirely surrounded by mountains, and they wanted to see it for themselves.

It was not that they scoffed at the cryptic warnings of the Indians or the strange tales of the trappers and hunters who roamed this untamed tangle of mountain wilderness, but they were possessed of an overwhelming desire to do something dangerous and exciting. They wanted to go into the Valley of Death and come back to tell their story.

Each summer their appeals to their parents fell on deaf ears, but now, old enough for military service, husky and confident, they were not to be denied. Reluctantly, their parents consented to the expedition.

And thus it was they were on their way one July morning in their new aluminum canoe, prepared to camp out for several weeks. Their staple supplies could be supplemented by fish, game, berries and other wild edibles well known to such experienced woodsmen as Roger and Jack.

They both had their rifles as well as fishing gear and all necessary camping equipment, and their hearts were light and gay as they drove their sturdy canoe up the Dark River. For some miles, as they knew from long acquaintance, the Dark River wound leisurely through the foothills before entering (actually coming out of) Murmuring Gorge.

Murmuring Gorge was aptly named. Either because of its peculiar formation with close leaning mountains, or its many pine trees, or the wind currents, or the rushing of the Dark River itself around sharp bends in its course, or some combination of these, anyone in the gorge was aware of an almost constant murmuring sound. This murmuring was especially noticeable at night.

Some hunters declared that when they lay in their blankets at night, and all was still, other than the murmuring, they could make out definite words—even messages. Some said they heard their own names mentioned, or the names of persons they knew. Others claimed that past incidents in their lives had been referred to, or prophesies made or hinted. Still others spoke of threats and warnings against further travel up the Dark River.

The year before Roger and Jack had gone as far as Murmuring Gorge, but had not stayed overnight. This was as far as they had been up the Dark River. Beyond the gorge, the river came through a wild, rough region called "The Shadows," because of the towering mountain ledges which overshadowed the river as it flowed through the rocky canyons. Camping spots along here were few and tiny. However, there were not many men who could speak with much authority regarding this desolate stretch of river since it was generally shunned by the trappers and hunters who had little to gain from forcing their way up against the strong current.

The Shadows eventually gave way to the Tunnel of Fear, where the Dark River bored right through the mountain. It was possible to go through the tunnel, it was said, when the river was low enough; but in the Spring, when the snows were melting the river completely filled the tunnel. Roger and Jack had heard all sorts of wild yarns about those who had ventured into the Tunnel of Fear, but could find scarce half a dozen men who had actually been into it themselves, and all of these had admitted turning back before going all the way through.

There could be no doubt it took a long, hard paddle against a swiftly flowing river to make it, with the danger of striking rocks below, or one's head against the low ceiling above. The Indians said it was death to defy the Spirit of the Mountain by entering the Tunnel of Fear, and that none had ever returned who went through into the Valley of Death beyond.

Roger and Jack paddled steadily most of the day, with just a short stop for lunch. About six they pulled over to the bank and made camp. They caught some fish for their supper, and turned in early, since they were weary from their long day's paddle up the river and wanted to be up with the dawn.

About noon the next day they reached Murmuring Gorge and, after lunch, set out to explore it. They were curious to see whether they could discover any definite explanation for the strange murmuring sounds. However, after a long afternoon's investigation of its many recesses, caves and twistings and turnings, they were no wiser than when they began. Always there was the murmuring. Sometimes it was so faint they almost felt rather than heard it. Again it became so loud they fancied they could distinguish actual words.

But not until they were in their sleeping bags almost asleep were Roger and Jack able to make out anything that might be considered a message. Roger heard it first and nudged his friend. Both of them listened, bodies tense, resting on their elbows as they raised their heads and shoulders to hear better.

It came as a blood-chilling warning, repeated several times, each time more faintly than the time before.

"Roger and Jack—go back—go back—go back."

The boys tried to convince each other it was merely their imagination, but they were disturbed more than they cared to admit. How was it they both heard it? The same words? And their own names?

There had to be some natural, reasonable explanation they told themselves, but still . . .

They listened, but did not hear the warning again, although they thought they could detect the word "Shadows." It was most disquieting.

But eventually Roger and Jack fell asleep.

The next day dawned bright and fair, and the boys forgot their forebodings as they shoved off their canoe for the hard fight they knew awaited them in their journey through The Shadows.

The Dark River was narrower now, the current stronger. As they paddled their way, more slowly, through the alternate patches of gloom and light, they thought of all the stories they had heard of fear, and mystery, and death, in these dark waters. Certainly it would be a fearful place to be in the Spring flood. In fact, it would be impossible to paddle against it.

Even then, in July, it took strong backs and arms, and skillful handling of paddles, to keep the canoe moving forward. The boys had some close escapes from upsets and swamping. Every time they spotted a bit of low ground, safe for stopping, they pulled over and rested. Thus they found some odd little niches in the mountain wall, but after surprising a nest of rattlesnakes in one of them, they approached each new spot with watchful caution.

They had hoped to see The Tunnel of Fear before stopping for the night, but when they came upon the pleasantest little spot of all toward the end of the afternoon, they dared not pass it up. There was no telling what, if anything in the way of a campsite, lay ahead.

Wearily they pulled their canoe up on the bank and made camp. They were in wild country indeed, and as night came swiftly, it seemed as though the darkness came down upon them as great shadows closing in to seize them. Not a star pierced the gloom, and their little fire was hemmed in on all sides by a blackness that was most ominous. And terribly still.

The boys talked quietly and listened much. But all was silent about them. This fearful stillness was more menacing than even the murmuring of the night before. It was as though, having been warned, and having chosen to disregard that warning, they were now waiting for some awful consequence to overtake them—some fearful punishment for their defiance.

Roger and Jack were uneasy, but refused to give in to the fears that so naturally came to them. Putting more wood on the fire, they smiled reassuringly at each other, and promised themselves that the next night they would camp in the Valley of Death itself. Common sense told them that there was nothing that could harm them as long as they did not panic. Still . . .

The boys got into their sleeping bags, and, once again, their tired young bodies relaxed gratefully in the deep sleep of youth.

The fourth day was dark and glowering. Roger and Jack wondered whether they should go on, or stay where they were and prepare for bad weather. They decided to go on. There appeared to be various places along the river where they could improvise some shelter, if need be, and they were anxious to reach the mysterious Tunnel of Fear.

Shortly after lunch, they came upon it. They were going through a narrow gorge, where the banks on either side seemed to reach over closer and closer, so that the trees and bushes almost touched to form an arch. They were paddling hard against the swift current, when they came around a slight bend in the river and saw the tunnel not fifty feet ahead.

Almost before they could adjust their thinking to the fact that they had finally reached the tunnel, they were entering it. Quickly Roger lit the power hand light they had mounted in the bow of the canoe for this purpose. They paddled on into the stygian darkness except for the path of light on the water ahead.

This, then, was the famous Tunnel of Fear, a swiftly flowing river far down under the great mountain that sought to block its path.

They felt a terrible oppressiveness as they sweated to keep their canoe going forward against the powerful drag of the current which sucked at their canoe as though trying to pull it under.

Sometimes they had to bend over quickly to avoid striking low-hanging rocks. At such times the canoe threatened to swing around and overturn. Several times they almost ran into rocks that almost seemed to float into position before them.

Their progress was painfully slow, and it seemed as though they had been going for hours through this dark tunnel, when Jack saw a little alcove ahead. They pulled into it and rested, chests heaving, arms aching, as they watched the Dark River flow by them.

How much farther was it?

They shoved off and again fought their way, yard by yard, up the dark, mysterious river, far down under the wild mountain that guarded the Valley of Death.

It was almost four by Roger's watch when they found a second alcove in which to rest, and none too soon. For their forward motion had almost stopped.

The boys had no idea how far they had come, or how much farther they must go. They could not help but realize that the return journey back would be perilous indeed. If they came back.

Resolutely, they put such thoughts aside, and, once again, pushed their canoe forward.

The current appeared to slacken a little and then the river became wider. A faint lightness relieved the darkness of the tunnel. Then they rounded a bend and saw daylight ahead.

The boys paddled out of the Tunnel of Fear into a wild, gloomy depression in the mountain—the Valley of Death.

Slowly they made their way over to the bank, and got out. The long, mournful howl of a wolf floated down from the mountain. Was it a signal that the evil spirits knew of their coming?

But the boys had no time to reflect on the weird tales of the Indians for a wind was coming up and dark clouds dimmed the feeble light that made its way down through the crags and fir trees to the Valley of Death.

A hurried investigation resulted in their finding a cave a short ways off, and here they packed their gear and supplies, after securing their canoe against the coming storm.

Roger and Jack had barely reached the shelter of the cave when the storm broke in all its tempestuous fury. Trees moaned and went down before the great blasts of wind; branches were sent hurtling through the air, and thunder exploded through the mountain passes. While blinding streaks of lightning thrust themselves down into the valley as though seeking out some trembling prey.

Then came the rain. Hard and relentless. What little daylight there had been quickly faded into night as the rain came down in torrents. Roger and Jack waited and watched from the mouth of the cave until the storm was over.

Then they went out to gather wood. They had little desire to spend the night in the Valley of Death without even a fire to guard them against the evil spirits of the Indians.

It was a strange thing, but the boys had not been conscious of being afraid while the storm lasted. Only a sense of wild excitement and thrilling adventure. But in the sudden stillness (except for dripping trees) that followed, a great, inexplicable fear came suddenly upon them.

This fear was unlike anything either boy had ever known before. It was a cold, terrible thing that crawled right into the mind so that each boy felt an awful, sickening sense of impending doom. Hastily they found wood and brought it back to the cave. Once they had a fire going they would feel better.

They looked for their hand axes to split the wet wood and get at the dry centers for kindling. There were no axes. Puzzled, they searched through their packs and camping gear. The axes were not there. Jack decided they must somehow have been left with the canoe, and, taking the power light, he hurried away into the darkness.

Roger was very uneasy. The axes should have been with their other gear. He decided to check their guns and make sure they were dry and ready for use.

He could not find the guns.

Had they, too, been left with the canoe? It didn't seem possible.

Fear grew in him as he sought in vain for his hunting knife. He usually wore it. As a matter of fact, he always did. He felt again. His sheath was on his belt all right, but there was no knife in it. He couldn't recall using it for anything all day. Something very strange was going on. First the axes, then the guns, now his knife.

Anxiously Roger looked toward the Dark River, but could see no sign of Jack's light. That was odd.

He felt an unreasoning panic building up within him. He fought to beat it down. He must not let the evil spirits of the Valley of Death claim another victim through fear of the unknown. That was all it was—fear of the unknown—he told himself.

Just then his flashlight went out. He struggled with it a minute or so, snapping it on and off and tightening the lens and spring. He was badly frightened now. He told himself it must be the bulb. That was it, the bulb had gone out.

But why then? Still, it had to give out sometime. But why was everything disappearing? Why couldn't he see Jack's light? Why didn't Jack come back? Where was he?

"Jack!" he called, in panic. But he got no answer. There was no sound at all in the Valley of Death beyond his own panting breath. His own throbbing heart.

Was Jack gone for good? Had "they" gotten him in the darkness?

Desperately Roger groped for his pack. He had a small flashlight in the pouch. He struck his hand against a sharp rock and brought blood. He could not see it in the darkness, but felt it flowing from the wound.

His hands were trembling and wet with sweat and blood when he found the little flashlight, and snapped it on.

Its tiny beam of light reassured him a little. He had never realized before what a world of difference one small light could make. With it he could defy the evil spirits.

His hand was bleeding freely, so he got out his first-aid kit. He balanced the flashlight on a small rock while he opened the kit.

Suddenly, the light rolled off the rock and down the slope from the mouth of the cave. Roger jumped to get it. The light evidently rolled into a hole a short way down the slope for all was suddenly dark again.

In his wild haste to get the flashlight, Roger ran into a

small tree, or bush, scratching his hands and face. Terror gripped him.

He must find the light before "they" got him. "They" were coming for him. The Evil Spirits of the Valley of Death were after him. But if he could find the light be could hold them off.

But where was it?

Frantically, he groped his way down the slope. "They" were all around him now. "They" were reaching for him. "They" were going to get him.

Ah! The light!

He saw a faint gleam down among some leaves in a small hole. He dropped on his knees to reach for it. "They" couldn't get him now! He would be safe!

But even as he reached for the light, blood from his hand fell on it, and *it went out!*

The light was out and he was in darkness!

AND THAT'S WHEN THEY GOT HIM!

* * * *

CROOKED ARROW AND HIS GHOST WOLVES

The only facts connected with this story are these: the Delaware Indians did live in the section described, there is an island owned by the Philadelphia Boy Scouts called Treasure Island, and they once did have lantern patrols, but I am not sure why.

Many years ago, before the white men came, the Delaware Indians lived in that part of America we now know as the states of Pennsylvania and New Jersey. They camped and had settlements along the Delaware Valley, where they raised crops, hunted and fished, and mostly lived in peace with their fellowmen and with the Great Spirit, who ruled over all.

One small settlement of the Delawares was located on a

beautiful island in the Delaware River, called "The Island of Many Birds." This island was well named. It was indeed a favorite of the birds, and it seemed that The Great Spirit of All Life looked with special favor on this happy spot and the friendly Indians who dwelled there.

For all up and down the Delaware Valley and to far distant regions The Island of Many Birds was known as a place of peace and plenty. And beauty. No war parties going up or down the river would think of violating its hospitality. It was recognized as a place where all could meet in peace and friendship.

Thus it was through many generations that all went well on The Island of Many Birds.

Until one day a shadow, at first no larger than a swallow's wing, appeared and the Indians of the Island were disturbed. For a strange boy was growing up among them. A boy who was one of their own, and yet not one of them.

For when this boy began to make arrows, as all Indian boys did, he insisted on making them all crooked. "I like them this way," he said, when the tribe's arrow makers tried to show him how to make arrows that were straight and true. "They shoot better this way," the boy insisted. And the old men shook their heads. No good would come of a thing like that.

The boy became known as Crooked Arrow, and more and more he went his way alone. He cheated and quarreled so much the other boys did not care to play with him. Or compete with him in trials of strength and skill. Crooked he became in his speech, his actions and his thoughts.

It seemed strange that anyone on The Island of Many Birds should be so unfriendly, but Crooked Arrow evidently did not care. So he went his way alone.

Had an evil spirit come to live among them? Had the tribe sinned against the Great Spirit? Were the spirits of their fathers angry with them?

So the Indians questioned one another. And when none could answer these questions, some of the braves went to talk with Grey Duck, the wise old medicine man of the tribe. Grey Duck went up to the north end of the Island to talk with the spirits of their fathers.

In the gathering darkness of twilight he crossed the North Channel to the Island to the North, the resting place of their fathers, a place that was sacred to the dead.

For it was the custom of this tribe, when anyone died, to lay the body on the shore at the north end of the Island of Many Birds. There at twilight they prayed to the Great Spirit for the safe journey of the soul of the dead to the happy hunting grounds of all good Indians.

Then they would leave the body on the shore in the gathering darkness and in the morning the body would be gone. For the spirits of their fathers came during the night and carried the dead to the Island to the North. Thus the Island to the North was sacred to the dead and no one but the medicine man dared cross the North Channel.

All night Grey Duck communed with the spirits of their fathers on the Island to the North. All night the tribe waited, sitting in the council circle.

With the dawn Grey Duck returned.

"Hearken well," said the old medicine man, "for the words I now speak to you were given to me by the spirits of our fathers."

"Speak on, Grey Duck," said the braves of the tribe.

And a great silence descended upon the council circle as they listened to his words.

"There comes a time to all men and nations when they must make hard decisions. This has not been so with us for a time beyond the memory of any living warrior. Now the Great Spirit has sent Crooked Arrow as a test of our courage. He is not one of us though born among us. He is a child of the evil spirits and must be sent away. He must be placed in a canoe, with all his crooked arrows, and banished from this island forever. So all will go well on The Island of Many Birds.

"Should he ever return, he must die. The Spirits of Our Fathers have spoken it."

"No! No!" cried the father and mother of Crooked Arrow. "He is our boy. He means no harm to the tribe. Let him stay."

Grey Duck warned the tribe of evil to come should they ignore the warning of the spirits of their fathers, while the parents of Crooked Arrow pleaded for their child. In the end the tribe could not find the courage to banish Crooked Arrow. And so he stayed.

But his ill nature increased as he grew to manhood, and dark days did come to The Island of Many Birds. Passing Indians stole from them, something unknown to the island before. The deer came less frequently, the birds became fewer, crops failed, and many other evil things came to pass.

Then the parents of Crooked Arrow died, and he went to

live alone at the northern end of the island. This action greatly disturbed the tribe. For Crooked Arrow's lodge faced the very spot where they always laid their dead in the twilight.

Some of the men went to talk with Crooked Arrow. "You must not dwell here," they said. "It is not good."

"I will dwell here," said Crooked Arrow.

The men returned to the tribe with the report of Crooked Arrow's decision. There were many who murmured at the evil news, but none spoke out until a youth cried:

"Let us force him to move. Let him live at the south end of the island, if he must live alone."

But while there was much talk, no decision was reached, so accustomed had they become to ways of peace. So Crooked Arrow lived alone on the north end of the island.

And then, one day, a boy brought back news that sent a shudder through the tribe. Crooked Arrow had now moved his lodge to The Island to the North, the place sacred to the spirits of their fathers.

Again there was much talk, and this time there were those who urged the banishment or death of Crooked Arrow. But again, no decision was reached. Nothing was done.

It was not long after that, on a night when the moon was on the wane, that the howl of a wolf was heard from the Island to the North.

The tribe was much disturbed. No wolves had ever been known on the islands. Surely no wolf would swim the river. Perhaps they had misjudged the sound. Perhaps it had come from either side of the river farther up and the wind had made it seem as though it came from the Island to the North. But the tribe was uneasy. It was a bad omen.

The next night, as the moon waned further, they heard again the howl of a wolf from the Island to the North. And then another. And another. There was no mistaking the source.

Then it was said that Crooked Arrow, having the soul of a wolf, had leagued himself to the wolves, and had brought them over at night in his canoe. Certain it was the wolves now hunted with Crooked Arrow on the Island to the North. Would they cross over to the Island of Many Birds?

The answer came all too soon. The very next night a little girl, Chirping Bird, vanished from the camp. All the next day the tribe searched the island but no trace of the girl was found. They did find the tracks of wolves and so it was said that Crooked Arrow and his wolves had carried her away.

The parents of Chirping Bird were dead and, while her old grandmother wept, no one dared suggest they cross the North Channel to the Island to the North.

But from that night on guards were posted for the first time in generations. Keen eyes watched for any further threat from the north. Ears trained to catch the slightest sound listened in the woods at night. A new moon came and all was still on the Island to the North.

But when the moon had passed its fullness once more, the wolves of Crooked Arrow were heard again. And as the moon waned the wolves seemed to come closer, crossing the North Channel to the Island of Many Birds.

And then—on a night when the moon had reached its last quarter, a small boy, Happy Beaver, vanished as mysteriously as the little girl the moon before. The guards had seen and heard nothing, but Happy Beaver was gone, and the tracks of wolves were found again.

A great anger filled the hearts of the Indians, for Happy Beaver had been well loved by the tribe for his friendly ways and happy laugh. Now, at last, the men began to sharpen their flint knives, to look to their tomahawks and their bows and arrows. Not for many years had such warlike preparations been seen on the Island of Many Birds.

That night the men painted their faces. The war drums sounded and the men danced—awkwardly at first—a war dance almost forgotten by even the oldest members of the tribe. Fires burned brightly as the dance increased in fury.

Suddenly, the howl of a wolf came from the north. The dancers froze in their places. The war drums became silent.

And then—a great shout of anger arose. The braves, for so they truly were now, snatched up their weapons and sped on silent feet to the north.

When they reached the North Channel they saw Crooked Arrow and his wolves facing them across the water. Arrogant at first, Crooked Arrow shouted his defiance, thinking they would not dare to cross the channel.

But when the braves raised their war cry and plunged into the water, Crooked Arrow and his wolves fled into the woods of the Island of the Dead. Angry braves tracked them down. One by one they slew the snarling wolves until only two remained with Crooked Arrow.

On the northernmost tip of the Island to the North, Crooked Arrow and his two favorite wolves stood at bay. The braves closed in. They cast aside their bows and arrows. Nothing but knife and tomahawk, tooth and claw could settle the battle now.

Fighting furiously, Crooked Arrow and his wolves went down before the onslaught, and the death chant rose in the night air.

Dragging all the bodies of the wolves together, the Indians built a huge funeral pyre. They threw the bodies of the wolves upon it and the body of Crooked Arrow on top. With pine torches the fire was lighted and roared a great flame into the sky. Around it the braves danced and shouted in victory.

But suddenly one cried, "Look!"

The dance stopped and a deep silence came upon the Indians. For as they watched in horror, the great cloud of black smoke ascending into the greyness of the coming dawn seemed to take shape. They could distinctly see the form of Crooked Arrow escaping into the sky, with his pack of wolves behind him.

It was an evil omen indeed.

The tribe knew they had waited too long to rid their island of this evil, and now the ghosts of Crooked Arrow and his wolves would return to haunt them. The terrible warning was written in the sky.

It was even so.

For the next time the moon began to wane, the howling of wolves was heard again from the Island to the North. Only it was not the same. These wolves howled with a ghostly quality that chilled the blood and clutched at the heart with cold fingers of deadly fear. For these wolves were dead and yet they roamed the woods of the Island to the North. The ghosts of Crooked Arrow and his wolves had returned.

Great fires were built around the camp and guards with torches peered fearfully into the night. Nothing was seen. Nor in the nights that followed.

"Fire is your weapon," said the old Grey Duck. "The dead fear the light. Fire must guard the camp from this time forth at night. No man must go into the woods at night when the moon is on the wane unless he carries a torch. Fire must always go with you."

And so it was. Though they might hear the ghostly howling of the wolves from the north, and though they might see the strange glowing of eyes in the darkness or hear the soft padding of ghostly feet, no harm ever came to the Indians who carried torches.

But once, when a young brave spoke his scorn of ghosts and went into the North Woods in the darkness, his body was found the next day lying beside a path. There was no wound upon it, and no mark. Save the faint impression of teeth at his throat.

Another time, a brave whose torch went out was found dead on the north shore. He, too, bore the faint impression of teeth at his throat.

Fear ruled the island. It was no longer a place of peace and happiness. It was a place to be shunned by birds and Indians alike.

The years rolled on and the Indians went away. The white men came, but few ventured upon and none lived on the island, although it was said that Crooked Arrow and his ghost wolves had long since departed to the Land of Evil Spirits.

And then, one bright summer day, new life came to the island. For Boy Scouts from Philadelphia came to camp there. They named it Treasure Island and soon the place rang with their shouts and bugle calls. Boys swam in the cool waters of the Delaware and roamed the woods by day, while songs rose from their campfires at night.

Then it was that Crooked Arrow and his ghost wolves returned. They were displeased to see happiness there again and so they came back.

Scouts who knew nothing of the old Indian legend reported hearing the faint ghostly howling of wolves on the Island to the North when the moon was on the wane. Others said they saw strangely glowing eyes when walking through the north woods and heard the soft padding of ghostly feet. From some Indians of New Jersey they learned the old legend of the Island of Many Birds, and while many scoffed at it, others felt something should be done.

They thought of the words of the old medicine man, Grey Duck, and it was decided to post a watch at night. It was agreed that two boys with a lantern should patrol the woods and thus keep away the ghosts of Crooked Arrow and his wolves. And so, each night during the summer, from ten until six, eight scouts patrolled the woods, two at a time for two hours each, carrying a lantern between them.

Many boys' hearts grew fearful as they advanced into the North Woods particularly when the moon was on the wane. Some turned back before they reached the northern end. Then, it was said, Crooked Arrow and his ghost wolves would become bold and cross the channel to roam the north woods of Treasure Island.

But when the scouts who carried the lantern went forward in spite of their fear until they reached the northernmost end of the island, Crooked Arrow and his ghost wolves came not across the channel. The powers of evil were helpless against the light of courage.

Strange eyes might glow in the darkness across the channel and the prowling of ghostly forms might be heard in the woods, but all was well on Treasure Island.

The years went by and it was said that Crooked Arrow and his ghost wolves became discouraged and went away. Because the Boy Scouts came in increasing numbers and would not be frightened away. No longer did anyone hear the ghostly howling of wolves, or sense the soft padding of feet, or see the strangely glowing eyes. The lantern patrols were discontinued.

And then a great war came upon the world. Former boy scouts who had camped on Treasure Island went off to serve their country in faraway places.

On an island in the South Pacific, in a steaming jungle one night, two former Treasure Island campers, Jerry and Guy, sat with a third soldier. The three had become lost while on patrol and were waiting for dawn to find their way back to their company. They lit no fire for the enemy might be very close. Jerry and Guy talked in whispers of their boy scout days.

"Remember how scared we were when we carried that lantern in the north woods?" asked Jerry.

"Boy, I'll say," said Guy, "but I'm a lot more scared now. I only wish we were back on Treasure Island with that lantern."

"Me, too," said Jerry. "I'd give anything in the world to be walking through those north woods right now with that good old lantern between us."

Those were the last words either soldier spoke. For an enemy automatic rifle stuttered in the darkness, and Jerry and Guy were dead. Alone, the third soldier hugged the jungle earth and waited for dawn. Then he made his way back to the company and told his story.

A burial detail went out, but, strange to say, no trace of Jerry or Guy could be found other than some blood stains where they had lain. Their bodies had vanished as completely as had those of the Indians many years before when laid upon the north shore of The Island of Many Birds.

When the third soldier returned home after the war, he told his story of Jerry and Guy, the former Treasure Island campers, and how they died.

A few years later, one August night on Treasure Island, two boy scouts were walking in the north woods. Their only flashlight was burning low. The moon was at its last quarter.

Suddenly they heard, or thought they heard, the faint howl of a wolf from the Island to the North. They had just reached the North Channel and, as they peered across the water, their flashlight flickered, and went out.

Almost at once they saw strangely glowing eyes across the channel. Fearfully they turned and hurried back down the path toward their troop camp. Then they heard, or thought they heard, the ghostly padding of feet behind them in the woods. They hurried faster, but dared not run lest their very panic bring something, they knew not what, upon them.

Strangely glowing eyes could now be seen in the woods to either side of the path, and a deadly fear clutched at their hearts. Camp seemed far away and some awful danger very close.

And then, coming toward them along the path, they could see a lantern. As it came closer they saw two scouts carrying it, talking quietly together. The boys who were hurrying back to their camp were sure they heard the disappointed whimpering of the ghost wolves of Crooked Arrow as they slunk away into the woods before the advancing lantern.

The boys went to greet the scouts with the lantern but as they came close they observed some mystic quality to both scouts and lantern. While they hesitated, in some confusion, the scouts with the lantern came right up to them and seemed to pass through them although they felt nothing.

They turned long enough to see the unknown scouts with the lantern pass out of sight up the path, and then they ran back to camp as fast as they could to tell their story.

Their fellow scouts laughed at them. "Aw, you're crazy with the heat," they said. "There are no ghosts and no scouts carrying a lantern on patrol. You've been seeing things."

Maybe so, but other scouts have reported hearing the faint howling of wolves from the Island to the North when the moon was on the wane. And others have seen strangely glowing eyes in the darkness across the North Channel. Or, if their lights burned low they might see the strangely glowing eyes in the north woods of Treasure Island itself. Or even hear the soft padding of ghostly feet. While still others have reported seeing a lantern moving through the North Woods. Some said the lantern simply floated along. Others claimed it was carried by two scouts.

However this may be, it is said that Crooked Arrow and his ghost wolves still prowl the darkness when the moon is on the wane. But it is also said that the ghosts of Jerry and Guy now carry a lantern of courage through the night, and as long as they keep their faithful patrol no harm can ever come to the scouts who camp on Treasure Island.

* * * *

THE GHOST TRAIL

If the second, explanatory ending is used, you will probably get more questions for additional explanations than you will for "The Valley of Death" where everything is left up in the air.

It all began as a practical joke, or, to be more exact, it started because Peter Randall boasted he was not afraid of the Ghosts of Dead Men's Tree.

Dead Men's Tree was a huge white oak on the outskirts of Marlinville, where the road forked, the left branch swinging around White Cat Mountain on its way to Rock City while the right fork ran through the swamp. The right fork was rarely used any more, since the lumbering operations beyond the swamp had ceased some years before. Thus it was a much neglected road, full of ruts and holes, and hemmed in on both sides by the swamp.

Many years before the right fork also led to Swamptown, a disreputable place where all sorts of thieves and criminals congregated until a hard-riding vigilante committee finally scattered them once and for all. Then it was that the ring leaders were hung on the big oak tree at the fork in the road as a drastic warning to all other evildoers to stay away from

Marlinville. The warning was most effective, and ever since that fateful day the old oak was known as Dead Men's Tree. It became a place to be shunned, particularly at night.

Indeed, there were those who said the ghosts of the dead bandits haunted the place, and more than one person claimed to have seen them hanging there in the moonlight, swinging slowly from side to side. Others claimed the ghosts of the murderous outlaw gang lurked along the right fork to Swamptown, and might stalk anyone going that way by night. Some even swore they had seen the flash of knives and to have heard the stealthy movements of the outlaws, stalking them along the edge of the road.

Certain it was no one relished traveling that road at night. For that matter, there were few who cared to follow its twisting course even by day, what with the gloomy swamp on either side. And then there was no good reason why anyone should.

However, the group of boys in their early teens of which Peter Randall was one had several times traveled the old right fork to Swamptown, and had poked about through the tumbled-down old shacks that made up the bandit town so many years before. On one occasion they had even followed the Ghost Trail up over Cemetery Hill back of the town, and then down through the swamp on its tortuous, treacherous way to the River Road, which came into Marlinville on the other side of the swamp.

Of course, this had been in the daytime—a bright, sunny day at that. Even so, it had been an experience none of the boys would ever forget.

The Ghost Trail had been made by the outlaws and, so far as anybody knew, was the only safe way through the swamp from Swamptown to the River Road. It began, as stated, at

Cemetery Hill, where the bandits buried their dead in those long ago days. As the crow flies it was possibly a mile or so from the far side of Cemetery Hill to the River Road, but the Ghost Trail probably ran three miles or more, winding and turning as it did in a search for secure footing.

The trail was so much overgrown during the years since last used by the outlaws the boys would never have been able to follow it except for two things. The bandits had not only succeeded in finding the safest natural way through the swamp, but had greatly improved it by the use of cedar logs and many stones which they had dragged in with what was, undoubtedly, the greatest expenditure of toil and sweat of their evil lives.

They then marked the trail with the bones of animals nailed to trees along the way. It was rumored that some of these markers were human bones, victims of the outlaws, but whatever their origin, many of them could still be seen along the winding trail when the boys made their way from Swamptown to the River Road. Small wonder it was a trip that none of the boys cared to repeat in a hurry.

Afterward Spike asserted that he thought he had glimpsed a human skull at one spot, a little ways down what might have been a side trail. None of the others had seen it, however, and it was more or less agreed that Spike was laying it on a bit.

Anyhow, it was about a week after this eerie experience that Pete boasted he did not believe in any ghosts and was not afraid to carve his initials on Dead Men's Tree alone at night. This had been the test of a boy's courage when their fathers were their age, or so some of their fathers said.

The rest of the gang promptly challenged Pete, so that, rather reluctantly, he felt obliged to make good his brave words. It was agreed he would return at ten-thirty that night, and one boy was detailed to watch him so that he did not come sooner, when it was more likely that cars would be coming by. Actually, the others only wanted to make certain Pete did not arrive before they had fixed up a couple of dummies to hang up in the old oak, fastened by ropes that led over some branches and down into the bushes behind the tree. Thus the dummies could be lowered at the right moment. The boys then hid in the bushes and waited for Pete.

Pete came right on time, secretly trailed by Stumpy Williams, the boy assigned to watch him. Pete was whistling as he arrived at Dead Men's Tree, and was congratulating himself on his lack of fear—almost. He had walked all the way in the dark, as the boys had stipulated, but now, switching on his flashlight, was dismayed to see its feeble glow. How could that be when he had gotten new batteries only that afternoon? What he didn't know was that Stumpy had switched these new batteries for old ones, the boys' insistence upon his walking in the dark having been intended to cover up this bit of treachery.

Well, he just had to make the best of it, so he hooked the flashlight in the left pocket of his flannel shirt, got out his pocket knife and began to carve his initials. He was just finishing the "P" when he thought he heard something in the tree overhead. He flashed his light upward, but saw nothing. Or did he? Had something moved up there?

Alarmed, Pete stepped back to get a better view, craning his neck and holding his light higher. To his horror the faint beam picked up the body of a man swinging from a rope, high up in the branches. And then he saw another. This was no trick of his imagination. He could see them swaying slightly in the wind that was beginning to blow toward town from the west.

As he stared, mouth suddenly dry, heart pounding, the swaying figures dropped toward him. At the same time he heard a rustling noise in the woods back of the tree. This was too much.

Pete bolted down the road, somehow catching the flashlight which bounced from its perch on his pocket. He ran

harder than he had ever run in his life. He ran fast and far before slowing down to catch his breath, which was now coming in great, gasping sobs. His legs were ready to buckle under him as he came to a stop, head hanging, panting for breath.

Then he made a terrible discovery. In his fright he had run down the right fork through the swamp—away from Marlinville. That meant he was headed for Swamptown, with Dead Men's Tree down the road behind him. What on earth was he to do now? The road ahead went on for miles with no way to turn off except into the old outlaw town or the trackless swamp itself. He certainly did not want to keep going farther away through the swamp, but neither did he relish going back past Dead Men's Tree.

While he hesitated, torn between two fears, he seemed to sense rather than hear something that made his very flesh begin to creep. Something was coming toward him through the brush alongside the road behind him. He could hear—he was sure of it now—a soft rustling made by whoever or whatever it was that was evidently following him.

Then he heard something or someone else on the other side of the road. By the feeble light of his flash, he thought he saw the glint of metal in the bushes. Could it be an outlaw knife? Were all those stories true?

Pete bolted up the road. He tried to listen for footsteps in pursuit but he could not be sure because of the noise of his own running feet and his own breathing. Almost before he realized it he was opposite Swamptown.

A horrible thought came to him. If he had actually seen the ghosts of the outlaw leaders hanging from Dead Men's Tree, then perhaps the whole gang was after him along the dark road.

As little as he cared to venture into Swamptown, wouldn't it be better to go that way and try to follow the Ghost Trail to the River Road, and then back to town? He could hardly keep going mile after lonely mile through the swamp. It didn't appear as though there was any other way out.

It was a badly frightened Peter Randall who groped his way along the path that led into Swamptown, where he was soon frantically seeking the beginning of the trail which would take him up over Cemetery Hill. Everything was so overgrown it was hard to find it in the darkness, with only the light of the moon and his dim flashlight beam. Hurrying between two of the old shacks he struck his head against a piece of timber swinging loose from what was once a roof.

Stars whirled before his eyes and then a deep blackness came up and gathered him into its embrace.

When he came to he had no way of knowing how long he had been lying there unconscious, but despite his aching head, he remembered what had happened, and listened for any sounds that might tell him where the ghosts of the outlaws were. He heard nothing.

Maybe it had all been his imagination after all. In that case the only sensible thing to do was go back down the road past Dead Men's Tree, and so on to his home. He would have to get his head attended to as soon as he could.

But just as he regained his feet he heard the sounds of voices and feet coming along the path into Swamptown from the Right Fork.

It was the whole gang of outlaws! He knew it! He had to get out of there!

Crouching, so as not to be silhouetted against the rising moon, he made his way up Cemetery Hill. If he could only get over the brow of the hill without being seen, he might have a chance to escape them. But he had just reached the top when he heard a faraway voice crying, "There he goes!" The very sound of it made him shiver.

They were after him now for sure! He ran down the other side, stumbling around the turns in the path. His hands were sweating so he could hardly hold onto his flashlight. He could hear the sounds of pursuit behind him as he reached the beginning of the Ghost Trail itself, and struggled to find his way along the slippery, old path, with only the aid of the feeble beam of his light. For the moon's rays did not penetrate the thick growth of the swamp.

After a bit he realized he had gained on them, but this knowledge did not reassure him for long. They must know the trail by heart while he had to blunder his way along. They probably knew of short cuts and couldn't ghosts move silently, if they wanted to? Maybe they would be lying in wait for him somewhere ahead.

But there was nothing to do but keep going. Whatever happened he must stay on the trail. From time to time his light gleamed on one of the bones fastened to a tree, and every time it did so, his heart beat faster.

Once he thought he did see a human skull. It was a little way down a faint path just as Spike said it was. Pete didn't linger to investigate.

Several times his feet slipped off logs into the muck, and once he fell headlong. If he broke a leg or turned an ankle, he would be done for.

He dropped his flashlight but managed to grab it before it sank into the swamp. Between the blood from his cut head and the mud and mire of the swamp he must be a sight to scare somebody himself. But that was nothing if he could only get out of the place alive.

Always he listened for sounds behind him. At times he felt he heard them coming and again he felt they were lurking somewhere along the trail before him. His light was getting very dim now. What would he ever do if it went out?

He fell again. And when he picked himself up he heard it. Something was close behind him. Real close!

He ran on in a wild panic. If he could only make the River Road, some car might be coming by. At least he'd be out of the swamp. And the road couldn't be much farther.

He heard the sound again! It was even closer! He ran blindly now, slipping and stumbling. Sobbing for breath!

The River Road! It was right ahead! He could see the headlights of a car! And it was standing still! If he could get there before it started up he would be saved!

But what was that? Was there something in front of him, too? Between him and the road?

He stumbled once more and dropped his light. It was gone in the muck. But he could see the road! It was right ahead of him! Gasping for breath, he had almost made it when two shadows loomed out of the darkness.

One reached for him! But he got away!

"Help! Help!" he cried. "Help me!"

BUT THE OTHER ONE GRABBED HIM!

Now I wouldn't want you to think the ghosts really got poor Peter Randall after all his trouble. Because his friends, frightened at the way things turned out, and unable to catch up with him, ran back into town and told their families. Pete's father and some of the others piled into cars and went up the Right Fork to Swamptown where they got out and started into the old outlaw village, reasoning he wouldn't keep going through the swamp. That was when Pete came to and heard them.

In the meantime his older brother and twin sister had gone out the River Road to where the Ghost Trail came out, and they had just started to make their way in, when they heard Pete coming. They had turned out their lights for fear of scaring him back and were also afraid to call to him for the same reason. Pete's brother knew he would be frightened crazy by that time.

Therefore, they had just waited and Pete's brother had tried to catch him, but he got away and ran right into the arms of his twin sister. He almost fainted when she grabbed hold of him, but when he found out who it was he was so relieved he kissed her.

And she fainted.

* * * *

WHEN A LITTLE GIRL MEETS A BIG GHOST

Just creepy enough to afford some nice shivers, this story is more whimsical than the others—a good tale for younger children and general family-type audiences.

This is a good ghost story, which can be told with regular lighting, for cub scouts and other groups of this age range, or for general family audiences. It can and should be both humorous and just a little creepy, with the story teller's voice assuming a suitable hollow ghostly tone for "The Big Ghost."

It is my practice to introduce the story somewhat as follows:

"When a Little Girl Meets a Big Ghost" is for all boys and girls, and grownups too, who do not believe in ghosts, but who, should they chance to meet one in a graveyard at night would run like the dickens first, and then, sometime the next day say, "Aw, I'm not afraid of any old ghost."

Sometimes I have arranged to have two cubs (if telling it to a cub scout and family audience) take the parts of the little girl and big ghost. Thus, as soon as I finish the above introduction, the first cub, wearing a girl's dress, comes skipping out saying, "I'm the little girl." Then the second cub, with a sheet and ghost mask on, comes out, saying "I'm the Big Ghost." Naturally the little girl runs off with the ghost after her (him).

Then I have to wait for order to be restored before I can proceed with the story.

Once upon a Thursday a little girl named Nancy Lee moved into a new house with her mama and daddy. That is, it was a new house to Nancy Lee and her parents, but actually it was a very, very old house. Not only that—it was a haunted house!

Or anyhow, that's what everybody said. They said the Ghost of Kunkleman walked around in the kitchen. And they said you could hear strange noises coming from way down in the cellar. But mostly it was the Ghost of Kunkleman walking around in the kitchen. People said it made them feel goose-bumpy all over.

Naturally, with things like that, nobody wanted to live in the old haunted house. In fact, nobody did live in it for a long, long time.

Until Nancy Lee and her mama and daddy moved in. They had to move in because they had just come to town and there was no other place to move into. And they didn't want to live in the woods with the squirrels and chipmunks.

Nancy Lee didn't like the idea of living in a haunted house.

With the Ghost of Kunkleman walking around in the kitchen. And strange noises coming from way down in the cellar. Even if the boy up the street did say:

"Gee, but you're lucky! Imagine living in a genuine haunted house with your very own ghost!"

"But I don't want my very own ghost," said Nancy Lee. "I'd rather have a puppy dog."

"Just like a girl!" said the boy up the street. "Never satisfied!"

Of course, Nancy Lee's mama told her there was no such thing as a ghost. "I don't care what the boy up the street said," said her mama, "there are no ghosts and that's that!"

And Nancy Lee's daddy also told her there were no ghosts. "Ghosts!" laughed Daddy. "Don't be silly, Nancy Lee. There are no such animals."

Naturally Nancy Lee believed her mama and daddy, rather than the boy up the street. Especially in the daytime. And when all the lights were lit downstairs at night. But when it was real dark outside, and the house was awfully still inside. And Nancy Lee was up in her own little room. All by herself. Why then, well, Nancy Lee wasn't so positively sure about there not being any ghosts.

Of course, she knew there weren't any—really. But suppose there was just one. Suppose that just that one lived in that very house. Suppose it was the Ghost of Kunkleman.

And with all that supposing, it's no wonder that when the big grandfather's clock boomed way downstairs. And the wind moaned through the trees outside her window. And Nancy Lee listened real hard. She was sure she could hear strange noises coming from way down in the cellar.

And then! And then she knew she could hear the Ghost of Kunkleman walking around down in the kitchen.

And Nancy Lee got frightened.

"Mama! Mama!" she cried. "Daddy! Daddy!"

And mama and daddy came hurrying to see what was the matter. And to tell Nancy Lee once more that there just weren't any ghosts.

Of course, with mama and daddy there, and the lights all on, Nancy Lee wasn't afraid any more. So everything was all right again. Except that mama and daddy didn't like being called like that in the middle of the night all the time. For which you could hardly blame them.

Still, that is just the way it went, until one day when Nancy Lee decided that if the boy up the street could climb trees she could too. Only she tumbled out of the tree right into their best rose bush.

She didn't break any bones. Or anything like that. But she did get all scratched and stuck up by the thorns. Besides that, she was almost scared out of her wits. As who wouldn't be?

So mama and daddy took her to Dr. Brown to get patched up. Then, while Dr. Brown was doing this, they went out to the store to buy some things. Which gave Nancy Lee a chance to ask Dr. Brown about ghosts.

"Tell me, Dr. Brown," said Nancy Lee. "Do you believe in ghosts?"

"Well, now," said Dr. Brown, "that's a question . . ."

"Mama says there aren't any. And daddy says so too. But the boy up the street says there are. He says one lives right in our house. He says it's the Ghost of Kunkleman. And he walks around in the kitchen at night. The Ghost of Kunkleman, I mean, not the boy up the street.

"Of course, he can't be, if mama and daddy say he isn't. But sometimes I wonder just the same. And whether he is or isn't, I get awful scared when I hear the grandfather's clock go boom-boom-boom. And it sounds like funny noises coming from way down in the cellar. And then, I'm almost positively sure I can hear someone walking around in the kitchen. Do you really think it could be the ghost of Kunkleman?"

"Well, Nancy Lee," said Dr. Brown, "when I was just about your age I used to wonder about ghosts, too. Especially when I had to pass the graveyard at night . . ."

"You had to go by a graveyard at night?" gulped Nancy Lee.

"I certainly did," replied Dr. Brown.

"All alone?"

"Quite often. You can bet your boots I walked very fast and whistled as loud as I could."

"Why didn't you run?"

"Sometimes I did. What's more, I never went any closer to that graveyard than I could help. Until the night I was looking for my dog . . ."

"Your dog was lost?"

"He had been hit by a car."

"Aw, the poor little doggie," sympathized Nancy Lee.

"Of course, I didn't know it when I started out to look for Spike. Spike was my dog's name," explained Dr. Brown. "Anyhow, one of Spike's legs was broken and he had dragged himself into the graveyard. He was trying to get home."

"That's when I came looking for him. Naturally I didn't want to go into the graveyard, but when I heard Spike in there, whimpering, I said to myself, 'That's Spike, and he needs me, and no old ghost is going to stop me from getting my dog.' And I marched right straight into that graveyard and got Spike and took him home."

"And no old ghost tried to stop you?"

"Well, I didn't see any," said Dr. Brown, "but if one had tried to stop me I would have walked right smack through it, and you can bet your boots on that."

"And so would I if my dog needed me," said Nancy Lee fiercely. "Only I haven't got any dog," she added sadly.

"Is that so?" said Dr. Brown, more to himself than to Nancy Lee. "Well, I guess we have you all fixed up now, so suppose I write out a little prescription for your mama and daddy to have filled."

"Not any nasty old medicine," protested Nancy Lee.

"No, nothing like that," said Dr. Brown, and then he wrote out a prescription. And what do you suppose the prescription said?

It said, "One puppy dog for Nancy Lee."

Naturally, with Dr. Brown's prescription saying they should, mama and daddy bought their little girl a puppy dog. It was the cutest little black and white puppy you ever saw. With the softest velvety ears. Nancy Lee named it Snuffles. Because of the funny way it wrinkled up its little nose.

Nancy Lee thought the world of Snuffles and wanted to take him up to her room when it was time for bed. But daddy said:

"Nothing doing, young lady. Snuffles sleeps on the back porch."

"But, Daddy," protested Nancy Lee, "Snuffles will get lonesome back there, and, besides, what if the Ghost of Kunkleman should get him?"

"The Ghost of Kunkleman won't get Snuffles," said daddy firmly, "because there is no Ghost of Kunkleman."

"But, Daddy!"

"But nothing," said Daddy. "You go upstairs to bed and Snuffles goes to the back porch."

Which is the way it was. Because mamas and daddies know best. Even if it doesn't always seem so to a little girl.

Anyhow, Nancy Lee soon fell asleep. Because she was very tired. What with falling out of the tree, going to see Dr. Brown, getting Snuffles, and all.

But sometime in the middle of the night Nancy Lee woke up. And at first everything was very, very still. Then suddenly, she heard Snuffles barking—very faintly—from way down on the back porch. Was something wrong, she wondered.

Just then the grandfather's clock began to boom downstairs, the echoes sounding all over the house. It boomed twelve times while Nancy Lee shivered. It was so scary-like.

After that she thought she heard strange noises from way down in the cellar. And then—and then, she was sure she could hear the Ghost of Kunkleman walking around in the kitchen.

"He's after Snuffles," thought Nancy Lee. And with that she hopped out of bed, grabbed her little flashlight, and started downstairs to rescue her dog.

At first she wasn't scared a bit because she was so worried about Snuffles. But then the steps began to squeak under her bare feet. And she was more than ever sure she could hear funny noises from way down in the cellar. And it began to sound more and more like the Ghost of Kunkleman was walking around in the kitchen . . . why then . . . why then, Nancy Lee began to be afraid.

"It's so dark," she gulped, "and so s-scary. I w-wish Daddy was w-with me. Or M-mama. But they would send me back to bed. And I just have to save Snuffles. N-no old ghost is going to k-k-keep me from my d-dog. If he tries it, I'll j-just walk r-right smack through him. I w-will so. I w-w-will."

So Nancy Lee made her way down the stairs and through the long, dark hall that led to the kitchen. She was a mighty frightened little girl, but she was determined to save Snuffles from the Ghost of Kunkleman.

So she came to the kitchen door. She was afraid to open it at first, because she just knew that the Ghost of Kunkleman was in there. But if she didn't, she wouldn't be able to save Snuffles.

So Nancy Lee opened the door to the kitchen.

And sure enough!

By the light of her little flashlight she could see a big ghost right in front of the door to the back porch. It was an awful big ghost.

"Are y-you the G-Ghost of K-K-Kunkleman?" she asked.

"Yes, I am," said the ghost. "Now get that light out of my eyes. Do you want to blind me?"

"N-no," said Nancy Lee, "b-but I w-want my d-dog."

"Then for Pete's sake go and get him," said the ghost. "He's making enough noise to wake the dead."

Which was true, for Snuffles was barking like anything.

"I w-will get him if you'll move out of the way," said Nancy Lee.

"Who's in your way?" asked the ghost.

"You are. You're standing right in front of the door to the back porch."

"What of it? You can walk right through me, can't you?"

"I g-guess so, but would it be polite?"

"Who cares?"

"I do. Mama says I mustn't walk into people."

"Well, I'm not people. I'm a ghost."

"Just the same I don't think Mama would approve."

"Did she ever say you mustn't walk through a ghost?"

"N-no, but . . ."

"Maybe you're afraid to."

"W-well, I-I-I . . ."

"Or maybe you don't care what happens to your dog. I guess I'll just take him with me."

"You just better not," said Nancy Lee fiercely, starting for the door to the back porch. "You just try to take Snuffles and I'll, I'll . . . Why! I walked right through you."

"Of course you did," said the ghost. "Anybody can walk through a ghost if they're not afraid. Because there are no ghosts."

And with that the Ghost of Kunkleman disappeared.

And the next thing Nancy Lee knew it was morning. The

sun was shining in her window, the birds were singing outside, and Snuffles was cuddled up beside her on the bed.

Now how did Snuffles get up to her room from the back porch? Did she go walking in her sleep to get her dog? Or did she really wake up and go downstairs and walk right smack through the Ghost of Kunkleman?

Nancy Lee wasn't sure. But one thing she did know. She was not afraid of the Ghost of Kunkleman any more. Or any other ghost. Because, of course, there are no ghosts. As everybody knows.

But still, Nancy Lee didn't exactly have any desire to go walking in a graveyard alone at night.

Ending number one:

But then, there really isn't any *good* reason why a little girl *should* go walking in a graveyard at night.

Now is there?

Ending number two: How about you?

NOTE: *Ending number one may be preferable where young children are present or for other reasons when it seems desirable to end on a whimsical note. Generally speaking, ending number two is better for most children's groups, such as cub scouts.*

In either case, the sentence "But still, Nancy Lee didn't exactly have any desire to go walking in a graveyard alone at night" should be done in a real ghostly-type voice, especially the last few words. An extra scary quality should go into the question, "How about you?" and, at the same time, the story teller can point one index finger at the group, slowly moving it from face to face.

At this point someone dressed for the part may enter and make like a ghost. Of course, the action would be best in a dim light and the ghost's presence should be very brief.

* * * *

THE GHOST OF THE LOST HUNTER

There is no reason we cannot teach a lesson with a ghost story, and this one really ought to accomplish something for those organizations with "firewood" troubles. With several endings, you can tell it differently "the second time."

It is traditional among hunters and campers to leave a pile of wood for the next person or group who may use a campsite after they have gone. The next campers may arrive at night, or in the rain and a ready supply of wood may mean a great deal. Moreover, it is but ordinary out-of-doors courtesy, a part of the code of the woods.

Indeed, a good woodpile is one of the surest signs of a real camper. He checks his wood supply when he arrives and from then on makes sure it is always adequate and protected against bad weather. He is particularly careful there is enough wood for the night and the following morning. Only a greenhorn runs out of firewood or moves on without leaving a neat pile for those who follow.

But there are greenhorns—poor campers who know no better or, knowing, do not care. Thus comes the tale of the Ghost of the Lost Hunter.

It was in the summer of 1925 that Al and Jack were sitting by a campfire near Eaglesmere in the Allegheny Mountains of Pennsylvania, with some 90 other boy scouts from Philadelphia who were getting a summer of camping by caddying for their board.

Al and Jack had made sleeping bags of their blankets

and ponchos, and had stowed them behind a tree near the campfire circle in order that they might spend the night there in the woods, instead of returning to camp with the others. This was to be one of their nights in the open for their camping merit badge.

However, Al and Jack were a little sorry they had picked that particular night as they watched the flashlights of their brother scouts move farther away down the winding trail to Camp Kerodoki. The closing story had been a creepy one so that, as sure as they were that there were no such things as ghosts, they could not help wishing the night were not quite so dark and that they did not feel so awfully far away and alone up there in the woods by themselves. Besides, were they really certain there were no ghosts or anything like that?

Those fire tenders would have to soak the fire down so carefully that there was not one single spark left. A few glowing embers would have been so cozy. Their pleas of "We'll watch it good" had been countered with "You're going to sleep like good boy scouts, so what do you need a fire for?"

And so there they were in the dark. Except for their flashlights. There was really nothing to do but go to bed; so they placed their improvised sleeping bags side by side, took off their sneakers, loosened their socks and crawled in.

"Well, anyhow," said Al, "we can talk as loud as we want because they won't hear us up here, taps or no taps."

"Yeah," Jack agreed, "we don't have to talk in whispers."

Yet, strangely enough, that is exactly what they did. Perhaps it was habit. Or maybe they were tired and sleepy. Or could it have been because they didn't care to be heard by anyone, or anything, that might be prowling around in those woods? But then, there was nothing in the woods that would harm them. Or was there?

Whatever the reason, they talked in whispers, and listened to all the sounds around them—the wind rustling through the branches, the katydids, and a whip-poor-will. Soon even the whispering ceased.

Suddenly Jack started as a hand brushed across his face.

"Just wanted to make sure you were still there," whispered Al nervously. "It's so dark and creepy, I'm scared."

"You're not the only one," said Jack.

The boys wriggled inside their blankets until they could feel the outline of each other's bodies. They whispered a bit more, and then were silent, listening to each other's breathing. Finally they fell asleep.

It was sometime during the night when Al woke up. Forgetting where he was, he sat up, feeling for the familiar board side of his tent platform, but finding nothing more substantial than air. Then he remembered. He could hear Jack's even breathing beside him. This calm evidence of his friend's nearness reassured him somewhat, but it was so dark and still. If only he could see something! But there was not a star in the sky, not one tiny bit of light anywhere.

And then, almost as if in answer to his unspoken wish, the clouds parted abruptly and the light of the full moon came down through the trees to light up the campfire circle.

And that's when Al saw it!

A figure was moving silently around the far side of the council ring, stepping carefully over the logs the scouts used as seats. The figure was carrying something in both arms. Oddly enough it appeared to Al as though he were carrying a load of firewood. Al's instinctive fear was mingled with astonishment as he watched this mysterious figure make his way to the place where they kept their supply of wood for the campfire, where he slowly knelt to place the load he was carrying between the beech tree and the two stakes that had been driven into the ground to serve as the other end of this outdoor woodbin.

In the bright moonlight Al could plainly see it was a heavy-set man, dressed as for cold weather and wearing a hat such as his grandfather wore on the farm in an old picture in the family album. The man seemed to be looking around as though he had lost something, or wasn't quite sure where he was. He rubbed the back of his hand across his forehead and eyes.

Then he started to leave but paused to pick up several

pieces of wood that were lying scattered on the ground. These he placed neatly with the wood he had brought. Then he silently left the way he had come.

Al woke Jack as quietly as he could, holding one hand over his friend's mouth, but by the time Jack had struggled into a seeing position the mysterious figure had vanished.

"But there was somebody," Al insisted to his sleepy and dubious friend. "I saw him carry a load of firewood and set it down right where we always store wood for the campfire. You know, over there by the beech tree. I saw him as plain as anything."

"In that case the wood must be there now," said Jack, "and I can tell if it is because I was sitting right next to that woodpile and there were only three or four pieces left and they were scattered around where somebody dropped them. So, we'll just go take a good look."

Clouds now obscured the moon once more, leaving the campfire circle in darkness.

The boys groped for their flashlights, crawled out of their warm blankets and, stepping gingerly in their stocking feet, made their way over to the beech tree.

Their flashlights clearly revealed a neat pile of wood where only several loose sticks had been left when they had turned in for the night. Even these loose sticks had been placed on the pile, just as Al had claimed.

Al and Jack stared at each other in alarm. How explain a thing like that? Who or what did it? And why?

They played their lights all around them, but saw nothing other than the trees and shrubs, and the logs around the campfire circle. It was now so still in the woods one might think that everything was listening with them.

"Do you think we better go back to camp?" Jack asked.

"N-no," said Al, trying to convey a firmness he was far from feeling. "We'd just have the pants laughed off us, and besides, whoever it was didn't do anything but leave some firewood. No harm in that, is there?"

"No, I guess not," Jack agreed, "if that's all he does."

Two thoughtful boys climbed back into their blankets and lay quietly listening in the darkness. Admittedly frightened, they nevertheless stayed where they were and, in the morning, agreed to say nothing about it to the others. Al was positive about what he saw; Jack was just as certain the wood wasn't there when they turned in; but it was all so fantastic.

Therefore they kept it a secret until a year later when two other scouts, sleeping out by the campfire circle, had come running back into camp at night, scared stiff and claiming they had seen a man dragging a log through the woods.

When they calmed down a little, Al questioned them closely about the man's appearance. Their description, though a little confused, due to their obvious fear and not as good a light as Al had enjoyed the year before, tallied somewhat with his own observation.

Al and Jack, and some of the other scouts, went back with the two boys who had seen the figure, to check on the log. A log was found right where the boys said the mysterious figure left it, which was the exact place they always chopped their wood for campfires, but there was more or less disagreement as to whether or not it was there before.

It was then Al told the story of what he saw the year before. Completely bewildered, the scouts returned to camp, some skeptical, some scared, the others not certain what to think.

The next day Al mentioned both incidents to an old mountaineer, who worked on the grounds of the golf course, and from him he got the story of the Ghost of the Lost Hunter.

It was back about the turn of the century, according to the story, when four hunters made camp one December day near Laporte, across the mountain from Eaglesmere. It was late in the afternoon when they arrived at the rough cabin that served as their camp, and, to their dismay, discovered very little firewood on hand.

As a storm was obviously brewing, they had no time to lose. While one of the Lane Brothers started a fire and got supper under way, the others scattered to bring in more wood. They had hardly begun this chore when the snow began to fall.

After several trips back with wood it suddenly occurred to the Lane Brothers and Jerry Anderson that none of them had seen Jordan Bates for some time. Charley Lane recalled seeing him dragging a small log along a gully about the second time he had gone out for wood. No one else recalled seeing him at all. It was now quite dark and the snow was falling heavily.

Worried, the men went out to search for Jordan, calling his name continually, in the hopes he might hear them, and also to keep contact with one another. Once Jerry Anderson thought he heard a faint "Halloo" in the distance, but he got no reply to his shouts and was unable to definitely fix any point of origin for the voice he thought he heard.

Taking turns watching the fire, the men continued their search until exhausted. With the morning they sought help and a posse was formed to comb the woods. The snow was very thick by this time and, with the passing of another day, little hope of finding the lost hunter alive remained. Still the search was continued for two more days, by which time it was generally agreed there was little likelihood of locating Jordan's body until the snow melted in the gullies and hollows.

As a matter of fact, no trace of Jordan Bates was ever found; that is, no one ever discovered his body, or clothing, or any personal effects. But it was not the end of the story of Jordan Bates.

For it wasn't long until hunters began to tell strange stories of seeing a man who looked like Jordan dragging a log through the woods at night, or carrying a load of firewood. Most often he was seen in the woods, but sometimes appeared around camps. When seen in camps he would usually be bringing firewood, and more than once men swore that firewood had actually been left, piled neatly, where little or none had been present when they turned in for the night; just as Al and Jack had claimed for the figure Al saw at Camp Kerodoki.

The first few years after his disappearance Jordan, if it was he, seemed to confine his activities to the region right around Laporte and Eaglesmere, but it wasn't long before his wanderings took him farther afield, although he always returned to his old stamping grounds. As the years went by the stories of the Ghost of the Lost Hunter came from all over Pennsylvania and New York. And then from surrounding states, until reports came from as far west as the Rockies.

Apparently there was no method nor reason behind his wanderings, other than a never-ending search for wood to replenish neglected supplies and, perhaps, an equally fruitless search for the companions and camp he had lost in the darkness and the snow, so many years before.

That wood had really appeared where none was known to have existed at bedtime is a matter of much dispute.

There are those who assert that it is true, and also those who swear it simply cannot be.

And then there is a further question as to whether the Lost Hunter has ever been heard. Some have said he mutters to himself while dragging a log through the woods, or that he mumbles threats against campers who have let the woodpile go down. It has been said that at such times his face is dark, like a thundercloud, and woe to anyone who crosses his path at such a time.

From the earliest days it has been rumored that it was the blackness of his anger that led to Jordan's getting lost. It seems but reasonable to believe the Ghost of the Lost Hunter has little patience with those who fail to keep a good supply of firewood on hand.

Some scoff at this, but one thing is sure. No report has ever come of the Ghost of the Lost Hunter where a good pile of firewood sits neatly in its place. Which may explain why some veteran hunters and campers have never seen him while others have seen him more than once.

Still he searches for firewood and the campsite he can never find. Sometimes his faint "Halloo!" may be heard—out in the woods at night. If you should ever hear it, answer him, and then, if it is indeed the Ghost of the Lost Hunter, you will get no reply. Nor will you see him—if you have a good woodpile.

(Assume a real creepy tone, speaking slowly, in a low voice.)

But campers who turn in for the night with their woodpile low may receive a visit—from the Ghost of the Lost Hunter. He comes silently in the dark—a heavy-set figure—in an old-fashioned hat. Groping his way—through the woods—into your camp.

(Three endings are given for the story teller's selection.)

He—is looking—searching . . .

FOR YOU!

(or)

If you see him, lie still. Do not shine your light in his face, because . . .

IT'S NOT POLITE!

(or)

If you have neglected your firewood supply—close your eyes—and repeat slowly—to yourself, "I will never, never neglect the woodpile again. So, Ghost of the Lost Hunter, go away—go away."

Repeat this three times—slowly. Then open your eyes—and the Ghost of the Lost Hunter will be gone.

(Voice dies away at the end, but, if you wish, you can suddenly yell, "or he will grab you." Those who enjoy "Big Boo" endings like to be fooled by the story teller. I often get comments such as, "Gee, Bob, I was all set for you to jump at us, and then I thought it was going to be a creepy, die-away ending, and then—boy, was I scared!")

Section Six

INDIAN STORIES

Section Six is for scout troops and other groups putting on an all-Indian evening or who would like to have an Indian story as the high point in a more general program, whether indoors or at a campfire.

"The Old Ones" or "The Trail of Friends" may be used simply in narrated form or may be dramatized while read. The narrator should have a good speaking voice and read or tell the story in the dignified manner usually associated with Indian story telling and speaking. If no dramatization is used, it is particularly desirable that the story be told rather than read, which means reading it many times in order to learn it well enough to do a really good job of it. Indian stories are, of course, extremely effective when the story teller is in costume.

Either of these stories may be dramatized and a few suggestions along this line are offered with each. However, the possibilities depend to a large extent upon the personnel, Indian costumes and properties, and general setting at your disposal. Action, for the most part, may be slow and a fair amount of silent posing is good where costuming and the setting tend to make this effective.

There is a commendable trend to be more authentic in Indian lore activities than was formerly the case. Many groups endeavor to learn as much as they can of the costumes, traditions and activities of some tribe which actually lived in the same section of the country, while others adopt a tribe which happens to appeal to them.

In view of this I must offer an apology, perhaps, for stories that are completely my own imagination dealing with a fictitious tribe, but, as with ghost stories, I find it difficult to locate the type of stories that seem to me best fitted for this purpose. I am curious as to what others may think of my experiment in Indian story telling and will welcome any reports or pictures from scout troops or others using "The Old Ones" or "The Trail of Friends."

THE OLD ONES

Whether used as part of an evening's Indian program or simply as a more serious portion of a general program, "The Old Ones" may be told as a story or dramatized as here indicated. Even though told without any dramatization, some effort should be made to create the proper mood—by dimming the lights, having the story teller appear in Indian costume and so forth.

The following dramatization is offered as one possibility, using pantomime, partly on stage and partly by shadow play. For the shadow play portion a large sheet, or sheets, are suspended toward the rear of the stage and necessary lights set up for use at the proper time. An artificial fire and any other Indian props on the stage in front of the sheet, as well as the actors on the stage, must be arranged so as not to interfere too much with the audience's view of the shadow play. This may mean sitting the Indian boys in a short arc to one side of the stage with the story teller facing them across the stage (if distance is not too great) or toward the rear, where he can easily step aside a bit to give an unobstructed view of the sheet.

The curtain opens on a group of Indian boys around their lodge fire, Burning Fox seated with them but a little apart. The narrator, whether seen or invisible, can read the entire story, or Burning Fox can actually take over when it is his time to speak. In this case, however, he must know the story well enough to give it substantially as it is. Otherwise, it is better for him to go through the motions of speaking, mouthing the words with the narrator.

Likewise, the boys can actually say their lines, "Speak to

us of Singing Arrow. Burning Fox, we wait before you," or one boy with a clear voice can speak for them all.

The lights on the stage should be dimmed as Burning Fox begins his story (The stage should not be brightly lighted at any time), while a spotlight shines on the sheet.

Costuming may vary considerably depending upon what you have or can secure or make. Certainly Burning Fox should look very much like an Indian story teller. The boys can have very simple costumes, especially if fairly young. The number of boys used may be only a handful or a good-sized group.

A few branches of fir or pine may be extended inward at both ends of the sheet to give an impression of a forest, being waved, as though blown by the wind, at the proper time.

The spotlight can go off at any time to facilitate the shadow scene changing or when it is difficult to portray the action described in the story. In these cases the dim light of the fire in front will show enough of Burning Fox and the boys to afford some visual interest in addition to the narrator's voice. The suggestions for action given here are very sketchy and are subject to change to best suit the plans and capabilities of any group.

The spotlight might go on about the time the narrator, or Burning Fox, says "The Old Ones were not of the Towedoes," showing several of the returning hunters and Singing Beaver. He talks with them until they brush him aside and go off stage. The light can go out as he gets ready for his journey, coming on again with "So Singing Beaver went out . . ."

The light goes out again just before he gets to the cave, making it possible to get the Old Ones in their places, and so it goes. Needless to say, every effort should be made to do this shadow play in silence, so far as the actors are concerned. Generally speaking, actions need not be hurried and posing, done in Indian costume and as shadows, is quite acceptable.

It is not necessary to show anything for the deer until after it has been slain, or for the wolves, the actions of Singing Beaver and The Old Ones being sufficient. The spotlight goes out as Singing Beaver goes to meet his father.

The final council lodge scene should not be difficult. However, actions must be properly synchronized with the narrator. The spotlight goes out and the lights on the stage come up somewhat for the final words of Burning Fox.

The costuming of the actors participating in the shadow-play and the actual number acting are subject to variation in accordance with the group's desires.

The foregoing merely attempts to point out some possibilities. I should be very happy to receive any reports or pictures from groups staging such a program as "The Old Ones."

THE OLD ONES

(A Tale of Burning Fox)

The Great Cold Bear of the North was growling through the forest and shaking the lodges of the Towedoes, but within the Boys' Council Lodge there was warmth, and friendship, and a happy feeling of well-being.

No other lodge in all the village was so well built or so skillfully designed as this second home of the young braves-to-be of the Towedoes. A large fire burned in the center, yet a strange thing was seen. For despite the winter wind that howled all around and over the lodge the smoke still flowed up and out of the smoke hole.

The boys knew that in their own lodges the breath of the Cold Bear oft times drove the smoke back into their faces.

How he must rage to know that Burning Fox, the Teller of Tales, had outwitted him.

The boys sat cross-legged, watching the flames slowly fall back into a great glowing heap of embers. They had sung their tribal songs and boasted of their deeds in contest and hunt, and the things they had seen and done out in the forest. They had danced and acted out their tales of adventure, even as did the braves of the tribe in the Warriors' Council Lodge.

Now a great stillness descended upon them as each boy sat wrapped in the golden dreams that come only to those who sit before the fire of friendship. They knew Burning Fox would not speak until the chosen moment and there must be no sound to disturb his spirit's sitting in council.

As living embers flamed and faded within the mass of glowing coals, creating wondrous pictures of animals, and birds, and men, the chosen moment came for Burning Fox to speak.

"Braves-to-be of the Towedoes, Mighty Warriors of the Future, Fathers of the Men-Who-Will-Be, I would speak of Singing Arrow."

"Speak to us of Singing Arrow," said the boys, all eyes upon him. "Burning Fox, we wait before you."

"Then listen well and I will tell you of Singing Arrow and The Old Ones, before his name was Singing Arrow; when he, as you, was still a youth, a brave-to-be, a not-yet-warrior. Listen well and I will tell you . . ."

Long, long ago before the days of the fathers of our fathers' fathers, there lived a young brave-to-be of the Towedoes, known to all as Singing Beaver. Mischief loving, happy hearted, friend to all was Singing Beaver.

It was the time of snows and the Great Cold Bear was on the prowl through the forest, even as he is now. His cold, icy breath was bringing snow and wind from out of the North, and there was much hurrying to and fro in the village of the Towedoes.

The lodges were being prepared to meet the full rage of the Cold Bear, the children gathered in, the braves returning from their hunting. Some came back to the village bowed by the weight of game, others walked straight with all their arrows and empty hands. All were glad to seek the shelter of their own lodges.

It was even then that Singing Beaver went out into the forest alone, into the very teeth of the Great Cold Bear of the North. For Singing Beaver had heard of the Old Ones, who had been left to die in the Half-Way Cave where the River of Pines came down the Black Mountain.

The Old Ones were not of the Towedoes. They were members of a wandering tribe from a land far into the sunset, and now, too old to earn their place by the fire, they had been left behind to die when their people moved on. Singing Beaver heard some of the returning hunters speak of the leaving of the Old Ones, and his heart quickened with angry sorrow.

How could they leave behind them the Old Ones who through so many moons and snows had kept the fire burning for others? It was a very bad thing to do, and nothing good could come of it.

But the Towedo braves would not heed his words.

"It is not of our doing," they told him. "They have never sat before our fires. They are not of the Towedoes."

"But they are children of the Great Spirit," cried Singing Beaver. "They have kept the fire when they were able. They should be warmed and fed now that they are old."

"Trouble us not," said the returning warriors, impatient to get to their own lodges. "We have our own people to warm and feed. Those Old Ones will soon sleep. The Great Cold Bear will see to that. He will come for them. Never fear."

So the warriors brushed the boy aside, and went their way to their lodges.

Singing Beaver hurried to his father's lodge, but only to get food, warm robes, and bows and arrows. Buffalo pack and quiver on his back, bow in hand, he stole quietly away, and no one marked his going.

Never before had he taken leave of his father's lodge without his father's word, and his heart was heavy within him. Yet he dared not risk the question that might bring the words of refusal he could not disobey.

So Singing Beaver went out to follow the River of Pines through the forest to where it comes falling down the Black Mountain, close by the Half-Way Cave.

Ever more fiercely the Cold Bear growled as Singing Beaver made his way, head bowed against the wind and driving snow. If the snow breath of the Great Cold Bear were not so thick he would have taken another, shorter, trail he knew, but he dared not leave the river. As long as the river lay on his bow side all was well, he reasoned.

Later he wondered if even this could be true, as the Great Cold Bear roared with such fury he feared he might lose the river itself. Once he almost plunged into it when he suddenly found it right before him. His body grew colder at the very thought of falling into its icy waters.

He lost all sense of space and time. Somewhere behind him lay the village of the Towedoes. Somewhere ahead was the Half-Way Cave where the Old Ones had been left to die. All around him raged the Great Cold Bear of the North. From tree to tree Singing Beaver slowly fought his way, as darkness came to swallow up that little of day not already hidden by the fast-falling snow.

But now he was nearing the Half-Way Cave. The trail by the River of Pines was twisting upward, and there were rocks against which he stumbled. And fell. Suddenly, a glowing eye winked at him through the snow. It was the faint, flickering fire of the Old Ones. They had been left without food or warm robes and now sat huddled before their dying fire, waiting patiently for the coming of the Great Cold Bear of the North.

Singing Beaver wrapped warm robes around them and then went out to find more wood. Piece by piece he wrestled precious fuel from the very jaws of the Great Cold Bear. He fed the fire until its warmth brought new life to the Old Ones. He brought more wood to keep the fire during the long night.

Though cold and very weary from his journey along the River of Pines against the full wrath of the Great Cold Bear, Singing Beaver worked hour after hour to find enough wood to keep the fire however great might grow the fury of the Cold Bear.

Then he fed the Old Ones from the food he had brought with him. And then, with the fire standing guard against the cold and the snow, Singing Beaver lay down and slept beside the Old Ones. The three slept together under the warm robes the boy had brought from his father's lodge.

By morning the growling of the Cold Bear had ceased and all was still as the forest lay sleeping under its heavy blanket of snow.

While sharing his food before the fire, the Old Ones told Singing Beaver he should not have come. "You have saved us once from the Great Cold Bear of the North," they told him, "and our hearts are grateful. Yet we must die. You cannot stay with us; you must return to your father's lodge. Our people have forsaken us. Our time has come."

"Not so," said Singing Beaver. "The Towedoes will welcome you to their lodges. You will find warmth and food and shelter with us. You shall be as our own Old Ones, honored and respected." Yet his heart was cold within him, for he feared his people would not receive the Old Ones. For they were not of the Towedoes.

Singing Beaver brought in more wood, seeking it out under its covering of snow. Then he went in search of game.

Down where the River of Pines stretched away from the Black Mountain there was a hollow thick with pines, firs and hemlocks. There the boy came upon a deer, struggling to escape through the snow. Singing Beaver's arrow sped true, and the deer's life blood leaped forth to darken the snow.

Singing Beaver bowed his head to ask forgiveness of the deer's spirit and in thankfulness to the Great Spirit of All Life.

Then he prepared to drag the deer back to the Half-Way Cave. He cut branches of fir and bound them together until he had enough to support the deer. He placed the deer upon this fir drag and made it secure with another deerskin thong from his belt pouch.

Then he bent his shoulder to the task of dragging the deer up through the snow to the Half-Way Cave. The Old Ones came out to meet him. The Old Man helped him skin the deer while the Old Woman busied herself cooking the fresh meat. Then they feasted and rested.

The gaunt grey wolves were almost upon them before they sensed their danger. Maddened by the scent of the freshly killed deer, the hungry wolves had forgotten their natural fear of man, and now came charging up the slope toward the cave. Singing Beaver and the Old Ones knew these terrible wolves would not stop for the fire that burned in the cave's mouth.

The boy strung his bow with the sure speed his father, Great Bow, had taught him. The Old Man handed him an arrow. With one swift motion the youth bent the bow and the arrow fairly sang its way into the first wolf.

The Old Man was ready with a second arrow, and again the bow bent swiftly, as this arrow, too, sped true to its mark. But the wolf pack had reached the mouth of the cave and Singing Beaver and the Old Ones might have gone down before them had not the Old Woman seized several burning brands and flung them right into the faces of the hungry wolves.

Howling with pain and fright, the wolf pack broke and fled. Before they could come on again, Singing Beaver heard shouts from down the slope. His father, Great Bow, was hurrying toward them, with several other warriors. The wolves quietly vanished into the forest.

Singing Beaver went forth to meet his father. The Old Ones hastened to rebuild the fire and cook more meat.

* * * *

In the Council Lodge of the Towedoes, Singing Beaver came before the assembled chieftains and warriors, all the braves of the Towedoes.

Singing Beaver's father went with him to the Council Lodge of the Towedoes, but once inside Great Bow took his place among the warriors. Singing Beaver stood straight as a young pine, waiting for some sign of recognition.

Loping Wolf, Chief of the Towedoes, turned his head toward One-Eyed Owl, the Medicine Man, who beckoned to

Singing Beaver. Singing Beaver came forward and stood before One-Eyed Owl, the Medicine Man of the Towedoes.

"As an arrow, you went forth into the storm from the lodge of Great Bow, your father," said One-Eyed Owl. "Straight and true you went to save the Old Ones from the Great Cold Bear of the North. With courage and skill you fought your way through the wind and the snow. With arrows that sang you slew the deer for food and the wolves that would drag down you and the Old Ones.

"The boy that was Singing Beaver is no more. He is gone from us forever. You are now a brave-in-being; you are now Singing Arrow, one who dares to fight for what he knows to be right; one who stands strong for what is good and true. You are a worthy son of your father, Great Bow. May he ever be as proud of his Singing Arrow as he is this day. May the blessing of the Great Spirit of All Life be ever with you, Singing Arrow, as you go your way along the trail your soul shall lead you."

Singing Arrow knelt before One-Eyed Owl, and the Medicine Man placed around his neck a necklace from which hung a bright arrow of porcupine quills. The Medicine Man took his place, and Loping Wolf placed a scarlet feather in the scalplock of Singing Arrow. Then the Chief touched the shoulder of the new brave of the tribe, and Singing Arrow stood erect before him.

"Great Bow, your father, has lost a boy, but the Towedoes have found a new warrior. Take your place in the Council Circle, Singing Arrow."

Thus it was, oh Braves-to-be of the Towedoes, Mighty Warriors of the Future, Fathers of the Men-Who-Will-Be, that manhood came to Singing Beaver, that he grew into Singing Arrow.

All was still in the Boys' Council Lodge as Burning Fox finished his tale. All eyes shone brightly with the dreams of those who would also be as Singing Arrow — braves who dared to fight for what they knew to be right, warriors who would stand strong for all that was good and true.

THE TRAIL OF FRIENDS

(A tale of Burning Fox)

Young Otter lay on the ground, the back of his head resting on his hands, the bleakness of winter on his face though the Spirit of Summer Sun warmed all the forest. Young Otter's eyes were dark pools of brooding sadness.

So lost was the boy's spirit in the blackness of his own making his ears did not note the coming of Burning Fox, until the Teller of Tales stood close by him. Slowly the eyes of Young Otter climbed from feet to head of the one who had thus come silently upon him. Suddenly realizing who it was and the respect due Burning Fox by a young brave-to-be of the Towedoes, the boy arose in haste and raised his hand in greeting.

"Be seated," said Burning Fox. "I would sit with you in council."

Young Otter waited until the Teller of Tales had taken his place. Then he sat facing the counselor and friend of the young braves-to-be.

"Speak as you will," said Burning Fox.

"I have no will to speak," replied Young Otter. "My words are hidden in darkness. My Spirit wanders in the Caves of Lost Spirits." The boy's head sank upon his chest.

Burning Fox looked upon him in silence for a moment. "Am I not Young Otter's friend?" he asked.

And the boy answered without raising his head from his chest, "Young Otter boasts proudly that Burning Fox is his friend."

"Then look at me," said the Teller of Tales.

The boy raised his head.

"When friend speaks to friend, the spirit of he who listens walks hand in hand with the spirit of the one who speaks.

This is the way a friend may help a friend over the broken words of his saddened spirit as he would over uneven ground when his friend's body is stricken and weak, and he cannot make his way alone."

"But if Young Otter speaks, Burning Fox who tells such wonderful tales of courage and manhood, will no longer be his friend. He will scorn this one who is not worthy to be a warrior of the Towedoes."

"Is the friendship of Burning Fox, then, so small—so weak a thing?"

"Not so. It is Young Otter who is small and weak. This one . . ." The boy fell silent, his head sinking once more upon his chest until the stirring words of Burning Fox brought it up once more upon his shoulders.

"We walk the Trail of Friends together," said the Teller of Tales, "together we speak, together we stumble and fall, together we rise and again follow the Trail. Not alone, but together we come out of the Caves of the Lost Spirits and climb the mountain to where the warmth of the Great Spirit awaits all who seek His Will. The Spirit of a friend may go with a friend because all are but parts of the Great Spirit of All.

"Burning Fox would join his spirit with that of Young Otter, his friend, serving him as truly as he would serve himself. This is what it means to walk the Trail of Friends."

In the silence that followed these words the hand of the boy's spirit reached out for the hand of his friend's spirit, and even so they followed the Trail of Friends together while Young Otter told his story.

Young Otter was but a rabbit, faint-hearted and afraid to meet the testing of a warrior. That very morning the other braves-to-be had laughed at him when he had failed to play the part of a warrior in mock battle. Led by Little Crow, the braves-to-be had gone on a practice war party during which they pretended to come upon their foe, the remains of the old Towedo lodges by Beaver Lake.

Stealing close, like shadows through the woods, they had first fired their arrows into the crumbling sides of the old lodges, and then, at Little Crow's signal, had charged with their tomahawks, hacking with savage fury at the bark sides and upright poles. But Young Otter had hung back.

So real had been their pretense that he could see the old lodges as Indian boys like themselves and his very spirit rebelled against attacking boys he did not hate, boys who might be his friends, boys who were also children of the Great Spirit of All Life. He could not tell the others how he felt. They did not care.

Little Crow had spoken hot words of scorn and, with a final gesture of disgust, had turned away from him. The others

had done the same, all showing their disapproval of Young Otter. He was left alone in his disgrace.

He longed to be as one of the others, true braves-to-be of the Towedoes, but he had no heart for war, no wish to slay his brothers of any tribe or people. He would live at peace with all. He was a coward, lacking the will to fight like a man.

So Young Otter told his story.

Burning Fox listened well before he spoke, waiting for the words of his young friend to take their rest in the council lodge of his spirit.

"The ways of peace are good ways," he said at length, "for we are indeed all children of the Great Spirit. It is not His Will that we should fight and slay one another. But bad medicine stirs in the hearts of men as well as good. Men sometimes follow the ways of darkness and tribes war with one another.

"A true child of the Great Spirit can only pray that his tribe will dwell at peace, that he may be a friend to all men, his brothers. But as surely as the green things go their way, the leaves fall and the snows come, so do men's hearts grow cold with hatred and a man must fight for his tribe. There is no time then to talk of peace. Not until hot blood has been shed in battle will men be ready to reason one with the other.

"Then it is, when the tribe is in danger, that a man's life is not his own. It belongs to his tribe and for his tribe he must fight. He does not slay then in the name of his spirit but for his tribe, his own people. He who will not fight at such a time does not help the cause of peace, pleases not the Great Spirit.

"For those men deride as faint-hearted sow seeds of bitterness within the tribe whose evil fruit is far worse than the sorrow that comes for those who die in battle. For know this well, my young friend, all men must sometimes do things they would not because it is their duty. Few men wish to fight, to shed the blood of their brother men, to slay those who might have been their friends. And when they must, for the sake of their tribe—their people—they have naught but scorn and ill-will for any who will not fight.

"Men know that their tribe lives only in the hearts of the brave; that their children are not safe in the hands of the faint-hearted."

So Burning Fox reasoned with Young Otter. So he told him that a warrior must always fight for what is right and good, and that the well-being of the tribe must always be good in the eyes of every true warrior. For the children of the Great Spirit live together as families, as clans, and as tribes.

"Ask the Great Spirit for good counsel," said Burning Fox. "He will guide you in the way that you should go. Ask for strength when strength you need, for a brave heart in time of danger. Ask for peace if it be His Will but always for the courage to do what must be done. Now go your way as a brave-to-be of the Towedoes, knowing that the spirit of your friend, Burning Fox, goes with you, for we have walked the Trail of Friends together."

The Teller of Tales arose and Young Otter stood to face him. Their hands were raised in silent token of the ending of their sitting in council. Young Otter bowed his head. When he raised it, Burning Fox was gone.

Young Otter had told his father he would not return before the next day's sun, that he had need of being alone in the forest. He wrapped his deerskin about him and lay down to sleep. The hours of darkness passed slowly.

Young Otter awoke.

Three enemy warriors stood over him, weapons ready to strike at his slightest move.

"Little dog of a Towedo," said one, "guide us to your camp if you would live to see tomorrow's sun."

The spirit of fear clutched at the boy's heart. What must he do? What could he do? He prayed to the Great Spirit for the courage to defy his enemies and die. He could not betray his people though his life be spared.

He was dragged to his feet; a knife was at his throat. "Will you guide us to your camp?" asked the Indian who held the knife.

The hand of Young Otter's spirit groped for the hand of the Spirit of Burning Fox, but the sharp point of the knife at his throat was very real and very close—the Trail of Friends a thing of shadows and far away.

"Will you guide us?" growled his enemy.

The boy felt his blood beginning to flow as the knife pushed through his skin. It was then he made his decision.

"Promise that I will live if I show you the way?" he asked in a voice of fear.

The scornful grunts that greeted his question spoke more eloquently than the replies his enemies put in words.

"Your life is yours," said the one who held the knife.

"Who would want it?" asked another.

"I will guide you," said Young Otter. He knew these three must be advance scouts for a war party coming to surprise his people. They would strike without warning in the first faint light of dawn. His tribe would not be ready for they were at peace with all around them. Only one tribe could be so treacherous—their ancient foes, the Ginowas.

"I will show you the way through the Black Swamp," Young Otter told them. "There are no guards on that side of our camp for none but our own know the trail."

He felt the eyes of Burning Fox's spirit upon him as he spoke these words, but he also felt the presence of his foes close around him.

"The Black Swamp begins here," he said after they had gone a little way. "Keep close watch and be sure of foot lest the mud that swallows things seize you in its jaws."

Young Otter led the way into the Swamp with the sureness that comes with long acquaintance with every foot of the trail.

"Keep close," he would say. "Jump quickly and jump again." The light of moon and stars was not much to go by, but the boy knew what he was doing and his enemies stayed close by him. They were well pleased with their good fortune in coming upon this one who would betray his own people.

"Now!" cried Young Otter. "Leap fast and hard to that dark mound ahead and then again quickly to that next one to the right."

Young Otter leaped and his foes leaped with him. Two of them leaped again to the right but Young Otter's second leap was to the left where he landed on firm ground. His enemies felt the jaws of the mud that swallows things close greedily upon their legs and struggled to escape. Their struggles but forced them deeper into the swamp.

The third Ginowa scout saw the boy's quick change of direction and, even as he made his second leap, turned also to the left. But he had not expected to turn this way and the sudden change threw him off balance. He landed just short of the firm ground where Young Otter was. Dropping his tomahawk, he seized the boy's right ankle.

The boy twisted himself free but his enemy was now

struggling up onto the solid ground. Young Otter knew he would be no match for the man-grown strength of the enemy scout once he had sure footing beneath him.

Turning swiftly, he seized his enemy's right arm at the elbow, pulling him forward hard and turning his body so as to reach for the knife at his enemy's side. Off balance from his desperate struggles to climb out of the mud, the Ginowa scout strove to keep on his feet and swing around to face the boy he now knew to be a brave and resourceful foe.

Too late he saw the swift thrust of his own knife. Without a sound he fell forward at the feet of Young Otter, the boy he had scorned as a coward.

The other Ginowas called vainly to their dying companion as they slowly sank deeper into the clinging mud of the Black Swamp.

With prayers of sadness for his enemies and of thankfulness for his own deliverance in his heart, Young Otter hurried to carry the warning to his tribe. His spirit knew no joy at the death of his enemies, but he was very sure he had done the only right thing he could do as a brave-to-be of the Towedoes.

Many things were in the mind of Young Otter some time later, after the battle had been fought and won, when he stood before his Chief in the Council Lodge of the Towedoes and heard the words of praise for what he had done. No scared rabbit but a proud young brave bowed his head to receive the headdress of a warrior.

"Leaping Wolf shall be your name," said the Medicine Man of the Towedoes. "For so it was you destroyed the enemy scouts and brought us warning of our danger."

"You may take your place with the braves," said the Chief.

Leaping Wolf looked toward Burning Fox, who had walked the Trail of Friends with him in his hour of weakness and despair. The Teller of Tales motioned to the empty place beside him.

Leaping Wolf lifted his arm in respect to his Chief and then made his way to sit beside his friend.

THE TRAIL OF FRIENDS

As with "The Old Ones" the suggestions given here for dramatization are sketchy and only indicative of the sort of thing that may be done.

The story may be shown entirely in shadow play or the parts involving Burning Fox and Young Otter and the final scene may be done in front of the sheet. This latter method is recommended where suitable Indian costumes and staging arrangements are available and is here briefly described.

The sheeting for the shadow play should be about halfway back on the stage. Nothing in the way of scenery is actually necessary for the front half of the stage. However, it may seem desirable to elevate Young Otter and Burning Fox so that they may be seen better when lying down and sitting as indicated in the story. For this purpose something to give the impression of a mound of earth, covered with green material, may be used for the boy and a log improvised for Burning Fox.

A reader, equipped with a shaded light, may stand or sit to one side of the stage, perhaps out of sight.

The curtain opens on Young Otter lying on the ground to one side of the stage. Burning Fox enters slowly and silently on cue, to take his place near the youth so that the boy's eyes can easily spot his feet first and slowly climb to his face. The action then follows the story until both sit down, which they do facing each other and sideways to the audience. By keeping to the one side of the stage, they will leave a clear view of sheeting for the shadow play.

The lights on the stage go out and the sheeting is lighted for the scene of Indian boys coming upon their imaginary foes. One or two shadow figures may be shown with drawn bows (no arrows) as the sheet lights up, others quickly draw their tomahawks and attack their imaginary enemies. One Indian boy who takes no part in this affair, standing back with a tomahawk in his hand, is subsequently denounced and scorned by the others who exit. He continues to stand there, drooping somewhat, after the others have gone, until the sheet goes dark, after the words, "He was a coward, lacking the will to fight like a man."

The stage is lighted again until Young Otter lifts his head to find Burning Fox gone, at which time the stage is darkened so that Young Otter may lie down behind the sheet. The light on the sheet comes on when Young Otter awakes to find the enemy scouts looking down on him.

It will take a bit of practice with lights and shadow movements to give a good interpretation of the enemy scouts following Young Otter and getting trapped in the mud, and also the fight between the boy and the third enemy scout. Whether this action is impressive or ridiculous will depend upon the willingness of all concerned to work together to achieve the right effect. The light on the sheet, of course, goes out as Young Otter starts off to give the warning to his tribe.

Since there should be a pause in the narration here anyhow, it will be quite all right to leave the stage in darkness until all are in their places for the final scene. If some Indian type music can be fitted into such intervals as this, it would not only help create the mood desired but also cover sounds made by the actors taking their places on the stage. Such music should begin softly as a background during the swamp shadow scene, building up during the pause, and fading slowly away during the final scene.

The final scene follows the story until the curtains close as Leaping Wolf makes his way toward Burning Fox.